T0092683

# Lecture Notes in Computer Science     **14397**

The series Lecture Notes in Computer Science (LNCS), including its subseries Lecture Notes in Artificial Intelligence (LNAI) and Lecture Notes in Bioinformatics (LNBI), has established itself as a medium for the publication of new developments in computer science and information technology research, teaching, and education.

LNCS enjoys close cooperation with the computer science R & D community, the series counts many renowned academics among its volume editors and paper authors, and collaborates with prestigious societies. Its mission is to serve this international community by providing an invaluable service, mainly focused on the publication of conference and workshop proceedings and postproceedings. LNCS commenced publication in 1973.

Davide Ceolin · Tommaso Caselli · Marina Tulin
Editors

# Disinformation in Open Online Media

5th Multidisciplinary International Symposium, MISDOOM 2023
Amsterdam, The Netherlands, November 21–22, 2023
Proceedings

 Springer

*Editors*
Davide Ceolin 🆔
Centrum Wiskunde & Informatica
Amsterdam, The Netherlands

Tommaso Caselli 🆔
University of Groningen
Groningen, The Netherlands

Marina Tulin 🆔
University of Amsterdam
Amsterdam, The Netherlands

ISSN 0302-9743        ISSN 1611-3349 (electronic)
Lecture Notes in Computer Science
ISBN 978-3-031-47895-6        ISBN 978-3-031-47896-3 (eBook)
https://doi.org/10.1007/978-3-031-47896-3

This Springer imprint is published by the registered company Springer Nature Switzerland AG
The registered company address is: Gewerbestrasse 11, 6330 Cham, Switzerland

Paper in this product is recyclable.

# Preface

Online media is a critical infrastructure that is economical, political, social and organizational. Interaction and civic participation can amplify access to political discussion. Diverse sources, huge amounts of information along with opinions and sentiments from the public are available to journalists through online media and all these contents can be part of their reporting. Online media can contribute to public opinion by affecting politicians, who can refine their positions and (maybe) change or maintain their actions while others can use these channels in order to circulate their views. Corporations and brands have their products reviewed by users who can contribute by securing a quality collective evaluation. In this context of digital transformation the Multidisciplinary International Symposium on Disinformation in Open Online Media (MISDOOM) is an important bridge to researchers from a variety of disciplines such as computer science, communication and media studies, computational social science, information science, political communication, journalism and digital culture, as well as digital activists and practitioners in journalism and digital media. The main essence of the symposium is its strong multidisciplinarity and its aims to provide a space of discussion for different fields and disciplines that gather around the idea of disinformation.

This volume contains the papers accepted at the fifth edition of the symposium, organized in 2023. This volume also includes the abstracts of the talks given by the two invited keynote speakers. Following the success of last year's fully virtual format, MISDOOM 2023 was also held completely in person on November 21–22, 2023. In total, there were 57 submissions: 19 papers and 38 extended abstracts. Reviews were single-blind. Each extended abstract was reviewed by at least two program committee members. Each paper was reviewed by at least three program committee members. The program committee decided to accept 13 paper submissions in the computer science track for publication in this LNCS volume. In addition, a total of 43 contributions were accepted for presentation at the symposium. Figure 1 shows a summary of the topics of all contributions to the symposium.

We want to express our gratitude towards all those who contributed to organizing and running this symposium. This includes the Program Committee, the MISDOOM Steering Committee, The National Research Center for Mathematics and Computer Science in the Netherlands (CWI) and the sponsor: the European Research Center for Information Systems (ERCIS). We hope that participants of all communities taking part in this multidisciplinary endeavor had a nice symposium and found some new insights and personal connections, especially between communities that usually do not meet so often in a symposium setting.

**Fig. 1.** Topics of MISDOOM 2023. Size is proportional to the frequency of the word in the titles of the submissions accepted to the symposium.

November 2023

Davide Ceolin
Tommaso Caselli
Marina Tulin

# Organization

## General Chair

Davide Ceolin      Centrum Wiskunde & Informatica,
The Netherlands

## Program Committee Chairs

Tommaso Caselli      Rijksuniversiteit Groningen, The Netherlands
Marina Tulin      University of Amsterdam, The Netherlands

## Communications Chair

Atefeh Keshavarzi Zafarghandi      Centrum Wiskunde & Informatica,
The Netherlands

## Program Committee

| | |
|---|---|
| Adriana Amaral | Universidade do Vale do Rio dos Sinos, Brazil |
| Alessio Maria Braccini | Universitá degli Studi della Tuscia, Italy |
| Alexandra Pavliuc | University of Oxford, UK |
| André Calero Valdez | University of Lübeck, Germany |
| Angela Chang | University of Macau, China |
| Angelo Spognardi | University of Roma "La Sapienza", Italy |
| Ansgard Heinrich | Rijksuniversiteit Groningen, The Netherlands |
| Bram van Dijk | Leiden University, The Netherlands |
| Budi Nurani Ruchjana | Universitas Padjadjaran, Indonesia |
| Carlos d'Andréa | Universidade Federal de Minas Gerais, Brazil |
| Christian Grimme | University of Münster, Germany |
| Dennis Assenmacher | GESIS - Leibniz-Institut für Sozialwissenschaften, Germany |
| Dina Pisarevskaya | Queen Mary University of London, UK |
| Emma Sarah van der Goot | University of Amsterdam, The Netherlands |
| Enes Altuncu | University of Kent, UK |
| Eric Araújo | Universidade Federal de Lavras, Brazil |

| Gerhard Weiss | Maastricht University, The Netherlands |
| Gerasimos Spanakis | Maastricht University, The Netherlands |
| Henna Paakki | Aalto University, Finland |
| Janina S. Pohl | University of Münster, Germany |
| Jeremie Clos | University of Nottingham, UK |
| Joshua T. Nieubuurt | Old Dominion University, USA |
| Jozef Michal Mintal | Matej Bel University, Slovakia |
| Juan Pablo Bascur | University of Leiden, The Netherlands |
| Kun He | Rijksuniversiteit Groningen, The Netherlands |
| Lena Frischlich | University of Münster, Germany |
| Lennart Schäpermeier | Technische Universität Dresden, Germany |
| Leon Fröhling | GESIS - Leibniz-Institut für Sozialwissenschaften, Germany |
| Liesbeth Allein | KU Leuven, Belgium |
| Lilian Kojan | RWTH Aachen University, Germany |
| Lina Buttgereit | University of Amsterdam, The Netherlands |
| Louis Michael Shekhtman | Northeastern University, USA |
| Lotte van Poppel | Rijksuniversiteit Groningen, The Netherlands |
| Lucia Passaro | University of Pisa, Italy |
| Łukasz Grzegorz Gajewski | Warsaw University of Technology, Poland |
| Ludovic Terren | University of Antwerp, Belgium |
| Luiza da Silva Bodenmüller | Universidade Federal de Minas Gerais, Brazil |
| Mariele de Almeida Hochmüller | Universidad de Valencia, Spain |
| Marilia Gehrke | Rijksuniversiteit Groningen, The Netherlands |
| Matteo Gagliolo | Université libre de Bruxelles, Belgium |
| Mehwish Nasim | University of Western Australia, Australia |
| Meysam Alizadeh | University of Zurich, Switzerland |
| Michiel van der Meer | Leiden University, The Netherlands |
| Mike Preuss | University of Leiden, The Netherlands |
| Monika Hanley | University of London, UK |
| Nicoleta Corbu | National University of Political Studies and Public Administration, Romania |
| Peter van der Putten | Leiden University, The Netherlands |
| Sophie Morosoli | University of Amsterdam, The Netherlands |
| Sthembile N. Mthethwa | Council for Scientific and Industrial Research, South Africa |
| Thiago Magela Rodrigues Dias | Federal Center for Technological Education of Rio de Janeiro, Brazil |
| Thorsten Quandt | University of Münster, Germany |
| Travis Coan | University of Exeter, UK |

# Keynote Talks

# From Opacity to Clarity: Embracing Transparent and Accountable Fact Verification

Pepa Atanasova

University of Copenhagen
pepa@di.ku.dk

**Abstract.** Automating fact-checking processes is of paramount importance in the era of abundant online misinformation. Although substantial progress has been made in developing accurate systems, the focus must now shift towards ensuring transparency and accountability. The lack of understanding in the decision-making process of machine learning models, acting as black boxes, raises concerns about their reliability and trustworthiness.

This invited talk will delve into the significance of explainability in automated fact-checking. We will explore the state-of-the-art transparency methods that provide textual explanations for models' predictions, improving trust among stakeholders and enabling the identification of potential errors or biases. The talk will also present novel approaches to generate fluent, easy-to-read explanations with logically connected multi-chain arguments.

By emphasizing the importance of explainability, this talk aims to shed light on the potential benefits of transparent fact-checking models. Attendees will gain insights into how such explainability systems can bolster the analysis of model outputs, enhance decision-making processes, and contribute to building a more informed and trustworthy online information ecosystem.

# The User and the Algorithm: A Tug of War or Allies?

Judith Möller

University of Hamburg—Hans-Bredow-Institut
j.moeller@leibniz-hbi.de

**Abstract.** The relationship between users and algorithms in digital spaces remains a complex area of study. Dr. Judith Möller's research sheds light on how users interact with and influence their algorithmically curated information environments. Contrary to the perception that algorithms solely define content and user experience, evidence suggests that users play a more active role in determining their information spheres, if they want to. However, the real challenge lies in motivating users to recognize and harness the power they possess within these systems. Therefore, this talk will address the potential of nudges in these environments to guide users towards informed decisions. The aim of this keynote is to provide a balanced perspective on the intricate dynamics between users and algorithms in the digital age.

# Contents

# Generative AI for Explainable Automated Fact Checking on the FactEx: A New Benchmark Dataset

Saud Althabiti[1,2(✉)] , Mohammad Ammar Alsalka[1] , and Eric Atwell[1]

[1] University of Leeds, Leeds LS2 9JT, UK
salthabiti@kau.edu.sa, scssal@leeds.ac.uk
[2] King Abdulaziz University, Jeddah 22254, Saudi Arabia

**Abstract.** The immense volume of online information has made verifying claims' credibility more complex, increasing interest in automatic fact-checking models that classify evidence into binary or multi-class verdicts. However, there are few studies on predicting textual verdicts to explain claims' credibility. This field focuses on generating a textual verdict to explain a given claim based on a given news article. This paper presents our three-fold contribution to this field. Firstly, we collected the FactEx, an English dataset of facts with explanations from various fact-checking websites on different topics. Secondly, we employed seq2seq models and LLMs (namely T5, BERT2BERT, and BLOOM) to develop an automated fact-checking system. Lastly, we used ChatGPT to generate verdicts to check its performance and compared the results against other models. In addition, we explored the impact of dataset size on the model performance by conducting a series of experiments on seven different dataset sizes. The findings indicate that our fine-tuned T5-based model outperformed other generative LLMs and Seq2Seq Models with a ROUGE-1 score of about 26.75, making it the selected baseline for this task. Our study recommends examining the semantic similarity of the generative models for automatic fact-checking applications while also highlighting the importance of evaluating such models using additional techniques, such as crowd-based tools, to ensure the accuracy and reliability of the generated verdicts.

**Keywords:** FactEx Dataset · Automatic Fact-check · ChatGPT · Generative LLMs · NLP · Artificial Intelligence · Computer Science · Disinformation

## 1 Introduction

Fake news is a form of false information that can be intentionally spread through various media sources, such as traditional media, social media, or news websites [1]. The purpose of fake news is often to manipulate public opinion or beliefs, typically for political or financial gain [2–4]. It can be spread by individuals, organizations, or even governments to discredit opponents or promote their interests [4–6]. The consequences of fake news can be serious, creating confusion and mistrust, causing discord among different groups,

© The Author(s), under exclusive license to Springer Nature Switzerland AG 2023
D. Ceolin et al. (Eds.): MISDOOM 2023, LNCS 14397, pp. 1–13, 2023.
https://doi.org/10.1007/978-3-031-47896-3_1

and even inciting violence [7, 8]. Hence, it is essential to remain vigilant and critical of the information we consume, particularly online, and fact-check sources to differentiate between real and fake news.

This is where fact-checking websites play a crucial role in ensuring the information presented to the public is accurate and reliable. Fact-checking websites provide a platform for individuals to verify the authenticity of news and information by checking sources and validating claims [9]. These websites not only help in maintaining the integrity of information but also in educating people about how to identify fake news and misinformation. With the rise of social media and the increasing spread of fake news, the need for fact-checking websites has become more necessary than ever before [10]. One of the most popular fact-checking organizations is PolitiFact.com. It offers a rating system that assesses the accuracy of factual claims, including True, Half True, False, and "Pants on Fire" [11]. Another valuable way of fact-checking involves investigators examining related data and documents to evaluate claims and then disseminate their verdicts to the public, such as Fullfact.org.

However, manual fact-checking is tedious and too slow to keep up with the speed of online information. To address this, the journalism community can benefit from automating the fact-checking process using AI and NLP tools. This will help validate large amounts of new details that appear and spread quickly, motivating the need for automated fact-checking systems [10].

Although many systems have focused on binary or multi-class classification problems, such as predicting a binary verdict from text [10, 12, 13], this study investigates the use of sequence-to-sequence (Seq2Seq) and large language models (LLMs) to predict a textual verdict that explains a given claim based on a given article.

In our objective of generating explanations, we were initially motivated to explore one of the trending LLMs, such as ChatGPT, to see if it could justify a claim from the information provided in an article. As shown in Fig. 1, the generated verdict closely aligns with the human-written explanation on the trusted FullFact.org website. This shows the potential of such models to deliver reliable and comparable explanations, supporting our goal of advancing the field of explainable automatic fact-checking.

The purpose of this paper is to present our three-fold contribution, which includes:

- Collecting FactEx, a new English dataset for fact-checking explanations from trusted websites containing news articles, claims, and corresponding textual verdicts.
- We secondly fine-tuned some LLMs and seq2seq models, namely T5, BLOOM, and BERT2BERT architecture, to develop an automatic explainable fact-checking system and compare the results obtained from these models. The best-performing one is then subsequently published. To the best of our knowledge, we are the first to explore such effective architectures for this purpose.
- Last but not least, we attempt to consider a sample of our dataset to evaluate ChatGPT's capabilities by generating verdicts. We compare the results with other models to measure performances using the ROUGE scores.

The subsequent section includes a literature review of fake news detection and related work. Section three describes the methodology, including dataset collection, pre-processing, applying seq2seq models, and the evaluation method used. The results

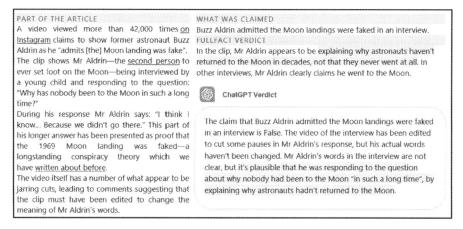

**Fig. 1.** Example from FullFact.org and a generated verdict using ChatGPT.

and discussion of the conducted experiments are detailed in the fourth section. Finally, we conclude this paper and suggest future work.

## 2  Related Work

Many NLP studies commonly view claim verification as a text classification task by building models that analyze a claim under investigation along with its retrieved evidence in order to reach a verdict regarding the claim. This verdict can typically be classified into different categories, such as support, contradict, or not enough information [14–19]. To implement classification tasks, various methods were used, including traditional machine learning algorithms, deep learning models, and Transformer-based models. These methods typically involve feature engineering and modeling steps, where text data is pre-processed, features are extracted, and a classification model is trained on labeled data [20, 21]. While in our study, we focus on seq2seq pre-trained models to provide an explanation rather than just a specific category.

Since the presence of textual justifications from journalists to explain verdicts is scarce in most available datasets [10], the study [22] expanded the LIAR dataset [11] by incorporating human justifications extracted from fact-checking articles. Although these justifications were initially intended as additional information to support claim verification and improve both binary and multi-classification tasks, it was also used by [23] to generate summaries. They employ an extractive method to generate justification summaries using DistilBERT. In contrast, the paper [24] adopted a joint approach involving both extractive and abstractive summarization. Additionally, they introduced the first dataset, which includes explanations crafted by journalists, fact-checking articles, and other news items related to public health claims [25]. Furthermore, [26] used the FEVER dataset [27] and a GPT-3-based system to generate summaries, resulting in a new dataset called e-FEVER consisting of 67,687 examples. On the other hand, this is the first study that investigates Seq2Seq models and compares them with generative large language models, such as ChatGPT, to generate claim verification explanations. Table 1 summarizes these studies regarding the utilized datasets and employed methods.

**Table 1.** Comparative of Related Studies: Datasets, Explanations (Ex), and Methodologies

| Study | Size | Topics | Explained by | Ex. Source | Model |
|-------|------|--------|--------------|------------|-------|
| [22] | 12,836 | Various | Humans | PolitiFact | ML models |
| [23] | 12,836 | Various | Humans | PolitiFact | DistilBERT |
| [26] | 67'687 | Various | Generated | Generated | GPT-3 |
| [25] | 11,832 | Health | Humans | Various | BERT |
| **FactEx** | 12,150 | Various | Humans | Various | T5, BERT2BERT, BLOOM, and ChatGPT |

# 3   Methodology

## 3.1   The FactEx Dataset

In order to train Seq2Seq models to predict explanations for fact-checking verdicts, we needed a dataset that combines claims, articles, and corresponding judgments. Therefore, we collected a new dataset named "**FactEx**"[1] (**Fact Ex**plained). The dataset contains 12,150 records from three trusted fact-checking websites, namely, FullFact.org, Politi-Fact.com, and BBC.co.uk, spanned from 2016 and 2023. This ensures that our dataset contains the most recent and relevant information from various reliable sources on different topics, such as health, economy, politics, education, and more. Initially, we used Google's fact-checking tool API, a tool that allows us to search for fact-checks previously published by fact-checking organizations, which provides a structured JASN file, as shown in Fig. 2. This streamlines the dataset collection process by handling JSON formatting.

We also collected the full articles related to each claim to make our dataset more informative by using the provided URLs with each claim, which yielded the following features to our dataset:

- URL [*string*]: The URL associated with the article.
- Title [*string*]: The title of the article.
- Text [*string*]: the claim text.
- TextualRating [*string*]: The verdict.
- Article [*string*]: The text content of the article.
- Article_HTML [*string*]: The text content of the article, including the HTML tags.
- Additional features such as, claimDate, claimant, and reviewDate.

---

[1] https://github.com/althabiti/FactEx.

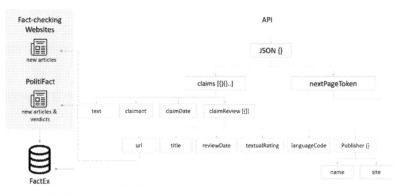

**Fig. 2.** The FactEx collection process using google API and NLP tools.

The FactEx dataset becomes more diverse and reliable by including content from different trustworthy sources. This makes it a valuable resource for researchers and practitioners working on automated fact-checking systems. Figure 3 provides an example from the FullFact.org website showcasing a claim, the related article, and a journalist's explanation of the verdict. While Fig. 4 presents a PolitiFact claim example and the relative website structure, which includes the title, article, and the verdict explanation, starting from the "Our ruling" section.

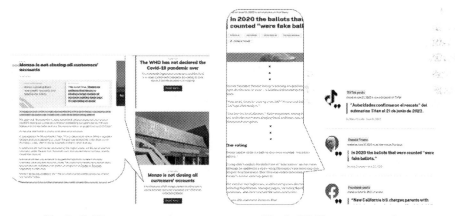

**Fig. 3.** FullFact.org example          **Fig. 4.** PlitiFact.com example

While retrieving the data, we encountered a challenge related to the inconsistent structure of the web pages. More specifically, the PolitiFact website has different styles that exhibit variations in the HTML tags and classes used to present articles and verdicts. This presented a significant obstacle in accurately extracting the desired content. To overcome this challenge, we adopted a two-step approach. Initially, we employed the BeautifulSoup library to scrape the entire web page, encompassing all HTML tags and content. Subsequently, we utilized NLP tools to selectively extract the relevant information, such as articles and verdicts, while filtering out irrelevant elements. This process allowed us to facilitate the impact of varying webpage structures and ensured the inclusion of all necessary information for our dataset. Furthermore, we included the URLs and HTML files in the dataset, enabling future enhancements as we aim to contribute to advancing research in the field of automated fact-checking. In addition, we excluded instances where the web pages contained lengthy explanations without explicitly mentioning the verdicts.

### 3.2   Preprocessing and Methods

In this study, we initially experimented with 900 claims samples from the collected FactEx dataset. We first split our dataset into three sets. Training: to train the model parameters; validation: for tuning hyperparameters; and testing: to check the performance of the tuned model. The sizes of the split data are 600, 150, and 150, respectively. Additional texts were prepended to each sample to help the selected models distinguish the contextual cues and establish a clear pattern for all samples. For example, *"claim:"* was prepended before each claim and *"article:"* before each new article. Secondly, a common practice when applying transformer models is to tokenize inputs and outputs. In this case, the article and a claim are the input, and the verdict is the target source we aim to predict.

It is generally challenging to train transformer-based models from scratch, requiring extensive datasets and high GPU memory. Therefore, to conduct the study, we decided to investigate four different models including T5, BERT2BERT, Bloom, and ChatGPT.

**T5** (**T**ext-**T**o-**T**ext **T**ransfer **T**ransformer) is a transformer-based language model developed by Google AI Language [28]. It is pre-trained on various natural language tasks using a text-to-text format, where the input and output are both text strings. As a result, T5 has achieved state-of-the-art results on various natural language processing tasks such as question answering, text summarization, and language translation [28]. We fine-tuned the T5-base model with learning rates of 4e-5 and 3 epochs.

**BERT** (**B**idirectional **E**ncoder **R**epresentations from **T**ransformers) is a powerful pre-trained encoder model that can be used to create a fix-sized representation of the text [29]. To use the model as a decoder, we followed the steps in a demonstrated architecture [30] that uses BERT to create an encoder-decoder architecture (BERT2BERT) for seq2seq models. We then fine-tuned the presented architecture on the 900 samples dataset using the default hyperparameters.

**BLOOM** is another open-source alternative for text generation. It is a recently released transformer-based large language model with about 176 billion parameters. We evaluated its performance on the 900 samples and compared it with the Seq2Seq models. Figure 5 illustrates the process structure of our experiments.

**GPT-3** (**G**enerative **P**re-trained **T**ransformer **3**) is a state-of-the-art language model developed by OpenAI [31]. It is a transformer-based language model that is trained on a massive corpus of diverse natural language data to generate human-like text.

**ChatGPT** is a fine-tuned model using reinforcement learning based on GPT-3 architecture [32]. It has a broad range of language capabilities, including language translation, question answering, text completion, and text summarization. OpenAI provides a full guide on how to fine-tune their models. Using their API, we integrated the "text-davinci-003" model and set the parameter "temperature" equal to 7 to increase the randomness of the generated texts [33], as we aim to predict an explanation rather than just a unique answer. Generative models, such as GPT3-based models can be effectively employed with minimal modifications, with or without fine-tuning as demonstrated by [26]. Therefore, we tested ChatGPT to see if it could provide a sound explanation when providing both the articles along with the claim on 180 samples with few-shot learning.

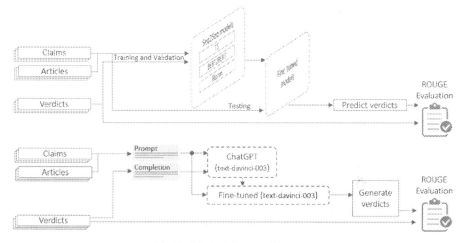

**Fig. 5.** Methodology architecture

To fine-tune the model, two main things should be provided: prompt and completion. Within each prompt $P$, we instructed the model to follow the steps that should be considered for the generation, along with claims $C$ and articles $A$ and provided the verdicts $V$ to be the completion appended with an ending tag. After training 20 samples, we tested the fine-tuned ChatGPT model on 160 samples to generate explanations by providing prompts, as the explained pseudocode in Algorithm 1, including the instruction $I$, claims, and articles only.

---

**Algorithm 1: Prompt used to instruct the fine-tuned generative model**

     **Input:** $C_i, A_i$   where $i \in FactEx$
     **Output:** $V_i$

1    $I \leftarrow$ "Given a text article starting from 'text_article:' and a claim starting from 'claim:', suggest a verdict based on possible evidence retrieved from the article."
2    **for** $i = 1$ **to** $n$
3        $M_i \leftarrow$ [{"role": "system", "content": "You are an automatic Fact Checker acting like a journalist" $+ I + A_i + C_i$}]
4        $P_i \leftarrow$ ({"role": "assistant", "content": $M_i$})
5        $V_i \leftarrow$ getCompletion($P_i$)
6    **end for**

---

## 3.3  Evaluation

The two widely used text generation tasks are machine translation and text summarization, evaluated by BLEU and ROUGE scores, respectively. BLEU (Bilingual Evaluation
Understudy) is mainly used for evaluating machine translation systems. It calculates
how well the generated translation aligns with one or more reference translations [34].
In contrast, ROUGE (Recall-Oriented Understudy for Gisting Evaluation) is a more
general metric for evaluating various NLP tasks, such as text summarization [35]. In our
task, the verdict generation is comparable to text summarization as it aims to convey
the article's essence to the reader; hence we will evaluate our results using the ROUGE
score [35, 36].

# 4   Results and Discussion

## 4.1  LLMs and Seq2Seq Results Comparison

As we initially split the dataset to train and validate, we tested them on the fine-tuned
models. The results of the predicted verdicts are evaluated using ROUGE-1, ROUGE-
2, ROUGE-L, and ROUGE-Lsum scores. ROUGE-1 is the overlapping of unigram or
each word between the human verdicts and the predicted explanations, ROUGE-2 is the
overlapping of bigrams, and ROUGE-L and ROUGE-Lsum are calculating the longest
common subsequent to capture sentence structure. While the ROUGE-L is computed
as the average of individual sentences, the ROUGE-Lsum is calculated over the whole
predicted text [35].
    One of the objectives of this paper is to test a sample of claims and articles to generate
verdicts using ChatGPT to compare its performance with journalists' verdicts and other
Seq2Seq methods. Table 2 indicates that the fine-tuned T5 model outperformed other
models when evaluating using the ROUGE score.

**Table 2.**  Testing results using ROUGE metrics.

| Used Model | rouge1 | rouge2 | rougeL | rougeLsum |
|---|---|---|---|---|
| **Our T5-based model** | **26.75** | **10.45** | **21.95** | **23.43** |
| BERT2BERT | 18.89 | 04.07 | 14.18 | 14.22 |
| Bloom | 03.54 | 01.84 | 02.84 | 03.24 |
| ChatGPT | 10.87 | 01.67 | 08.57 | 08.65 |

## 4.2  Model's Performance vs Dataset Size

To explore the impact of dataset size on the model performance, we specifically focused
on investigating the T5-small. We conducted a series of experiments on different dataset
sizes, ranging from 900 to 1500 samples. We fine-tuned using approximately four-sixths

of the dataset for training, one-sixth for validation, and the remaining for testing in each case and calculated ROUGE metrics. Upon analysis, we observed that the results exhibited a slight fluctuated increase with no significant difference among the dataset sizes tested. ROUGE-1 scores, for instance, range from approximately 23.4 to 25.3, as shown in Fig. 6. Given this, increasing the dataset size does not consistently lead to a considerable improvement in the model's performance. Therefore, we decided to use our trained T5-based model, presented in Table 2 as a baseline model for the task of automatic textual fact-checking explanations. Our model can be found on the HuggingFace.co repository[2].

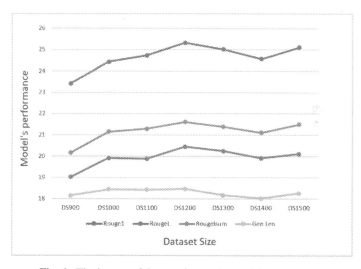

**Fig. 6.** The impact of dataset size on the model performance.

Table 3 presents two examples, each featuring a verdict and its source. In the first example, FullFact determined that the claim was true, and our model successfully classified the overall truthfulness of the claim, unlike the BERT2BERT model, which discredited the claim's credibility from the beginning. On the other hand, the second example compares a FullFact judgment with a verdict generated by ChatGPT. Although the claim is accurate for part of the claim, as the FullFact deemed, the generated text explained that by stating "Partly true", some of the chosen words align with those of the FullFact.

Despite the low scores, these instances showed promising outcomes. As seen in Table 3, T5 generates exact word matches, such as "correct" and "Switzerland", whereas the others generate meanings that may be more or less related but not the exact words. Since the ROUGE metrics are based on the same exact word matches and compute the overlap of n-grams (consecutive words of length n), it led to a significant difference between the results. Therefore, the meaning of the entire sentence must be considered in future evaluations.

---

[2] https://huggingface.co/althabiti/VerdictGen_t5-based.

**Table 3.** Two examples of human verdicts compared with generated verdicts.

| Source | Verdict |
| --- | --- |
| FullFact[3] | That's correct. Switzerland has some access to the EU's single market. It pays financially for this and takes on certain EU laws |
| **Our T5-based model** | It is correct. The EU imported a 20,000 of goods and services per person from Switzerland |
| BERT2BERT | It is not true, but it does not necessarily mean it would have to be used to contradict the uk. But it does not mean it can be used as a currency, … |
| FullFact[4] | This claim does not factor in people who identified as white but not white British, and so is not true for either London or Manchester. It is accurate for Birmingham, where 48.6% identified as white |
| GPT-3 based model | Verdict: Partly true: Minority group identified surveyed based across empty ethnic general become more usual England constituent cities nation |

## 5   Conclusion and Future Work

As online information increases continuously, it has become increasingly challenging for individuals to verify the truthfulness of claims they encounter. To address this problem, there is a growing interest in developing automatic fact-checking models that can analyze textual evidence and classify them into binary verdicts about the veracity of claims, for example, "True or False". However, fewer studies explored the problem of predicting textual explanations of claim credibility.

This paper has three main contributions, as we aim to develop an explainable automatic fact-checking model to assess the truthfulness of claims based on supporting articles. To achieve this goal, we first created the FactEx, a new dataset containing 12,150 samples on different topics from three trusted fact-checking websites. Each sample has various features, including a claim and a verdict (an explanation) paired with a corresponding article to serve as evidence for our model.

We then applied a seq2seq architecture to generate explanations for each claim by fine-tuning our models to achieve better performance. In the process, we conducted a comparison of different generative LLMS and seq2seq models, namely, T5, BERT2BERT, BLOOM, and ChatGPT, by evaluating their ROUGE scores. Based on our findings, we observed that the fine-tuned T5-based model outperforms other models with about 26.75 ROUGE1 score and made it publicly available for future use as a baseline model for this task. On the other hand, the discussion recommends investigating the semantic similarities rather than just the syntactic for the generative models, such as ChatGPT, which have strong potential for use in automatic fact-checking applications.

---

[3] https://fullfact.org/europe/vote-leave-facts-leaflet-exports/
[4] https://fullfact.org/immigration/nigel-farage-census-london-manchester/

We also concluded that increasing the dataset size does not always lead to a considerable improvement in the model's performance, as we utilized the T5-small model across seven different dataset size attempts.

While there is still much room for improvement in model robustness and evaluation technique, the results of this study provide a strong foundation for future research in this area. We also aim to extend this methodology to other languages, such as Arabic, since there are fewer fact-checking websites. In terms of evaluation, conducting a comprehensive human assessment to evaluate the extent to which ROUGE scores align with semantic similarity would be valuable. This could involve engaging experts in the field of misinformation, including journalists, social scientists, and politicians, to provide a more nuanced understanding of the quality of our model's explanations. As our main focus is on the automation parts of the task, joint efforts in this direction could significantly contribute to a deeper understanding of the relationship between automated metrics like ROUGE and human judgment, including assessing its accuracy and coherence. Furthermore, we aim to create a crowdsourcing tool for users to get a larger pool of evaluators to determine the generated verdicts and provide feedback.

## References

1. Shu, K., Sliva, A., Wang, S., Tang, J., Liu, H.: Fake news detection on social media: a data mining perspective. ACM SIGKDD Explor. Newsl. **19**(1), 22–36 (2017)
2. Tandoc, E.C., Jr., Lim, Z.W., Ling, R.: Defining 'fake news' a typology of scholarly definitions. Digit. Journalism **6**(2), 137–153 (2018)
3. Jahng, M.R., Lee, H., Rochadiat, A.: Public relations practitioners' management of fake news: exploring key elements and acts of information authentication. Public Relat. Rev. **46**(2), 101907 (2020)
4. Tejedor, S., Portalés-Oliva, M., Carniel-Bugs, R., Cervi, L.: Journalism students and information consumption in the era of fake news. Media Commun. **9**(1), 338–350 (2021)
5. Andorfer, A.: Spreading like wildfire: solutions for abating the fake news problem on social media via technology controls and government regulation. Hastings LJ **69**, 1409 (2017)
6. Rapti, M., Tsakalidis, G., Petridou, S., Vergidis, K.: Fake news incidents through the lens of the DCAM disinformation blueprint. Information **13**(7), 306 (2022)
7. Rocha, Y.M., de Moura, G.A., Desidério, G.A., de Oliveira, C.H., Louren-ço, F.D., de Figueiredo Nicolete, L.D.: The impact of fake news on social media and its influence on health during the COVID-19 pandemic: a systematic review. J. Public Health (Bangkok) **31**(7), 1–10 (2021)
8. Khan, S.A. Alkawaz, M.H. Zangana, H.M.: The use and abuse of social media for spreading fake news. In: 2019 IEEE International Conference on Automatic Control and Intelligent Systems (I2CACIS), pp. 145–148. IEEE (2019)
9. Zlatkova, D., Nakov, P., Koychev, I.: Fact-checking meets fauxtography: verifying claims about images. arXiv preprint arXiv:1908.11722 (2019)
10. Guo, Z., Schlichtkrull, M., Vlachos, A.: A survey on automated fact-checking. Trans. Assoc. Comput. Linguist. **10**, 178–206 (2022)
11. Wang, W.Y.: liar, liar pants on fire: a new benchmark dataset for fake news detection. arXiv preprint arXiv:1705.00648 (2017)
12. Zeng, X., Abumansour, A.S., Zubiaga, A.: Automated fact-checking: a survey. Lang. Linguist. Compass **15**(10), e12438 (2021)

13. Naderi, N., Hirst, G.: Automated fact-checking of claims in argumentative parliamentary debates. In: Proceedings of the First Workshop on Fact Extraction and VERification (FEVER), pp. 60–65 (2018)
14. Alanazi, S.S., Khan, M.B.: Arabic fake news detection in social media using readers' comments: text mining techniques in action. Int. J. Comput. Sci. Netw. Secur. **20**(9), 29–35 (2020)
15. Althabiti, S., Alsalka, M., Atwell, E.: SCUoL at CheckThat! 2021: an AraBERT model for check-worthiness of Arabic tweets. In: CEUR Workshop Proceedings (2021)
16. Köhler, J.: Overview of the CLEF-2022 CheckThat! lab task 3 on fake news detection. In: Working Notes of CLEF 2022—Conference and Labs of the Evaluation Forum, Bologna, Italy (2022)
17. Nakov, P., et al.: Overview of the CLEF-2022 CheckThat! lab on fighting the COVID-19 infodemic and fake news detection. In: Proceedings of the 13th International Conference of the CLEF Association: Information Access Evaluation meets Multilinguality, Multimodality, and Visualization, Bologna, Italy (2022)
18. Nakov, P., et al.: The CLEF-2022 CheckThat! lab on fighting the COVID-19 infodemic and fake news detection. In: European Conference on Information Retrieval, Springer, pp. 416–428 (2022). https://doi.org/10.1007/978-3-030-99739-7_52
19. Althabiti, S., Alsalka, M.A., Atwell, E.: SCUoL at CheckThat! 2022: fake news detection using transformer-based models. In: CEUR Workshop Proceedings, CEUR Workshop Proceedings, pp. 428–433 (2022)
20. Zhou, X., Zafarani, R.: A survey of fake news: fundamental theories, detection methods, and opportunities. ACM Comput. Surv. (2020). https://doi.org/10.1145/3395046
21. Althabiti, S., Alsalka, M.A., Atwell, E.: Detecting Arabic fake news on social media using sarcasm and hate speech in comments. Int. J. Islamic Appl. Comput. Sci. Technol. (IJASAT) **10**(4), 28–36 (2022)
22. Alhindi, T., Petridis, S., Muresan, S.: Where is your evidence: improving fact-checking by justification modeling. In: Proceedings of the first work-shop on fact extraction and verification (FEVER), pp. 85–90 (2018)
23. Atanasova, P., Simonsen, J.G., Lioma, C., Augenstein, I.: Generating fact checking explanations. arXiv preprint arXiv:2004.05773 (2020)
24. Kotonya, N., Toni, F.: Explainable automated fact-checking: a survey. arXiv preprint arXiv:2011.03870 (2020)
25. Kotonya, N., Toni, F.: Explainable automated fact-checking for public health claims. arXiv preprint arXiv:2010.09926 (2020)
26. Stammbach, D., Ash, E.: e-FEVER: explanations and summaries for automated fact checking. In: Proceedings of the 2020 Truth and Trust Online (TTO 2020), pp. 32–43 (2020)
27. Thorne, J., Vlachos, A., Christodoulopoulos, C., Mittal, A.: Fever: a large-scale dataset for fact extraction and verification. arXiv preprint arXiv:1803.05355 (2018)
28. Raffel, C., et al.: Exploring the limits of transfer learning with a unified text-to-text transformer. J. Mach. Learn. Res. **21**(1), 5485–5551 (2020)
29. Devlin, J., Chang, M.-W., Lee, K., Toutanova, K.: Bert: pre-training of deep bidirectional transformers for language understanding. arXiv preprint arXiv:1810.04805 (2018)
30. Falaki, A.A.: How to train a seq2seq summarization model using 'BERT' as both encoder and decoder!! (BERT2BERT) (2022). https://pub.towardsai.net/how-to-train-a-seq2seq-summarization-model-using-bert-as-both-encoder-and-decoder-bert2bert-2a5fb36559b8
31. Floridi, L., Chiriatti, M.: GPT-3: Its nature, scope, limits, and consequences. Minds Mach. (Dordr) **30**, 681–694 (2020). https://doi.org/10.1007/s11023-020-09548-1
32. Hassani, H., Silva, E.S.: The role of ChatGPT in data science: how Ai-assisted conversational interfaces are revolutionizing the field. Big Data Cogn. Comput. **7**(2), 62 (2023)

33. Zong, M., Krishnamachari, B.: a survey on GPT-3. arXiv preprint arXiv:2212.00857 (2022)
34. Papineni, K., Roukos, S., Ward, T., Zhu, W.-J.: Bleu: a method for automatic evaluation of machine translation. In: Proceedings of the 40th annual meeting of the Association for Computational Linguistics, pp. 311–318 (2002)
35. Lin, C.-Y.: ROUGE: a package for automatic evaluation of summaries. In: Text summarization branches out, pp. 74–81 (2004)
36. Wazery, Y.M., Saleh, M.E., Alharbi, A., Ali, A.A.: Abstractive Arabic text summarization based on deep learning. Comput. Intell. Neurosci. **2022**, 1–14 (2022)

# Multi-Modal Embeddings for Isolating Cross-Platform Coordinated Information Campaigns on Social Media

Fabio Barbero, Sander op den Camp, Kristian van Kuijk[ID],
Carlos Soto García-Delgado, Gerasimos Spanakis[ID],
and Adriana Iamnitchi[(✉)][ID]

Department of Advanced Computing Sciences, Maastricht University,
Maastricht, The Netherlands
{fabio.barbero,sjgm.opdencamp,kristian.vankuijk,
c.sotogarciadelgado}@student.maastrichtuniversity.nl,
{jerry.spanakis,a.iamnitchi}@maastrichtuniversity.nl

**Abstract.** Coordinated multi-platform information operations are implemented in a variety of contexts on social media, including state-run disinformation campaigns, marketing strategies, and social activism. Characterized by the promotion of messages via multi-platform coordination, in which multiple user accounts, within a short time, post content advancing a shared informational agenda on multiple platforms, they contribute to an already confusing and manipulated information ecosystem. To make things worse, reliable datasets that contain "ground truth" information about such operations are virtually nonexistent. This paper presents a multi-modal approach that identifies the social media messages potentially engaged in a coordinated information campaign across multiple platforms. Our approach incorporates textual content, temporal information and the underlying network of user and messages posted to identify groups of messages with unusual coordination patterns across multiple social media platforms. We apply our approach to content posted on four platforms related to the Syrian Civil Defence organization known as the White Helmets: Twitter, Facebook, Reddit, and YouTube. Results show that our approach identifies social media posts that link to news YouTube channels with similar factuality score, which is often an indication of coordinated operations.

**Keywords:** Information operations · Time/text/network embeddings

## 1   Introduction

While social media platforms may be independently attempting to detect nefarious information campaigns within their own platforms, the problems due to multi-platform coordination are not likely to be addressed in the current environment of legislature void and platforms' competition for user attention.

D. Ceolin et al. (Eds.): MISDOOM 2023, LNCS 14397, pp. 14–28, 2023.
https://doi.org/10.1007/978-3-031-47896-3_2

Previous research has shown that information operations online are now much more sophisticated than networks of coordinated bots that (re)broadcast some messages. Instead, such coordinated efforts i) are concurrently deployed on multiple social and alternative news media platforms [9, 14]; ii) promote the intended message by means specific to each platform (such as videos on YouTube and written news or opinion articles on alternative media websites) [5, 21]; iii) amplify the same message by repeating it in altered forms (such as including the same video footage in multiple videos posted on different channels on YouTube) [5, 14]; and iv) amplify the same content via platform-specific affordabilities, such as retweeting on Twitter vs. liking/commenting on YouTube to possibly manipulate the platform's content promotion algorithms [5, 12].

Due to limited datasets on such covert, often undetected operations, previous research focused on specific contexts (for example, the Russian Internet Research Agency's engagement in influencing the US 2016 elections) and on single platforms, typically the promotion of specific URLs on Twitter. Yet coordinated online information campaigns continue to be employed by various state, business, or social actors for various purposes, from disinformation and monetization to activism and public health campaigns. Although some are carried out by legitimate groups or individuals, many campaigns may be supported by entities with undisclosed motivations, such as foreign governments or political parties, and may not be transparent about their underlying goal [12, 15, 21]. While social media platforms reacted to some of such problems and typically blocked accounts seen to engage in coordinated information operations[1], coordinated operations deployed on multiple platforms can escape the vigilance of individual platforms if they keep a low profile on any particular platform.

This paper proposes a methodology that, given a multi-platform collection of social media posts, identifies a subset of such posts that are likely to be part of a coordinated information campaign and clusters them based on content and posting time locality. Clusters with only one post are likely to represent messages that do not participate in a coordinated campaign, thus ignoring them can reduce the dataset that needs to be further analysed by human operators or via computational means. We show on a multi-platform datasets that includes content posted on Twitter, Facebook, Reddit and YouTube that by using multi-modal approaches (text, network structures, and time) we can identify similar messages that not only link to the same URL (as previous work has been done) but link to different URLs of similar factuality as reported by the Media Bias/Fact Check website[2]. In the lack of ground-truth datasets that clearly mark which messages are part of a coordinated operation, we use agreement on factuality within a cluster as a performance metric.

Our approach can work on diverse combinations of platforms and on diverse topics without the requirement to identify whether messages are factual or not. This generality is due to the design of our approach that: 1) considers only messages that introduce new information on the platform (e.g., tweets on Twitter

---

[1] https://transparency.twitter.com/en/reports/moderation-research.html.
[2] https://mediabiasfactcheck.com/.

but not retweets; posts and comments on Reddit, etc.), thus not depending on platform-specific message promotion algorithms or functionalities; 2) it detects coordination in the absence of shared tokens (such as hashtags or URLs). However, our technique works under the assumptions that coordinated campaigns push semantically similar (but not identical) messages within a short time.

## 2    Related Work

Intentional spread of fake news with political or financial objectives has been studied for cases such as Brexit [3], COVID-19 [4,6] and the Syrian War [1,21]. Sometimes, these fake news are known to be posted and promoted by bots [9]. The behaviour of these bots has been studied, and different datasets exist for their activity [19] on platforms such as Twitter. Furthermore, such campaigns are also known to often be coordinated. Ratkiewicz et al. [17] describe a machine learning framework that combines topological, content-based and crowdsourced features of information diffusion networks to detect the early stages of viral spreading of political misinformation. Sharma et al. [20] investigates user activity embeddings to find coordination between accounts and is trained using labelled data. Because labelled data are not always available, others have looked at unsupervised clustering methods. Fazil and Abulasih [8], Pachero et al. [16] and Magelinski et al. [13] all explored creating a user network based on similarities in user profiles, activity, or post content. They cluster the resulting network to identify groups of users showing signs of coordination. These methods have each focused on one category of features but have not looked much at combining different modalities. In addition, all of them use single-platform data. However, there is significant evidence to suggest that these coordinated campaigns do not limit themselves to only one social media platform. Lukito et al. [12] explore the activity of the Internet Research Agency (IRA), a Russian company engaged in online propaganda and influence operations, on three social media platforms, Facebook, Twitter, and Reddit, to understand how the activities on these sites were temporally coordinated. Ng et al. [14] studied how coordinated campaigns occurred for the White Helmets across YouTube, Facebook and Twitter, and how they can exhibit certain patterns when studying time and relationships between users and posts. Our paper uses multi-modal data (text, network structures and time) to identify likely coordinated groups that post similar content in a synchronized manner on multiple platforms.

## 3    Datasets

One topic known to have been part of information campaigns is the White Helmets [14]. The White Helmets[3] (WH) is a volunteer organization that operates in rebel held areas of Syria. They perform medical evacuation, urban search and rescue in response to bombing, evacuation of civilians from danger areas

---

[3] https://www.whitehelmets.org/en/.

and often publish videos showing the human impacts of the conflict. The WH is known to have been a target of information campaigns by supporters of the Syrian president Bashar al-Assad and Russian state-sponsored media organizations such as Russia Today (RT) and Sputnik, for instance, accusing the WH of faking evidence of atrocities.

For this paper, we used data from the White Helmet campaign as described in [14], which we expanded with our collection of Reddit data and augmented with factuality scores from Media Bias/Fact Check. This dataset was originally built by collecting YouTube videos that include"White Helmets" in different languages in the video's title or description. The videos identified this way were posted between September 2006 and April 2019. Each video is uniquely identified by a *video ID* and contains information on the *video title, video channel name, published time* and *video captions* (which can be automatically generated by YouTube). Comments on the videos are not included, nor the number of users subscribed to the channel. Using the GNIP Twitter API in early 2019, tweets that include the YouTube videos URLs on White Helmets in our collection were collected. Later on, data was collected from CrowdTangle on Facebook messages posted between April 2018 and April 2019 that include the YouTube video URLs from the original dataset.

To collect Reddit data, we performed an identical platform search to NG et al [14] by fetching posts during the same time frame (April 1, 2018 to April 30, 2019) containing videos from our dataset. We used the Pushshift Reddit Dataset [2] in March 2023. Pushshift has collected Reddit data and made it available to researchers since 2015, updated in real-time, and including historical data back to Reddit's inception [2]. Pushshift includes submissions (posts) and comments that have since been deleted by Reddit or subreddit moderators. Because of the free availability of this data, we also do not have to limit our search to specific keywords, but can find every submission and comment made that includes any of the relevant URLs from the collected YouTube data. Nevertheless, shortly after our data collection, Reddit officially removed their API access. While Pushshift still retrieves Reddit data, access is only granted for moderation purposes to approved Reddit moderators.

Each message in our dataset is identified by a unique *post ID*, and has information on the *user ID, published time, platform, text content, action type* (whether it is a post or a reply) and linked *video ID*. Through a language detection model, we noticed that more than 83% of the posts are in English, with the second most used language being Arabic with 6.9% of posts. We present the characteristics of our dataset in Table 1.

Our cross-platform dataset thus contains posts from Twitter, Facebook and Reddit that include URLs to videos that have "White Helmets" in their descriptions or titles on YouTube. This dataset may include authentic messages in addition to messages that may be part of the well-documented coordinated campaign against the White Helmets. Since the dataset is unlabelled, we augmented it with the Factuality Score on the Media Bias/Fact Check (MBFC) website. The factuality score is an integer ranging from 0 to 5, with 0 being "Very Low" and 5

"Very High" that is assigned currently to more than 6,800 news websites based on information from fact-checkers that are either a signatory of the International Fact-Checking Network or have been verified as credible by MBFC.

We labelled ≈ 30 questionable video channels and ≈ 30 mostly factual video channels, with questionable sources being the most frequent in the dataset. In fact, the three most posted video channels have a very low factuality score. Clarity of Signal, RT and Vanessa Beeley are present in 2505 posts, 2073 and 1824 posts, respectively. A total of 9757 posts in our dataset posted a video labelled with a factuality score, with 7273 posts having a factuality score of 0 (74.5%) and 1888 posts a factuality score of 1 (19.4%).

**Table 1.** Characteristics of the multi-platform dataset on White Helmets. YouTube video URLs are used to collect relevant messages posted on the other social media platforms during the April 2018–April 2019 interval.

| Platform | Posts | YT URLs | YT channels | Users |
|---|---|---|---|---|
| Reddit | 481 | 113 | 63 | 266 |
| Twitter | 15,314 | 666 | 283 | 4927 |
| Facebook | 1,146 | 241 | 100 | 684 |
| YouTube | – | 667 | 283 | – |

## 4    Methodology

Our objective is to design an approach based on content similarity and time locality that identifies groups of messages that are likely coordinated. Because we do not have ground truth information at fine granularity—that is, we do not know which are the particular messages or the user accounts involved in a campaign—we need to find different ways to evaluate the likelihood that our groupings make sense.

The approach we propose makes some assumptions about coordinated information operations, listed in Sect. 4.1. It includes two clustering stages, one based on text and network embeddings and one based on the time lapse between posts on social media platforms. We experiment with two text embeddings techniques, Doc2Vec and BERTopic, as presented in Sect. 4.2. Furthermore, we define a user-to-content network and extract its network embeddings using Node2Vec [11] and, alternatively, MetaPath [7], that we append to our textual embeddings. Finally, we account for temporal dynamics by incorporating a final clustering component based on post time. The final pipeline leverages multimodal embeddings by combining text similarity, temporal information and the network structure of users, posts, and shared links. Figure 1 illustrates our processing pipeline.

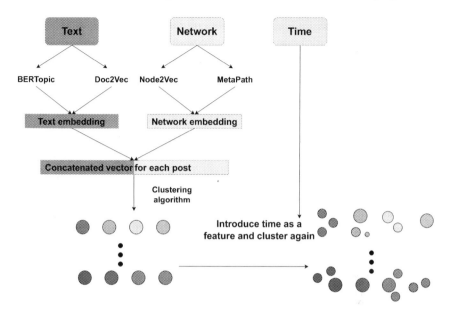

**Fig. 1.** Methodology pipeline overview. Textual and network embeddings are concatenated, after which we perform a first clustering on the produced embeddings and a second clustering on the time component.

### 4.1  Assumptions

Our approach makes the following assumptions:

*Coordinated campaigns are characterized by messages posted closely in time and that discuss similar topics.* This may not always be the case: a coordinated campaign may publish posts throughout a longer period of time, and mostly exploit liking each other posts to make them more visible.

*Text embeddings of posts across social media platforms are comparable.* This implies that the language used across social media platforms is similar, and that the language model used will encode them similarly. In practice, this may not always be the case: e.g., tweets are known to be shorter than Reddit posts.

*Links posted by coordinated campaigns are from sources with similar factuality scores.* The underlying idea is that a coordinated campaign is unlikely to be posting about sources with conflicting viewpoints. In practice, we might have reliable sources being discredited in a coordinated campaign, alongside other less reliable posts.

Apart from the Node2Vec method, all other methods assume that *past user's activity is not relevant for identifying coordinated campaigns.* This seems to differ among campaigns, and has been seen to be true in some campaigns, such as AIMS [9].

Given these assumptions, our methodology builds on temporal, network and textual proximity of posts with the goal of detecting potential coordinated campaigns. Having specific thresholds for the proximity allows us to identify groups (clusters) that are potentially part of the same campaign.

## 4.2   Text (Semantic) Similarity

We explored two approaches that can handle the text content of posts, namely Doc2Vec and BERTopic. They are both enhanced by a temporal component, as described in Sect. 4.4.

**Doc2Vec.** Our first approach combines Doc2Vec with K-means. The following steps outline the process. We start with a Doc2Vec representation of each post. This technique enables us to effectively capture the semantic relationships between posts, facilitating subsequent clustering. We then perform an initial clustering with $K$-means to group semantically similar posts together. We determine the number of clusters based on the characteristics of the dataset. To further refine the clustering results by accounting for temporal dynamics, we employ the Density-Based Spatial Clustering of Applications with Noise (DBSCAN) algorithm. We provide more details on the latter part in Sect. 4.4.

**BERTopic.** Our second approach involves BERTopic to obtain clusters for all posts with a topic representation of the clusters [10]. BERTopic uses Sentence-BERT to build 384 dimensional embeddings per document. We then apply UMAP for dimensionality reduction, mainly so the clustering is more efficient. For clustering, we employ HDBSCAN, a hierarchical density-based clustering algorithm. Lastly, we obtain our topic representations from clusters with c-TF-IDF, generating candidates by extracting class-specific words. To improve our topic representations, we end the pipeline with Maximum Candidate Relevance. Note, while we implement the same pipeline as the original paper, each component could be replaced by alternatives. For instance, one could employ PCA instead of UMAP for dimensionality reduction. As with Doc2Vec we apply DBSCAN to get clusters based on temporal information as well.

## 4.3   Network Similarity: Random Walks

We define a network that connects users across social media platforms as shown in Fig. 2. In this multipartite network, edges connect users to their posts, posts to videos, and videos to channels. While this definition is specific to the dataset and social media platforms we used, it can be generalised to, for example, (URLS to) online articles (instead of YouTube videos) and their hosting websites (instead of YouTube channels). This structure does not capture text or temporal information but only information on user interaction with content (URLs). However, this allows us to create graph embeddings for each post using Node2Vec, as nodes are only sparsely connected. We concatenate these network embeddings to the text embeddings described in Sect. 4.2. To align both embeddings, we perform

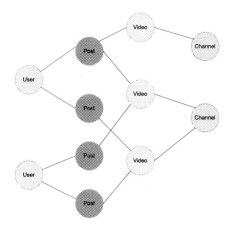

**Fig. 2.** Example network structure.

dimensionality reduction on both representations, such that both embedding vectors have the same length (64 in our case).

Node2Vec does not take into account the different typed of nodes in a network. In our network, there are four types of nodes: users, posts, videos and channels. Since this information might be important and to account for these different types of nodes, we apply meta-paths [7]. Meta-paths guide the random walks by only allowing a fixed set of paths. In this paper, we set the following paths: [user, post, video, post, user]; [video, channel, video]; [post, user, post] and [channel, video, channel]. This allows us to incorporate semantic information on node types into the network embeddings.

## 4.4 Temporal Dynamics

We assume coordinated campaigns occur within a short timeframe. By considering the temporal dimension, we ensure that we detect subgroups (subclusters) containing posts that are not only semantically similar, but also close in time (i.e. posted close in time). Hence, we subdivide clusters obtained from Doc2Vec and BERTopic to account for temporal dynamics through a DBSCAN algorithm. We choose $\epsilon = 52$ seconds as suggested by [14] for the same dataset we used. This is the inter-arrival time threshold in seconds between a video's first share on any platform (either Twitter or Facebook) and all successive shares. For more details on our choice of $\epsilon$, we refer to [14]. With this approach accounting for temporal dynamics, we aim to facilitate the discovery of underlying patterns and trends, shedding light on coordinated activities that may impact the analysed content and enhancing our understanding of the data and identifying potential coordinated efforts.

# 5   Results

In this section, we first describe the metrics we use to evaluate our methods. We then perform an ablation study among the three components (text, network and time) of our approach to evaluate how each affects the performance of our approach. Finally, we further investigate different values for certain hyperparameters.

## 5.1   Metrics

To evaluate the effectiveness of our approach, we employ two metrics: the standard deviation of factuality scores among clusters and the silhouette score for the clustering of Doc2Vec, BERTopic and Random Walks features before and after temporal subdivision. The following analysis provides insights into the performance and detection capabilities of our approach.

**Silhouette Score:** We assess the quality of the clustering results by computing the silhouette score [18]. The silhouette score measures the cohesion and separation of data points within clusters. A higher silhouette score indicates better-defined and more distinct clusters. We compute the silhouette score using the features before and after applying the temporal subdivision, providing insights into the improvement achieved through the incorporation of temporal considerations.

**Standard Deviation of Factuality Scores.** We calculate the factuality score for posts containing YouTube links, which rates the factual accuracy of the information in the respective YouTube channels. After executing the entire pipeline, we analyse the factuality score for each cluster. A low standard deviation among the factuality scores indicates that our algorithms cluster posts sharing videos of similar factuality, whether they are questionable or of high factuality, whereas a higher standard deviation suggests potential variations in the factual accuracy of the information within the clusters. We report the average, median, standard deviation, and proportion of 0 standard deviation in clusters among all clusters. We also provide the standard deviation of all posts.

## 5.2   Evaluation: Ablation Study

To evaluate the performance of our clustering, we compare the silhouette score and the intra-cluster standard deviation in factuality score. As mentioned in Sect. 4.1, we expect coordinated campaigns on social media to share sources of similar factuality, whether questionable or high factuality. As we end the pipelines of both methods by subclustering with regards to the posts' time, we compare the factuality standard deviation pre- and post-time clustering, and the effect of our graph embeddings on these metrics. Table 2 presents our results.

**Table 2.** Evaluation of different approaches. We calculate the factuality standard deviation on clusters of 2 or more posts. $\propto 0$ denotes the proportion of Factuality Standard Deviation of 0 obtained through all clusters. The total standard deviation in the dataset is 0.75. N2V denotes Node2Vec and MP2V Metapath2Vec.

| Methods | Silhouette Score | Factuality Standard Deviation | | | |
|---|---|---|---|---|---|
| | | Avg | Median | Std | $\propto 0$ |
| Doc2Vec | 0.04 | 0.61 | 0.65 | 0.49 | 0.26 |
| Doc2Vec+PostTime | −0.17 | 0.38 | 0.26 | 0.41 | 0.10 |
| BERTopic | 0.30 | 0.32 | 0.18 | 0.41 | 0.24 |
| BERTopic+PostTime | −0.26 | **0.02** | **0.00** | 0.13 | **0.96** |
| Doc2Vec+N2V | 0.23 | 0.52 | 0.41 | 0.48 | 0.05 |
| Doc2Vec+PostTime+N2V | −0.07 | 0.13 | 1.45 | 0.27 | 0.33 |
| BERTopic+N2V | **0.54** | 0.09 | **0.00** | 0.27 | 0.54 |
| BERTopic+PostTime+N2V | −0.61 | **0.02** | 0.00 | **0.12** | 0.96 |
| Doc2Vec+MP2V | 0.23 | 0.56 | 0.57 | 0.43 | 0.2 |
| Doc2Vec+PostTime+MP2V | −0.11 | 0.19 | 2.79 | 0.31 | 0.16 |
| BERTopic+MP2V | 0.31 | 0.27 | 0.00 | 0.40 | 0.37 |
| BERTopic+PostTime+MP2V | −0.44 | **0.02** | **0.00** | 0.15 | 0.94 |

The silhouette score drops after clustering the time component for both methods. This is because we obtain clusters of significantly smaller size. Post-time subclustering is computed on the time component, and not based on the original embeddings, while the silhouette score is still computed with respect to the original embeddings. Due to the temporal subclustering, the new clusters are no longer optimal in respect to the original embeddings (which are taking into account only the text content). BERTopic encapsulates the textual information better than Doc2Vec according to the silhouette score of the two methods. Still, the silhouette score is far from 1, the optimal value. Values close to 0 signify clusters that overlap. Negative results typically signify that a post was attributed to a wrong cluster because another cluster would have better fit the post.

All methods achieve a better average factuality standard deviation than the total standard deviation in the dataset. Clustering post-time strongly improves the factuality standard deviation. This highlights the temporal aspect plays a role in coordination campaigns, as this improves the clusters' factuality wise.

BERTopic+PostTime identifies 5,544 clusters of only one post. We drop those clusters for our analysis as we judge they are unlikely to be part of a coordinated campaign. Hence, we suspect the 587 clusters of size at least 2 ($\approx 10\%$ of the clusters) to be likely part of a coordinated campaign as they have similar textual and temporal information (the posts within a cluster have been shared within 52 seconds apart). Interestingly, the factuality standard deviation strongly reduces to an average of 0.01 post time ($\approx 97\%$ lower than pre time), with 98% of the clusters having a factuality score standard deviation of 0.

Overall, BERTopic+PostTime+N2V performs best in factuality standard deviation. BERTopic produces contextual embeddings that are accounting for the context of the document as opposed to Doc2Vec, a simple generalization of Word2Vec. In most cases, incorporating network embeddings improves performance, with Node2Vec scoring better. An explanation for the Node2Vec performing better than MetaPath2Vec could be that we bias random walks in Node2Vec to more likely be directed at nodes that had already been visited. We do this because coordinated posts usually reference the same or similar videos. These nodes will, therefore, be close together in the graph. Biasing the random walks to explore less puts more focus on these local subgraphs, which gives posts close together in this graph more similar embeddings. We considered $p = 0.25$ and $q = 4$. In the implementation of the meta paths we use, these cannot be set.

Not included here due to space constraints, we also considered different values for the hyperparameters $K$ and $\epsilon$. $K$ is used in the $K$-means algorithm. $\epsilon$ is the radius of the DBSCAN search algorithm, in seconds. Additionally, we considered two cases, Twitter, Facebook as the first case, and Reddit as the second case. We evaluated the factuality standard deviation for different value of $\epsilon$. The optimal values of $\epsilon$ with regard to the factuality standard deviation are in the interval $[30, 60]$ seconds, confirming our choice of 52 seconds is close to optimal $\epsilon$.

### 5.3   Coordinated Campaigns

BERTopic+PostTime+MP2V performs best in factuality standard deviation. The clusters obtained by this approach take textual information into account, through Sentence-BERT embeddings. Furthermore, temporal aspect is incorporated with our clustering where each post within a cluster must have another post in that cluster that was posted within 52 seconds. Lastly, it encompasses the social media interaction through the Node2Vec embeddings of our graph. Since our clusters incorporate all those aspects, and due to the strong factuality standard deviation scores, we believe these posts are highly likely to be part of a coordinated campaign. We analyse these clusters next.

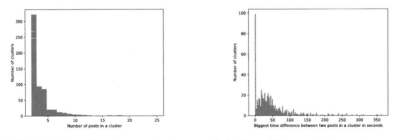

(a) Distribution of posts per cluster.     (b) Time difference between two posts.

**Fig. 3.** Distribution of posts and largest time difference between two posts within a cluster for clusters obtained by BERTopic+PostTime+N2V.

**Table 3.** The 10 most frequent video channels in the clusters computed by BERTopic+PostTime+MP2V. The description is from online sources (as of July 2023) shown in parenthesis and was not used in our framework.

| Video channel | # Posts | Description |
|---|---|---|
| Clarity Of Signal | 1, 204 | Focused on Syrian war, 8 videos and 200 subscribers. [YouTube description] |
| Vanessa Beeley | 455 | British activist/blogger known for sharing conspiracy theories and disinformation about the Syrian civil war and WH.[Wikipedia] |
| RT | 244 | "Questionable based on promoting pro-Russian propaganda, conspiracy theories, numerous failed fact checks, and a lack of author transparency." [MBFC] |
| Corbett Report | 76 | "Overall, we rate the Corbett Report a Tin Foil Hat conspiracy and Moderate pseudoscience website, based on the promotion of 9/11 conspiracies, False Flags, Chemtrails, and Deep State conspiracies." [MBFC] |
| RT UK | 20 | (see RT) |
| Corbett Report Extras | 16 | "This is the secondary channel of The Corbett Report." [YouTube description] |
| Syriana Analysis | 14 | "Overall, Syriana Analysis has a pro-Assad view [...]; therefore, we rate [it] Left biased due to their story selection and pro-Assad view. We also rate them Questionable due to poor sourcing, opinion-based commentary, lack of transparency, and a failed fact check" [MBFC] |
| The Last American Vagabond | 12 | Meanwhile deleted by YouTube |
| Sputnik | 11 | "Questionable based on the frequent promotion of conspiracies and pro-Russian propaganda, as well as the use of poor sources and numerous failed fact checks." [MBFC] |
| RT America | 11 | (see RT) |

BERTopic+PostTime+MP2V outputs 591 clusters with 2098 posts in total (1920 tweets, 141 Facebook posts and 37 Reddit comments), which represents 8% of the total posts in our dataset, hence an average of 3.37 posts per cluster. Figure 3a shows the distribution of posts per cluster. The distribution is right skewed, with a maximum of 24 posts within a cluster, despite a significant number of clusters with only two posts. Despite a low $\epsilon$ of 52 seconds in our DBSCAN algorithm, some clusters have posts separated by up to six minutes (Fig. 3b). This is still a very short timeframe, particularly considering the time span of our dataset over a year. As a matter of fact, most of the posts within a cluster are separated by 100 seconds or less. This strong time similitude highlights a coordination pattern between posts. Most of the clusters have posts with the exact same textual information and a different post time. We observe that 89% of the channels embedded in the posts had a factuality score of 0, hinting most coordinated behaviour covers questionable sources of very low factuality. We show the 10 most frequent video channels in Table 3.

### 5.4  Limitations

The limitations of this project can be categorized into two main areas: limitations related to the underlying models' structure and limitations of the results obtained from training the models on the given data.

Working with social media data is known to be particularly tricky, and this project is no exception. In particular, the patterns that our methods are trying to clusters are the result of controlled human behaviour, meaning that if these methods were put into place to identify clusters in an online scenario they would be working against"attackers" that will try to fool the system. Our solution would need a dynamically inferred time threshold like the one used to infer the 52 s interval in previous work [14].

A limitation of the results stems from the assumption that embeddings across different social media platforms can be directly compared within the same model, without considering the platform-specific language and behaviour. However, it is evident that the language used on Twitter greatly differs from that used on Facebook or Reddit, meaning the evaluation of our model acts as a lower bound. Furthermore, attackers are likely to employ different strategies tailored to each social media platform to exploit each social media's algorithm effectively.

As discussed in Sect. 3, there is no ground truth of what posts belong to coordinated campaigns. Our approach to use Media Bias Fact Check for evaluation has two limitations: first, not all channels are evaluated; second, the evaluation is at the news site granularity and not individual content (video, in our case). Thus, it is theoretically possible that a particular video in our dataset was fact-based while being hosted on a low factuality YouTube channel. That is why qualitative analysis of the content flagged by our approach is recommended.

## 6  Summary

This paper proposes an approach for identifying likely coordinated messages on multiple social media platforms that integrates different modalities in addition to temporal dynamics. We tested our approach on a dataset that includes content posted on Twitter, Facebook, Reddit, and YouTube related to the White

Helmets, the Syrian Civil Defence organization that was shown to be the target of discrediting information operations. Our method incorporates three key modalities relevant for a coordination campaign: i) textual information (through Doc2Vec and BERTopic); ii) temporal information, to detect social media posts with good temporal locality; and iii) content and user interactions represented as Node2Vec embeddings of a multi-modal network of users, posts, YouTube videos, and YouTube channels.

To evaluate the effectiveness of our approach in the absence of ground truth, we used metrics such as the standard deviation of factuality scores and the silhouette score. The standard deviation of factuality scores allowed us to assess the consistency of factual accuracy within clusters, while the silhouette score measured the quality of clustering results before and after incorporating temporal considerations. The results strongly hint we managed to find clusters of posts that are suspiciously coordinated in time and low-credibility content.

In the future we plan to test our approach on other multi-platform social media datasets, some that are likely to contain traces of coordinated information operations and others that do not. While in this paper we focused on designing an approach that includes the necessary elements of a multi-platform coordinated campaign—locality in content and in time—we plan to further evaluate the accuracy of our identification approach, and its adaptability to different platforms.

# References

1. Abu Salem, F.K., Al Feel, R., Elbassuoni, S., Jaber, M., Farah, M.: FA-KES: a fake news dataset around the Syrian war (2019). https://doi.org/10.5281/zenodo.2607278
2. Baumgartner, J., Zannettou, S., Keegan, B., Squire, M., Blackburn, J.: The pushshift reddit dataset (2020). http://arxiv.org/abs/2001.08435
3. Calisir, E., Brambilla, M.: Twitter dataset about brexit (2022). https://doi.org/10.7910/DVN/KP4XRP
4. Chen, E., Lerman, K., Ferrara, E.: Tracking social media discourse about the COVID-19 pandemic: development of a public coronavirus twitter data set. JMIR Public Health Surveill. **6**(2), e19273 (2020). https://doi.org/10.2196/19273
5. Choudhury, N., Ng, K.W., Iamnitchi, A.: Strategic information operation in youtube: the case of the white helmets. In: Thomson, R., Bisgin, H., Dancy, C., Hyder, A., Hussain, M. (eds.) SBP-BRiMS 2020. LNCS, vol. 12268, pp. 318–328. Springer, Cham (2020). https://doi.org/10.1007/978-3-030-61255-9_31
6. DeVerna, M.R., et al.: CoVaxxy: a Collection of English-language twitter posts about COVID-19 Vaccines (2021). arXiv:2101.07694
7. Dong, Y., Chawla, N.V., Swami, A.: metapath2vec: scalable representation learning for heterogeneous networks. In: Proceedings of the 23rd ACM SIGKDD International Conference on Knowledge Discovery and Data Mining, pp. 135–144 (2017). https://doi.org/10.1145/3097983.3098036
8. Fazil, M., Abulaish, M.: A socialbots analysis-driven graph-based approach for identifying coordinated campaigns in twitter. J. Intel. Fuzzy Syst. **38**(3), 2961–2977 (2020). https://doi.org/10.3233/JIFS-182895

9. Ganguly, M.: 'Aims': the software for hire that can control 30,000 fake online profiles. The Guardian (2023). https://www.theguardian.com/world/2023/feb/15/aims-software-avatars-team-jorge-disinformation-fake-profiles

10. Grootendorst, M.: BERTopic: neural topic modeling with a class-based TF-IDF procedure (2022). arXiv:2203.05794

11. Grover, A., Leskovec, J.: node2vec: scalable feature learning for networks. In: Proceedings of the 22nd ACM SIGKDD International Conference on Knowledge Discovery and Data Mining, pp. 855–864. KDD '16 (2016). https://doi.org/10.1145/2939672.2939754

12. Lukito, J.: Coordinating a multi-platform disinformation campaign: internet research agency activity on three U.S. social media platforms, 2015 to 2017. Political Commun. **37**(2), 238–255 (2020). https://doi.org/10.1080/10584609.2019.1661889

13. Magelinski, T., Ng, L., Carley, K.: A synchronized action framework for responsible detection of coordination on social media. J. Online Trust Saf. **1**(2) (2022). https://doi.org/10.54501/jots.v1i2.30

14. Ng, K.W., Horawalavithana, S., Iamnitchi, A.: Multi-platform information operations: twitter, facebook and youtube against the white helmets. In: Workshop Proceedings of the 15th International AAAI Conference on Web and Social Media. US (2021). https://doi.org/10.36190/2021.36

15. Nghiem, H., Muric, G., Morstatter, F., Ferrara, E.: Detecting cryptocurrency pump-and-dump frauds using market and social signals. Expert Syst. Appl. **182**, 115284 (2021). https://doi.org/10.1016/j.eswa.2021.115284

16. Pacheco, D., Hui, P.M., Torres-Lugo, C., Truong, B.T., Flammini, A., Menczer, F.: Uncovering coordinated networks on social media: methods and case studies. In: Proceedings of the International AAAI Conference on Web and Social Media vol. 15, pp. 455–466 (2021). https://doi.org/10.1609/icwsm.v15i1.18075

17. Ratkiewicz, J., Conover, M., Meiss, M., Gonçalves, B., Flammini, A., Menczer, F.: Detecting and tracking political abuse in social media. In: Proceedings of the International AAAI Conference on Web and social media, vol. 5, pp. 297–304 (2011). https://doi.org/10.1609/icwsm.v5i1.14127

18. Rousseeuw, P.J.: Silhouettes: a graphical aid to the interpretation and validation of cluster analysis. J. Comput. Appl. Math. **20**, 53–65 (1987). https://doi.org/10.1016/0377-0427(87)90125-7

19. Shao, C., Ciampaglia, G.L., Varol, O., Yang, K.C., Flammini, A., Menczer, F.: The spread of low-credibility content by social bots. Nat. Commun. **9**(1), 1–9 (2018)

20. Sharma, K., Zhang, Y., Ferrara, E., Liu, Y.: Identifying coordinated accounts on social media through hidden influence and group behaviours. In: Proceedings of the 27th ACM SIGKDD Conference on Knowledge Discovery & Data Mining, pp. 1441–1451. KDD '21 (2021). https://doi.org/10.1145/3447548.3467391

21. Wilson, T., Starbird, K.: Cross-platform information operations: mobilizing narratives and building resilience through both 'Big' & 'Alt' tech. In: Proceedings of the ACM on Human-Computer Interaction, vol. 5, no. (CSCW2), pp. 1–32 (2021). https://doi.org/10.1145/3476086

# FaKy: A Feature Extraction Library to Detect the Truthfulness of a Text

Sandro Barres Hamers[1] and Davide Ceolin[2]([⊠])

[1] Vrije Universiteit Amsterdam, Amsterdam, The Netherlands
[2] Centrum Wiskunde & Informatica, Amsterdam, The Netherlands
davide.ceolin@cwi.nl

**Abstract.** The transparency and explainability of fake news detection is a crucial feature to enhance the trustability of the assessments and, consequently, their effectiveness. Textual features have shown their potential to help identify fake news in a transparent manner. In this paper, we survey a list of textual features, evaluate their usefulness in predicting fake news by testing them on a real-world dataset, and collect them in a Python library called "faKy".

**Keywords:** faKy · Natural Language Processing · Fake News detection · Feature extraction

## 1 Introduction

Fake news has always been a phenomenon known to humankind [11]. Nevertheless, the Web and Social Network Systems (SNS) in particular, exacerbated the societal threats posed by misinformation for two reasons. First, people find it hard to distinguish information from misinformation [36]; this is becoming harder with the rise of state-of-the-art Artificial Intelligence (AI). Secondly, fake news can spread extremely fast on SNS [8]. Therefore fake news can reach a high volume of consumers quickly.

In this paper, we look at the interpretability of fake news assessments. While there are numerous Neural Networks (NN) and Large Language Models (LLM) that can accurately classify fake news with very high accuracy, in some cases up to 99% [34], these models, most of the time, lack interpretability: their reasoning is hardly interpretable by humans. Recent work shows that very accurate models tend to be less interpretable [7]; this phenomenon is called the interpretable accuracy trade-off.

We study whether linguistic features, obtained using Natural Language Processing (NLP), can provide a basis for assessing fake news. Among such features, we consider Readability, which measures the ease with which the text is read. Additionally, we investigate the Information Complexity (IC), which quantifies the amount of information contained in the object, and conduct sentiment analysis to assess the emotional tone of the text. Subsequently, we analyze Named

© The Author(s), under exclusive license to Springer Nature Switzerland AG 2023
D. Ceolin et al. (Eds.): MISDOOM 2023, LNCS 14397, pp. 29–44, 2023.
https://doi.org/10.1007/978-3-031-47896-3_3

Entity Recognition (NER) to identify instances where the object represents specific individuals, places, or other proper nouns in the text. Lastly, we employ Part of Speech (POS) Tags to determine a sentence's grammatical category or syntactic function. These features are carefully selected and based on existing literature, which we elaborate on in the related work section.

The novelty of our contribution is in faKy[1], an extensive library that collects a comprehensive list of NLP features known to have shown a correlation with fake news assessment. These features (and, consequently, the faKy library) are here aggregated, tested, and evaluated on real-world datasets. In this manner, faKy provides a validated toolkit for extracting features from a text that are potentially correlated to fake news, thus contributing to the explainability of the assessment process.

The overarching research question that we address is:

>   RQ: Can the truthfulness of textual information be accurately predicted using specific linguistic features, and how do these linguistic features contribute to distinguishing between truthful and untrustworthy textual content?

We decompose this question through the following subquestions:

>   SRQ1: *Does the readability measure of a text provide a basis to predict its truthfulness?*
>
>   SRQ2: *Does the IC measure of a text provide a basis to predict its truthfulness?*
>
>   SRQ3: *Does the sentiment of a text provide a basis to predict its truthfulness?* n n jb
>
>   SRQ4: *Do the of Named Entities recognized in a text provide a basis to predict its truthfulness?*
>
>   SRQ5: *Do the POS tags in a text provide a basis to predict its truthfulness?*

The rest of the paper is structured as follows. Section 2 introduces related work. Section 3 introduces the research methodology and the experimental design. Results are discussed in Sect. 4, while Sect. 5 concludes the paper.

## 2   Related Work

The fake news research body is extensive and much work has been done to understand and classify fake news. This is not surprising as this phenomenon threatens our society's foundations.

A recent study presented a comprehensive review of methods for detecting fake news on SNS. They include multiple techniques like ML, NLP, and information propagation analysis, which looks at how the different agents behave in the SNS ecosystem. They discuss content-based, network-based, and hybrid

---

[1] faKy repository.

approaches, as well as machine and deep learning models. The paper also high-lights the challenges and limitations of fake news detection. The authors found that readability features impact fake news detection and recommend considering them in developing detection systems [5].

Subsequently, a benchmarked study of 19 ML models on three different datasets, including the Liar dataset, demonstrated the superior performance of BERT-based models with the best f1-score of 62% for the Liar dataset. Additionally, they show an F1 score of 57% for a Naive Bayes and an F1 score of 51% for tree-based models for the Liar dataset. The researchers evaluated the models on accuracy, recall, precision, and F1-score. However, the researchers did not use k-fold-cross validation, which could have improved their evaluation [28].

Another popular method to extract information from a text object is NER and POS tagging, which looks at an object's structure, style, and content. A recent study proposes a linguistic method to detect fake news that can be applied to any language. They compare news articles using POS Tags and NER and train four ML models. They evaluate the model's performance with the F1-score and show that a Gradient Boosting model has the highest score, with an average of 70.83%. The paper presents a novel approach that delivers high-level performance using POSTag+NER features [39].

Lastly, using morphological tags and n-grams in decision tree-based ML algo-rithms demonstrates superior accuracy, precision, and F1 score performance in the scope of fake news [26]. The authors extract n-grams from the tags and use them for training decision trees in machine-learning algorithms where an n-gram is the probability distribution for the following word, given the corpus size. They use several n-grams (1-gram, 2-gram) for words and POS tags. Where a 2-gram considers two words, and a 3-gram three words, their approach outperforms other models in accuracy, precision, and F1 score. They argue that future work should explore more sophisticated models and linguistic features. However, these linguistic features have also shown promising results in predicting a broad set of information quality aspects (beyond the mere veracity prediction considered in fake news detection) by supporting argument computation [13].

## 3    Research Methodology and Experimental Design

As is common in many NLP problems, the classification of fake news can be formulated mathematically as an optimization task, represented by Eq. 1. This equation captures the essence of the language processing algorithm's two main modules. The search module's objective is to discover the optimal output $y^*$ that maximizes the scoring function $\Psi$ given an input $x$ and the possible outputs $y$ from the set $Y(x)$. The learning module is responsible for iteratively adjusting the parameters $\theta$ to minimize a loss function, $L(y, y*)$ which quantifies the disparity between the true outcomes $y$ and the generated ones $y^*$ during the learning process [17].

$$y^* = \arg \max_{y \in 0,1} \Psi(x, y; \theta) \tag{1}$$

We will employ an incremental experimental design, allowing for a step-by-step breakdown of the various variables. The experimental design is based on the methodology presented in [2] and has been slightly modified to align with the requirements of this specific experiment. The experiment comprises four main parts, visually depicted in Fig. 1: data collection, experimental pipeline, classification, and validation. The subsequent subsections will provide a detailed examination of these components.

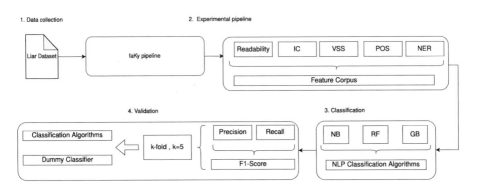

**Fig. 1.** Experimental Design

### 3.1 Data Collection

We use the Liar dataset, obtained from Hugging Face[2]. The Liar dataset is a publicly available resource for fake news detection and consists of 12.8 thousand manually labeled statements collected from various contexts. These statements were originally sourced from PolitiFact, a non-profit organization known for fact-checking the accuracy of claims. PolitiFact provides detailed analysis reports and links to source documents for each case. Furthermore, each statement in the dataset has been evaluated by PolitiFact editors for its truthfulness. By utilizing the Liar dataset from Hugging Face, we aim to reduce label bias in our research [21]. We categorized the statements into three categories: **True, False,** and **In Between (IB)** claims. We classify True claims as the 'negative class' (0), False claims as the 'positive class' (1), and IB claims as (2). It should be noted that we assigned these labels on a qualitative rationale. The Liar train dataset consists of 10239 rows; Table 1 provides an overview of the distribution of claims in the dataset. The Table includes four columns: "Label," "Claim," "Number of statements," and "Percentage of total."

---

[2] https://huggingface.co/datasets/liar.

**Table 1.** Number of claims

| Label | Claim | Number of statements | percentage of total |
|-------|-------|----------------------|---------------------|
| 0 | True | 1676 | 16% |
| 1 | False | 2833 | 28% |
| 2 | IB | 5730 | 56% |

## 3.2 Experiment Pipeline

This subsection discusses the NLP pipeline, which involves converting text objects from the Liar dataset into a machine-readable format using the spaCy library[3]. By applying the spaCy nlp function, the text objects are transformed into doc objects, which undergo tokenization and processing through the spaCy pipeline. Features are computed and integrated into the pipeline, creating the feature extraction library faKy. FaKy utilizes spaCy extensively and is therefore named after it. The spaCy library offers comprehensive NLP and linguistic capabilities, ensuring efficient and accurate execution. The subsequent paragraphs illustrate the computation of different features.

**Readability.** The readability of a text tells us how easy it is to read and understand a particular text. A text with low readability indicates that the text consists of complex and unique words; this can be, for example, an academic paper. We compute the readability via the Flesch-Kincaid Reading Ease (FKE) score; we chose FKE for three reasons. First, the FKE score can be computed with the spaCy readability object[4], enabling the spaCy pipeline's use. Secondly, the FKE score is developed for English text, the target language for this study. At last, FKE is ubiquitous and the standard test of readability for documents and forms for the US military [29], insurance policies [40], and word-processing programs [1].

$$\text{FKE} = 206.835 - 1.015\frac{\text{TW}}{\text{TS}} - 84.6\frac{\text{TSL}}{\text{TW}} \qquad (2)$$

The FKE score is computed based on the equation represented in Eq. 2. The FKE is established on the total number of words (TW), the total number of sentences (TS), and the total number of syllables (TSL). The FKE estimates a text's readability by estimating the ratio of words to sentences and syllables to words. A higher FKE score thus means that a text consists of shorter sentences and fewer syllables per word and is thus easier to read, enhancing readability.

**Complexity.** In fake news research, linguistic features have been the primary focus for distinguishing fake and True objects. However, we propose a novel

---

[3] https://spacy.io/.

[4] https://spacy.io/universe/project/spacy_readability.

approach by incorporating the concept of IC derived from algorithmic information theory. We posit that the IC encapsulates crucial information and can be computed relatively easily, making it an interesting feature for investigation.

We use the Kolmogorov complexity to compute the IC of an object; the IC tells us how much information an object conveys. We define the Kolmogorov complexity $C(x)$ of a string $x$ as the length of the shortest program $p$ that processes $x$ running on a universal Turing Machine $U$. The formula conveys the following idea: A string with low information complexity is highly compressible as the information it contains can be encoded in a program much shorter than the length of the string itself [47].

$$C(x) = min_p\{\text{length}(p) : U(p) = x\} \tag{3}$$

We mathematically represent the Kolmogorov complexity in Eq. 3. Nonetheless, $C(x)$ is proven to be uncomputable because finding the shortest program is equivalent to solving the halting problem, which is undecidable [43]. This means that no general algorithm or formal system can accurately determine the halting behavior of all programs and inputs, making the computation of $C(x)$ impossible [24]. We can thus only approximate $C(x)$ due to its uncomputable nature. We do this by using a compressing algorithm since the $C(x)$ may be roughly described as the compressed size [38]. The IC is thus computed by applying a compressing algorithm to the object and returning the compressed size of that object.

**Sentiment.** We conduct the sentiment analysis using the Vader Sentiment Scores (VSS). VSS measures the polarity (positive, negative, neutral) and the intensity of the emotion for a given text. A very negative sentiment will thus have a different score than a moderately negative object. VSS relies on a lexicon of words and phrases with known sentiment values, as well as rules to capture sentiment in context. VSS has demonstrated superior performance in detecting sentiment intensity compared to other sentiment analysis models [22], and it has also proven effective in fake news detection systems [6]. Computation of VSS was implemented using the NLTK library[5].

**Sequence Labeling.** We adopt two sequence labeling tasks, NER and POS tagging. As discussed earlier, NER and POS tagging have proven valuable in detecting fake news. Furthermore, NER tags provide semantic representations, such as identifying events and relationships [25]. On the other hand, POS tagging is the first step toward syntactic analysis (which, in turn, is often helpful for semantic analysis).

We compute both the total number of NER tags as well as the count per NER category. We represent this by means of a numerical vector.

$$\text{NER vector} = [0, 0, 0, 0, 1, 0, 0, 0, 0, 0, 0, 0, 0, 3, 0, 0, 0, 0] \tag{4}$$

---

[5] https://www.nltk.org/howto/sentiment.html.

The initialized vector represents the frequency of each unique NER tag, where the first position corresponds to the 'CARDINAL' tag, the second corresponds to the 'DATE' tag, and so on.

*Syntactic labeling* Unlike NER tagging, POS tagging is a dependent feature that relies heavily on the context and placement of words within a sentence. To illustrate this point, let us examine the same object used in NER tagging but apply dependency parsing, which results in specific POS tags. Within dependency parsing, we describe the syntactic structure of a sentence in terms of directed binary grammatical relations between the words [25].

We compute the POS tags similar to the NER tags, except we are only interested in the sum of individual POS tags per object since computing the total count of the pos tags will count approximately every tokenized word, giving us no relevant information in the structure or style of the object.

## 3.3   Classification

The classification is a 3-way multi-class text classification problem classifying, True, False, and 'IB' claims. We employ three machine learning models: Naive Bayes (NB), Random Forest (RF), and Gradient Booster (GB). We choose these models since an NB performs highly due to the computation of conditional probabilities [4], an RF has shown superior performance in classifying fake news [2], and at last, a GB since it is advantageous in cases of unbalanced datasets and outperforms an RF with its robustness [31]. We use the Python-based ML algorithms from sci-kit-learn[6].

Since the dataset is unbalanced, we use an oversampler to avoid poor performance of the minority class, after oversampling the minority class, the train and test data are equally distributed; the distributions of these claims are presented in Table 2.

**Table 2.** Train instance counts before and after oversampling

| Label | Class | Counts (initial) | Counts (after oversampling) |
|-------|-------|------------------|------------------------------|
| 0 | True | 1676 | 4565 |
| 1 | False | 2833 | 4565 |
| 2 | IB | 5730 | 4565 |

Since the RF and GB are tree-based models, there is no need to scale the features; also, the NB does not need scaled features since it is a probabilistic model and thus only looks at the frequency of the features.

---

[6] https://scikit-learn.org/stable/.

## 3.4    Evaluation

We validate if the features $\theta$ significantly differ between the three independent groups corresponding to the labels (True: 0, False: 1, IB: 2). We first plot the distributions of the features and test if they are parametric through the Kolmogorov-Smirnoff Test (KST). We conduct the KST for the continuous features: Readability, IC, and VSS; discrete features, represented by POS and NER tags, are inappropriate for the KST since the discrete features are not used to measure some properties but solely as a count of tags [32]. The results are shown in this repository[7].

Next, we perform the Kruskal-Wallis Test (KWT) to validate the features. The KWT is chosen due to its suitability for analyzing data involving more than two independent groups, unbalanced datasets, and non-parametric distributions [46]. To determine significant differences between pairs of independent groups, we employ a post-hoc method. The Dunn test is selected as the most suitable post-hoc method for conducting pairwise comparisons [16]. We set the significance threshold at $p < 0.05$ since it is the industry standard [30]

Finally, a preliminary examination is undertaken, encompassing the computation of the mean, and standard deviations across the three labels for both continuous and discrete features, we compute the highest value for the continuous features. This analysis facilitates a fundamental comprehension of the data distributions, giving us a basic main difference between the different claims. We validate the performance of $\Psi$ in combination with $\theta$, and we conducted three validation methods. First, we assessed the performance of $\Psi$ without any feature selection, thus incorporating all the computed features. Next, we evaluated the performance when selecting two-way significant interaction features. These features demonstrate significance between at least two of the three groups, for example, (True; False or IB; False, and so on). Finally, we computed the evaluation of three-way significant features, which are significant across all three groups, denoted as (True; False, True; IB, False; IB). We evaluated the performance of $\Psi$ using the F1 score and k-fold cross-validation. The F1 score is selected due to its industry standard as the harmonic mean of precision and recall [20]. K-fold cross-validation divides the dataset into five subsets (k=5), which is considered a good compromise [19]. With k-fold cross-validation, we mitigate overfitting by applying $\Psi$ to the k subsets. We compute the Coefficient Variance (CV), depicted in Eq. 5; the CV considers the spread of the distribution for the variation. High variance, indicated by $CV > 1.0$ [27], suggests inconsistent performance across subsets and is, thus, sensitive to overfitting.

$$CV = \frac{Standard\ deviation}{Mean} \tag{5}$$

At last, we compute a baseline evaluation to put the model's performance into perspective; we employ the 'uniform' dummy classifier since it generates uniform random predictions based on the three classes. We compare the F1 score performance of the $\psi$ to the Dummy Classifier (DC) using Relative Improvement

---

[7] Feature distributions repository.

(RI). The RI returns a positive result if the $\psi$ F1-score is high in comparison to the DC F1-score, and a negative result if it is low, the RI is depicted in Eq. 6 [14].

$$RI = \frac{F1_\psi - F1_{DC}}{F1_{DC}} \tag{6}$$

## 4   Results and Discussion

We present the findings of the conducted research in two distinct parts, aligning with the overarching objective of the experiment: validate if the features $\theta$ can maximize the output $y^*$ through the natural language algorithm $\Psi$. The evaluation results for the features and ML algorithms are presented in the following repository[8]. Throughout this section, we will address the sub-research question of Sect. 1.

### 4.1   Distinguishing True and False Claims: Insights from IC, Readability, VSS, NER, and POS Tags.

The statistical results of the significant continuous features: Readability and IC are presented in Table 3 where we show the features corresponding mean, max, mode, and standard deviation associated with the three labels.

The IC is a significant feature between True, False, and IB claims since the p-value is lower than 0.05 between the three labels. Therefore, the truthfulness of textual information can be distinguished based on the IC. True claims convey more information compared to False claims as depicted in Table 3. Moreover, False claims demonstrate a greater distribution, suggesting that the information they convey is more scattered than True claims. This becomes more evident since the maximum value for the IC is higher for False claims while the mean is lower, indicating the scattered nature of the IC for False claims.

Similar to the IC, the Readability of an object is also a significant feature since the p-values are lower than 0.05; we thus conclude that Readability plays a crucial role in determining the truthfulness of a text. Our analysis further reveals that False claims tend to have increased difficulty regarding Readability, reflecting more complex word choices and sentence structures, see Table 3. This observation aligns with the existing literature [41]. However, comprehending the underlying factors contributing to this distinction needs interdisciplinary research. Additionally, we find a similar pattern observed for the IC, where False claims exhibit a greater degree of distribution, indicating a dispersed nature in their Readability compared to True claims. This discovery corresponds with the findings of [12], who demonstrated that deceptive content encompasses a wide range of readability levels.

The VSS are not significant between True and False claims since the p-value is greater than 0.05; thus, the VSS of a text is not suitable for determining

---

[8] Fake News Classification repository.

Table 3. Significant continuous features.

| Feature | Label | Average | Maximum | Mode | Standard Deviation |
|---|---|---|---|---|---|
| IC | True | 8555 | 149837 | 5592 | 4779 |
| IC | False | 8130 | 197589 | 5964 | 4929 |
| IC | IB | 8775 | 294076 | 5951 | 5112 |
| Readability | True | 60 | 127 | 74 | 21 |
| Readability | False | 56 | 124 | 60 | 22 |
| Readability | IB | 59 | 151 | 56 | 22 |

Table 4. ML models performance.

| Model | Feature Selection | F1 Score Test (%) | RI (%) |
|---|---|---|---|
| **Naive Bayes** | **Unselected** | **34.11 (+/− 6.44)** | **7.00** |
| Naive Bayes | two-way significant | 33.06 (+/− 11.07) | 3.71 |
| Naive Bayes | three-way significant | 27.35 (+/− 2.48) | −14.19 |
| Random Forest | Unselected | 27.59 (+/− 7.77) | −13.44 |
| Random Forest | two-way significant | 29.40 (+/− 6.09) | −7.76 |
| **Random Forest** | **three-way significant** | **31.72 (+/− 6.49)** | **−0.47** |
| Gradient Booster | Unselected | 30.48 (+/− 9.72) | −4.37 |
| **Gradient Booster** | **two-way significant** | **30.94 (+/− 12.86)** | **-2.93** |
| Gradient Booster | three-way significant | 28.92 (+/− 6.98) | −9.27 |
| Dummy Classifier Uniform | Nonapplicable | 31.88 (+/− 2.33) | 0.00 |

the truthfulness of a text. While we show that the VSS of text conveys no relevant information to determine the truthfulness of a text, it is essential to note that the VSS is tailored explicitly for analyzing SNS text objects. In contrast, this study's investigation subject is focused on political claims. Consequently, the utilization of VSS in this context lacks its specific purpose. This limitation deserves attention, and future research should consider exploring the significance of VSS on SNS objects or employing alternative sentiment analysis approaches to assess the truthfulness of the claims.

In the appendix we present an overview of the statistical results for the discrete features, we show a significant difference between False and True claims regarding NER tags. On average, True claims exhibit more NER tags than False claims, which aligns with the existing literature [37]. An explanation for this would be that False claims reference fewer existing entities due to their fictitious nature. However, we acknowledge that such a conclusion is overly simplistic, necessitating further investigation into the underlying factors driving this behavior. The only NER tags that are more present in False than True claims are 'PERSON' and 'ORG'; this may be related to the fact that fake news specifically targets political figures; think of the pizza gate incident or conspiracy groups like

Qanon [42]. Moreover, the emphasis on Organizations is reasonable, given that fake news commonly targets large pharmaceutical entities like Pfizer, as well as other major corporations and government institutions [10,15,23]. This phenomenon warrants comprehensive investigation to better comprehend its underlying causes. Lastly, we conclude that the specific style and syntax indicated by POS tags can distinguish the truthfulness of textual content. We do, however, not see that the specific POS tag groups: prepositions, adjectives, and nouns, appear more in False than in True claims; this contradicts the existing literature [26]. This may be due to the use of a different dataset or methodology than that adopted in the literature. Furthermore, our study demonstrates that True claims exhibit a greater prominence of POS tags, indicating greater linguistic diversity. Notably, False claims display a higher occurrence of 'Verb' and 'Part' POS tags (e.g., 'to go') when compared to True claims.

In summary, this study reveals notable differences between True and False claims. Consequently, False claims exhibit substantial distinctions in their linguistic structures. Additionally, empirical evidence demonstrates that False claims, on average, embody a higher level of distribution compared to True claims. This variation may be attributed to the fictitious characteristics inherent in False claims, in contrast to True claims that adhere to prescribed formats dictated by established standards.

## 4.2   Classifying Fake Claims: Insights from NB, RF, and GB

The outcomes of the three classification ML models with the corresponding feature selections are illustrated in Table 4. We show the mean F1-scores for the test data, acquired through k-fold cross-validation with k=5. Additionally, the Table includes the CV, as well as the model's RI in terms of the DC.

NB combined with no feature selection exhibited the highest performance, achieving an F1 score of 34.11%, with a CV of 6.44%. The high CV suggests potential overfitting, a finding further supported by the overperformance of the NB model on the training data. Compared to the DC, the NB model showed an RI of 7.00%. When applying an NB with the three-way significant features the model performance drops drastically, this could be because of the decreased number of features, Subsequently, we also notice that applying an NB with two-way significant features decreases the model's performance.

Subsequently, the RF model demonstrated the best F1 score when using three-way significant features, with a score of 31.72% for the test data, accompanied by a CV of 6.49%, indicating high variance. Notably, the training data significantly outperformed the test data in this instance, with a difference of approximately 45%, indicating extreme overfitting by the RF model. Next to the overfitting, the RF using three-way significant features showed a negative RI of -0.47% compared to the DI. We notice that the RF's performance declines when using two-way feature selection and reaches the lowest score when using no feature selection This can be attributed to the increased complexity introduced by the additional splits or the inclusion of potentially noisy or redundant features. Future research should analyze the importance of the individual features within the RF model and the way they interact with each other [9].

Lastly, the GB model achieved the poorest performance with the best F1 score of 30.94%, and a CV of 12.86%, when applying two-way significant features. Subsequently, the GB underperformed when compared to the DC, with an RI score of -2.93%. Based on our findings we thus conclude that the GB performs the best with two-way significant features however, this is a preliminary finding. Future research should focus on feature selection optimization [3,45].

Previous studies achieved F1 scores of 50–60% for similar algorithms, for binary classification tasks [28], where random performance is typically around 50% and tends to yield higher F1 scores [33]. In contrast, our study addressed a more challenging three-class classification task: True, False, and In Between. This distinction is vital for interpreting our results. While our models outperformed the baseline established by [44], it's important to note that our task was less demanding than the 6-way multiclass text classification problem in the same paper. Despite the inherent complexity of our task, our models achieved an accuracy of approximately 30%, showcasing promising results. Future research should explore the performance of different ML algorithms using our introduced features across diverse classification problems and different datasets.

All three models exhibited better performance on the majority class (TN) than on the minority class (TP). Moreover, they demonstrated better performance on the training data, indicating overfitting, and displayed high variances. Future research should prioritize improving the models by addressing overfitting through increased data volume and enhanced model robustness.

The model's performances align with the overall behavior of the models since NB classifiers can quickly learn to use high-dimensional features with limited training data compared to more sophisticated methods like the RF [18], therefore the NB will perform better with a higher number of features compared to the RF which achieves high results with the most relevant features. We thus conclude that the model's performance is dependent on the applied feature selection.

To conclude, our study presented the performance of three ML algorithms with F1 scores ranging from 27.35% to 34.11%. We showed relative improvement for the NB when applying two significant features and the NB when applying two-way significant features. However, it is essential to note that the observed relative improvement of the NB may not be statistically significant. The statistical difference between the two may not be large enough to discriminate the items effectively, as the two distributions may overlap.

### 4.3   Limitations & Future Research

The POS and NER tags are the first step in understanding text objects' lexical and syntactic information. However, more sophisticated methods can be employed to extract and leverage this information effectively. For instance, TF-IDF (Term Frequency-Inverse Document Frequency) is a numerical representation used in NLP that measures the importance of a term in a document by considering its frequency in the document and its rarity across the entire document collection. Furthermore, exploring advanced NLP techniques such as dependency parsers can enable the analysis of object styles and facilitate more advanced tasks like semantic parsing. Subsequently, the style of the objects could be further analyzed using dependency parsing, which, as a result, can be generalized to even more advanced NLP tasks such as semantic parsing, taking the text's actual meaning into account. Lastly, we propose using n-grams to analyze and model language patterns. Another area for future research is the optimization of the faKy library's runtime. While the current implementation utilizes the efficient spaCy pipeline, further improvements can be made to enhance its runtime capabilities. Investigating optimal data structures and pipeline components can significantly optimize the runtime performance, making the library even more efficient. Finally, it is crucial to recognize the ethical considerations surrounding this research, despite its aim to combat the spread of false information. The study introduces the concept of dual-use, where the same technology can be used for beneficial and potentially harmful purposes [35]. While FaKy has the potential to detect fake news, it could also be utilized by oppressive regimes to categorize dissenting texts, resulting in Orwellian practices. Therefore, the high risk of dual-use needs further examination and consideration.

## 5    Conclusion

Drawing upon the findings obtained from the addressed sub-research questions, we can respond to the main research question, RQ: Can the truthfulness of textual information be accurately predicted using specific linguistic features? Our study concludes that linguistic features can accurately predict the truthfulness of a text. We show that fake objects have a greater distribution across all the features, are more complex in terms of readability, convey more information, hold more Named Entities, and significantly differ between style and syntax regarding Part-of-Speech tags. Consequently, we reject the null hypothesis and accept the alternative hypothesis. Additionally, we introduce faKy, a comprehensive feature extraction library that computes relevant linguistic features for fake news detection. Our study highlights the significance of these features and shows that by combining them with machine learning classification algorithms the truthfulness of text objects can be predicted. While faKy is still in its early stages of development, our findings indicate its potential in combating fake news and advancing explainable AI.

**Acknowledgements.** This research has been partly supported by the Netherlands eScience Center project "The Eye of the Beholder" (project nr. 027.020.$G$15) and by the AI, Media & Democracy Lab (https://www.aim4dem.nl/).

# References

1. How to Use Readability Scores in Your Writing – Grammarly Spotlight (2020)
2. Abonizio, H.Q., de Morais, J.I., Gabriel Marques Tavares, G.M., Barbon, S.: Language-independent fake news detection: English, portuguese, and spanish mutual features. Future Internet **12**, 87 (2020)
3. Adler, A., Painsky, A.: Feature importance in gradient boosting trees with cross-validation feature selection (2021)
4. Albahr, A., Albahar, M.: An empirical comparison of fake news detection using different machine learning algorithms. Int. J. Adv. Comput. Sci. Appl. **11** (2020)
5. Ali, I., Ayub, M.N.B., Shivakumara, P., Noor, N.F.B.M.: Fake news detection techniques on social media: a survey. Wireless Commun. Mobile Comput. **2022**, 1–17 (2022)
6. Alonso, M.A., Vilares, D., Gómez-Rodríguez, C., Vilares, J.: Sentiment analysis for fake news detection. Electronics **10**, 1348 (2021)
7. Arrieta, A.B., et al.: Explainable artificial intelligence (XAI): concepts, taxonomies, opportunities and challenges toward responsible AI. Inf. Fusion **58**, 82–115 (2020)
8. Belloir, N., Ouerdane, W., Pastor, O.: characterizing fake news: a conceptual modeling-based approach. In: ER 2022–41st International Conference on Conceptual Modeling, Hyderabad, India (2022)
9. Biau, G.: Analysis of a random forests model. J. Mach. Learn. Res. **13**, 1063–1095 (2012)
10. Blaskiewicz,R.: The big pharma conspiracy theory. Med. Writing, **22**, 259–261 (2013)
11. Burkhardt, J.M.: Combating fake news in the digital age. Libr. Technol. Rep. **53**, 5–9 (2017)
12. Carrasco-Farré, C.: The fingerprints of misinformation: how deceptive content differs from reliable sources in terms of cognitive effort and appeal to emotions. Humanit. Soc. Sci. Commun. **9**, 162 (2022)
13. Ceolin, D., Primiero, G., Soprano, M., Wielemaker, J.: Transparent assessment of information quality of online reviews using formal argumentation theory. Inf. Syst. **110**, 102107 (2022)
14. college of san mateo. 250 i–2
15. Malaysian Communications and Multimedia Commission (2022). Accessed 14 Jun 2023
16. Dinno, A.: Nonparametric pairwise multiple comparisons in independent groups using Dunn's test. Stata J. Promoting commun. Statist. Stata **15**, 292–300 (2015)
17. Eisenstein, J.: Natural language processing (2018)
18. Fan, S.: Understanding the mathematics behind Naive Bayes – shuzhanfan.github.io. https://shuzhanfan.github.io/2018/06/understanding-mathematics-behind-naive-bayes/. Accessed 15 Jun 2023
19. Hastie, T., Tibshirani, R., Friedman, J.: The Elements of Statistical Learning. Springer New York (2009). https://doi.org/10.1007/978-0-387-21606-5
20. He, H., Ma,Y.: Imbalanced Learning. Wiley (2013)
21. Hovy, D., Prabhumoye, S.: Five sources of bias in natural language processing. Lang. Linguist. Compass **15**, 8 (2021)
22. Hutto, C., Gilbert, E.: VADER: a parsimonious rule-based model for sentiment analysis of social media text. In: Proceedings of the International AAAI Conference on Web and Social Media, vol. 8, pp. 216–225 (2014)

23. Reuters Institute. Types, sources, and claims of COVID-19 misinformation – reutersinstitute.politics.ox.ac.uk. https://reutersinstitute.politics.ox.ac.uk/types-sources-and-claims-covid-19-misinformation. Accessed 14 Jun 2023
24. James, M.: Programmer's guide to theory - kolmogorov complexity (2020)
25. Jurafsky, D., Martin, J.H.: Dependency parsing (2023)
26. Kapusta, J., Drlik, M., Munk, M.: Using of n-grams from morphological tags for fake news classification. PeerJ Comput. Sci. **7**, e624 (2021)
27. Kaufmann, J.: What do you consider a good standard deviation? (2014)
28. Khan, J.Y., Khondaker, M.T.I., Afroz, S., Uddin, G., Iqbal, A.: A benchmark study of machine learning models for online fake news detection. Mach. Learn. Appl. **4**, 100032 (2021)
29. Kniffin, J.D.: The new readability requirements for military technical manuals. Tech. Commun. **26**(3), 16–19 (1979)
30. Di Leo, G., Sardanelli, F.: Statistical significance: p value, 0.05 threshold, and applications to radiomics-reasons for a conservative approach. Eur. Radiol. Exp. **4**, 18 (2020)
31. Lyashevska, O., Malone, F., MacCarthy, E., Fiehler, J., Buhk, J.-H., Morris, L.: Class imbalance in gradient boosting classification algorithms: application to experimental stroke data. Stat. Methods Med. Res. **30**, 916–925 (2021)
32. Salvatore, S., Mangiafico. R.: Handbook: Introduction to Parametric Tests – rcompanion.org. https://rcompanion.org/handbook/I_01.html#:~:text=It%20is%20sometimes%20permissible%20to,data%20or%20other%20discrete%20data 2016. Accessed 15 Jun 2023
33. Del Moral, P., Nowaczyk, S., Pashami, S.: Why is multiclass classification hard? IEEE Access **10**, 80448–80462 (2022)
34. Nasir, J.A., Khan, O.S., Varlamis, I.: Fake news detection: A hybrid CNN-RNN based deep learning approach. Int. J. Inf. Manag. Data Insights **1**(1), 100007 (2021)
35. National Institute of Health. Dual-use research (2022)
36. Pennycook, G., McPhetres, J., Zhang, Y., Lu, J.G., Rand, D.G.: Fighting COVID-19 misinformation on social media: Experimental evidence for a scalable accuracy-nudge intervention. Psychol. Sci. **31**, 770–780 (2020)
37. Samadi, M., Saeedeh Momtazi, S., Fake news detection: deep semantic representation with enhanced feature engineering. Int. J. Data Sci. Anal. (2023)
38. Shen, A.: Around kolmogorov complexity: basic notions and results. CoRR, abs/1504.04955 (2015)
39. Spalenza, M.A.: LCAD - UFES at FakeDeS 2021: fake news detection using named entity recognition and part-of-speech sequences. In: IberLEF@SEPLN (2021)
40. Statutes, F.: Florida statutes section 627.4145 - readable language in insurance policies. (fla. stat. §627.4145) (2016)
41. Mohammadali, T., Harith, A., Grégoire, B.: On the readability of misinformation in comparison to the truth (2023)
42. Tuters, M., Willaert, T.: Deep state phobia: narrative convergence in coronavirus conspiracism on instagram. convergence: Int. J. Res. New Media Technol. **28**, 1214–1238 (2022)
43. Vitányi, P.M.B.: How incomputable is Kolmogorov complexity? Entropy **22**, 408 (2020)
44. Wang, W.Y.W.: liar, liar pants on fire: a new benchmark dataset for fake news detection, pp. 422–426. Association for Computational Linguistics (2017)
45. Eddie Xu, Z.E.X., Huang, G., Weinberger, K.Q., Zheng, A.X.: Gradient boosted feature selection (2019)

46. Zablotski,Y.: Kruskal-wallis test: compare more then two groups (2019)
47. Zenil, H.: A numerical method for the evaluation of Kolmogorov complexity, an alternative to lossless compression algorithms (2011)

# From Sharing Misinformation to Debunking It: How Coordinated Image Text Sharing Behaviour is Used in Political Campaigns on Facebook

Felipe Bonow Soares$^{(\boxtimes)}$ (iD)

London College of Communication, University of the Arts London, London, UK
f.soares@lcc.arts.ac.uk

**Abstract.** This study aims to understand how Coordinated Image Text Sharing Behaviour (CITSB) was used on Facebook during the 2022 Brazilian election, focusing on posts containing images about Lula da Silva or Jair Bolsonaro, the candidates in the Brazilian run-off election (n = 509,219 Facebook posts). The analysis is based on a script to identify CITSB on Facebook and includes social network analysis and a manual review of the most shared content. Findings show that both sides of the political divide engaged in CITSB to share promotional campaign-related content, which included criticising their opponents and promoting social media lives. Partisan accounts engaged in CITSB not only in their silos but also in other spaces on Facebook, such as local buy-and-sell Facebook groups. This indicates that CITSB was used to get the vote of undecided voters. Finally, while pro-Bolsonaro accounts engaged in CITSB to spread conspiracy theories and misinformation, pro-Lula accounts engaged in CITSB to debunk false claims about Lula.

**Keywords:** Coordinated Behaviour · Election · Misinformation · Political Campaign · Social Science

## 1 Introduction

Coordinated behaviour on social media has been widely associated with negative outcomes, such as misinformation spread and harassment campaigns. Coordinated behaviour refers to the coordination of social media accounts, usually malicious or fake users, to influence public opinion and online discussions [6, 7, 14]. Coordinated behaviour can be a problem for several reasons. Misinformation campaigns fuelled by coordinated behaviour can undermine trust in institutions and cause harm to individuals and communities [8]. When used to manipulate public opinion, coordinated behaviour can also influence elections and interfere with democratic processes [6]. Finally, coordinated behaviour can create a toxic online environment when used to promote hate or harassment campaigns [23].

Similar to this study, previous research has focused on coordinated behaviour behind link sharing on social media during elections. During the 2018 and 2019 Italian elections, coordinated behaviour was used by right-wing groups to promote links containing misinformation and partisan content in an effort to manipulate public opinion [6]. During the 2019 UK elections, another study found evidence of coordinated behaviour on both sides of the political divide and that not only inauthentic fake accounts were engaged in coordinated behaviour, but also political activists [14]. Many of the accounts involved in coordinated behaviour during the UK election were later suspended by Twitter. Similarly, most coordinated posts during the 2019 Philippine election were later removed or deleted, indicating that they contained content that violated Facebook moderation policies [25].

During the Covid-19 pandemic, one study identified that botnets mostly associated with right-wing and far-right sentiments often used coordination to promote conspiracy theories [7]. Another study related to Covid-19 identified that groups from both sides of the political divide engaged in coordinated behaviour, but content posted by right-wing accounts was more often deleted or removed from Facebook [8]. They also identified an international spread of links containing misinformation and partisan content, as accounts from Brazil, France, and some African countries also engaged in coordinated link sharing behaviour.

Building on previous research, this study focuses on coordinated behaviour around images on Facebook. This study uses a method called Coordinated Image Text Sharing Behaviour (CITSB). CITSB refers to the technique used to identify social media accounts that repeatedly share images with identical text in a short period of time from each other [4]. Previous studies mostly focused on coordinated link sharing behaviour [6, 8] and coordinated behaviour around specific hashtags [7, 14]. This study fills a gap by looking at how images are used in coordinated campaigns. Images have a powerful emotional impact [15], which can help them go viral on social media and mobilise online participation [2]. Additionally, previous research has found that visual misinformation can be seen as more credible than textual misinformation [9]. There is also a large prevalence of visual misinformation on social media. For example, a study on visual misinformation on Facebook found that 20% of their sample of images consisted of misinformation, which indicates that a large volume of misinformation has been potentially ignored by previous research that mostly focused on links [24].

To explore the role of CITSB, this research focuses on the 2022 Brazilian Election on Facebook. Political campaigns in Brazilian social media tend to be highly polarised, favouring the emergence of partisan content and misinformation from both sides of the political divide [18]. In 2022, incumbent Jair Bolsonaro ran against former President Lula da Silva. Jair Bolsonaro and his supporters were associated with misinformation campaigns during the previous election [11, 17, 22] and, particularly, during the Covid-19 pandemic [16, 19, 21]. This research focuses on Facebook because, at the time of the election, it was both the second most used social media platform in Brazil (67%) and the second most popular social media for news consumption in Brazil (40%), only behind YouTube [12].

Three research questions guide this study. *RQ1. What is the network structure based on accounts involved in coordinated behaviour?* Previous studies found mostly segregated networks of coordinated accounts involved in coordinated behaviour, indicating that each cluster is usually engaged in promoting different content from other clusters. In some cases, clusters were identified around different geographic locations or specific languages [7, 8]. Clusters of coordinated accounts were also identified around specific political ideologies or radicalised communities, such as QAnon groups [6–8, 14].

*RQ2. What are the political affiliations of Facebook accounts engaged in coordinated behaviour?* Coordinated behaviour has been mostly associated with right-wing accounts, particularly those promoting conspiracy theories and anti-vaccine content [6–8]. There is also evidence of left-wing accounts involved in coordinated behaviour, but previous research has identified that posts from right-wing coordinated accounts were more often deleted or removed [8, 14]. Overall, findings from previous studies indicate that both sides of the political divide might engage in coordinated behaviour, but the spread of misinformation and problematic content is more strongly associated with right-wing communities.

*RQ 3. What is the content shared in different clusters of coordinated accounts?* Coordinated behaviour is often used to spread partisan content, misinformation, hateful content, and spam [6, 7, 23]. Previous research identified that posts from coordinated accounts are frequently deleted or removed from the platforms, indicating the presence of problematic content [8, 14].

## 2  Methods

CrowdTangle was used to collect Facebook posts during the 2022 Brazilian run-off election. CrowdTangle is a Meta-owned tool that allows researchers and journalists to access and analyse public content on Facebook. It tracks the content of over 7 million influential Facebook pages, groups, and verified profiles, including all pages with 25K+ followers or likes, all public groups with 95K+ members (or 2K+ members for US-based public groups), and all verified profiles.

The search query for data collection was "Lula OR Bolsonaro", the names of the two candidates in the run-off of the election. While this means that posts that did not contain their names were excluded from the sample, it also narrows down the search query to make the analysis more focused on the two candidates. Data collection was also limited to the period of the campaigns in the run-off, 3rd-29th of October 2022. Posts removed by Facebook or deleted by users become unavailable on CrowdTangle. Therefore, data was collected on the 1st of November, soon after the election, to ensure the completion of the dataset. Finally, only posts containing images were collected for this analysis. In total, the dataset contained 509,219 public Facebook posts.

A specialised R script was used to identify coordinated accounts and the images they shared during the 2022 Brazilian run-off election. The R script called Coordinated Image Text Sharing Behaviour (CITSB) [4] reuses some of CooRnet [5] codes and logics to detect Facebook accounts repeatedly sharing images with identical text in a short period of time from each other. For this analysis, the coordination interval was set to 60 s, as established by previous research [7, 10]. This means that coordination is identified when two or more Facebook accounts share an image with the exact same text within 0–60 s of each other. Focusing on the image text poses some limitations, as this technique is less likely to identify manipulated images posted out of context as evidence for false claims. On the other hand, previous research in Brazil has identified that the most viral visual misinformation posts about Covid-19 on Instagram (an image-based platform) heavily relied on textual elements, such as posting screenshots of news headlines and posts from other platforms, overlaying text in front of images to provide context, and adding subtitles to videos [20].

Using CITSB, a network of coordinated accounts was created based on 126,730 coordinated posts. In the network, Facebook accounts (nodes) were connected when they shared images with the same text within the set threshold of 60 s. The resulting network consisted of 7295 Facebook accounts and 83276 edges connecting them. Gephi [1] was used to analyse the network, with a particular focus on the clusters of accounts that often shared images with the same text in a coordinated manner identified based on a community detection algorithm embedded in the CITSB script.

The community detection algorithm used by CITSB returned over one thousand clusters, most of them with less than 10 accounts within. Therefore, this analysis focuses on the main clusters of the coordinated network, based on an arbitrary threshold that only considers clusters containing at least 5% of the nodes in the network (i.e. at least 365 accounts). Three clusters met this threshold: cluster 1 (n = 1942 nodes, 26.5%), cluster 2 (n = 1224 nodes, 16.8%), and cluster 3 (n = 510 nodes, 7%). To make the analysis more focused, only accounts that engaged in coordinated behaviour at least twice were kept in the network, to avoid including accounts that might have coincidentally shared an image with the same text as other coordinated accounts on just one occasion. After the second filtering step, 1694 nodes remained in cluster 1, and they engaged in a total of 50,022 coordinated shares. Cluster 2 contained 1092 that engaged in 35,189 coordinated shares. Cluster 3 contained 465 nodes that engaged in 3,237 coordinated shares. The main accounts within each cluster, as well as the content they shared were manually reviewed to identify their political affiliation and provide insights about the strategies behind CITSB.

## 3    Results

### 3.1    What is the Network Structure Based on Accounts Involved in Coordinated Behaviour?

The network (Fig. 1) discovered in data analysis has a mostly polarised structure showing high segregation, especially between the two biggest clusters (1 and 2). To illustrate it, 96.6% of the edges of nodes within cluster 1 are internal (connecting two nodes within cluster 1), 94.1% of the edges of nodes within cluster 2 are internal, and 70% of the edges of nodes within cluster 3 are internal. Nodes within cluster 3 are similarly connected to cluster 1 (16.1%) and cluster 2 (13.9%). In response to RQ1, the segregated structure of the network indicates that most of the coordinated campaigns occurred within the clusters. This reflects on the political ideology of the cluster, as discussed below.

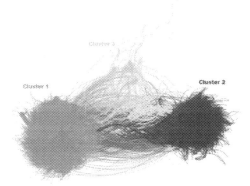

**Fig. 1.** Network of accounts that engaged in CITSB (3251 nodes, 64331 edges).

### 3.2  What are the Political Affiliations of Facebook Accounts Engaged in Coordinated Behaviour?

The polarised structure of the network reflects the political affiliations of Facebook accounts engaged in CITSB. While cluster 1 was mostly associated with the far-right politician Jair Bolsonaro, cluster 2 was mostly associated with the leftist Lula da Silva. Cluster 3, on the other hand, did not have a clear association with a political ideology, rather it is mainly composed of Facebook groups related to buying and selling products in specific locations. These types of Facebook groups are very popular in Brazil and have been found to be associated with misinformation spread during the Covid-19 pandemic [16].

The Facebook accounts with the highest degree (those that more often engaged in CITSB) within cluster 1 mostly make references to Bolsonaro (also referred to as "myth" and "Captain") and the political party he is trying to create (Alliance for Brazil), such as: "*Mito 22* (Myth 22)" (2253 degree), "*Aliança pelo Brasil 22* (Alliance for Brazil)" (1135 degree), "O Capitão Do Povo – Jair 22 (The People's Captain – Jair 22)" (1038 degree), "*Bolsonaro 2022*" (1007 degree), "*BOLSONARO ATÉ 2026* (Bolsonaro until 2026)" (909 degree). Some accounts also make general references to nationalism and conservatism, such as "*FORÇABRASIL* (Go ahead Brazil)" (1237 degree), "*Direita Politica* (Right-wing politics)" (1096 degree). Finally, there are also accounts linked to some of his supporters, such as the conservative polemicist Olavo de Carvalho, who supported Bolsonaro's campaign in 2018, but died in 2022 before the election: "*GRUPO OLAVO DE CARVALHO* (Olavo de Carvalho group)" (1040 degree).

The Facebook accounts with the highest degree within cluster 2 mostly include pro-Lula, pro-Workers' Party (his political party), and left-wing Facebook groups: "*APOIO A VOLTA DO LULA* (I support Lula's return)" (479 degree), "*Militantes de Esquerda* (Left-wing militants)" (449 degree), "*LULA PRESIDENTE* (Lula President)" (438 degree), "*A Gazeta Petista* (Workers' Party Gazette)" (429 degree), "*NOSSO ETERNO PRES-IDENTE LULA* (Our eternal President Lula)" (410 degree), "*Todos contra a globo e todos a favor do Lula* (Everybody against Globo and everybody pro-Lula)" (398 degree), "*Lula*" (389 degree). The Facebook group with the highest degree within this cluster was created to mock conservatives, pejoratively called "Coxinhas" (the term was originally used to mock military police and posh Brazilians): "*Perolas dos Coxinhas* (Gems from Coxinhas)" (530 degree).

Finally, most accounts within cluster 3 were Facebook groups associated with specific locations that aimed to be a space for buying and selling products. For example: "*CLASSIFICADOS DE MANACAPURU AMAZONAS* (Classified ads Manacapuru Amazonas)" (106 degree), "VUCO VUCO de NATAL GRANDE NATAL e RIO GRANDE DO NORTE (Mess in Natal, Greater Natal, and Rio Grande do Norte)" (62 degree), "*Compra, Venda e Troca – Tocantins* (Buy, Sell, Exchange – Tocantins)" (58 degree), "*Vila Velha – Vitória – Cariacica – VENDAS e TROCAS – ES27* (Vila Velha – Vitória – Cariacica – Sell and Exchange – ES27)" (57 degree), "*Desapega Tijucal e Região* (Let go Tijucal and Region)" (57 degree), "*Classificados Espírito Santo* (Classified ads Espírito Santo)" (52 degree), "*VENDA.COM – Feirão de Palmas-TO* (Sell.com – Sale in Palmas-TO)" (52 degree). Just one of the main accounts within the cluster was related to politics, but not to a specific party or ideology: "*POLÍTICA* (Politics)" (76 degree).

In response to RQ2, this analysis shows that both sides of the political divide engaged in coordinated behaviour, similar to findings from previous research [8, 14]. Nevertheless, CITSB was most prevalent within the right-wing cluster 1, composed of over half of the accounts in the final network (52.8%). Additionally, nodes within cluster 1 were also those with the highest degree in the network (as high as 2253 degree, meaning that the node engaged in CITSB with over two thousand accounts during the run-off election). Nodes within cluster 1 had an average degree of 44.5, compared to 37.5 within cluster 2 and 11.2 within cluster 3. One account within cluster 1 (*Mito 22*) engaged in as many as 6037 coordinated shares, while other eight accounts within this cluster engaged in over 500 coordinated shares. For comparison, only four accounts within cluster 2 engaged in over 500 coordinated shares (the account with the most coordinated shares engaged in CITSB 727 times), and none within cluster 3 (38 was the most coordinated shares by an account within this cluster). This shows that there were more Facebook accounts supporting Bolsonaro engaging in CITSB and that they were also more active than accounts supporting Lula. A somewhat unexpected finding was the presence of buy-and-sell local groups within cluster 3, but these were also engaged in political disputes, as discussed below.

### 3.3   What is the Content Shared in Different Clusters of Coordinated Accounts?

The most prevalent content shared from accounts within cluster 1 was promotional content related to Bolsonaro's campaign. Many images promoted live streams organised by Bolsonaro and his supporters (see Figs. 2 and 3 for example). There were also images criticising his opponent Lula da Silva and showing support for Bolsonaro (see Fig. 4).

Some of the most prevalent content within cluster 1 also included conspiracy theories and misinformation. In terms of conspiracy theories, the content most frequently shared in a coordinated manner focused on Brazilian electronic ballots and election fraud. This is a recurrent conspiracy theory reproduced by Bolsonaro and his supporters in Brazil [13]. Bolsonaro and his supporters claim that there is a conspiracy involving the left-wing Workers' Party, the mainstream media, the Brazilian Supreme Court, the Brazilian Superior Electoral Court, among others, to manipulate electronic ballots and

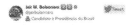

**Fig. 2.** Shared in a coordinated manner 213 times within cluster 1. In Portuguese: - Soon, at 19:00, we will make an important announcement on our social media. I ask you to share this invitation with all your contacts so that our announcement reaches all Brazilians. We'll be back soon!

**Fig. 3.** Shared in a coordinated manner 180 times within cluster 1. In Portuguese: Super Live. On the 22$^{nd}$ at 17:00. Lasting 22 h. With Neymar, Tarcisio, Silas Malafaia, Sergio Moro and +.

**Fig. 4.** Shared in a coordinated manner 190 times within cluster 1. In Portuguese: Minas Gerais, Rio de Janeiro and Sao Paulo governors declare support for Jair Bolsonaro's re-election against the Workers' Party.

the result of elections in the country. Figures 5–7 illustrates some of the images shared in a coordinated manner to spread such conspiracy theory.

In terms of misinformation, the main target of false and misleading claims was Bolsonaro's opponent Lula da Silva. Among the content most often shared in a coordinated manner, images reproduced a major misinformation narrative linking Lula to traffic and criminal factions in Brazil (see Figs. 8 and 9). During the campaign, Lula visited *Complexo do Alemão* (German's Complex), one of the largest groups of favelas in Rio de Janeiro, and wore a cap with the letters "CPX". They mean *Complexo* in reference to what neighbourhoods with a group of favelas are called in Brazil. Bolsonaro's son, Flávio, fuelled the spread of a misinformation narrative on social media by associating Lula's cap with criminal factions in the country. The narrative claimed that CPX referred to the word *cupinxa*, which refers to those who are friendly to criminal factions, and a clear indication that Lula was backed by *Comando Vermelho* (Red Commando), a major criminal faction in Brazil involved in drugs and arms trafficking. One of these images (Fig. 9) was fact-checked and identified as false by Facebook, so it appeared blurred to users with a message that it was false information and users would only be able to see it after clicking to see why it was false and then clicking to see the post.

Another piece of misinformation focused on Lula's corruption trial. Lula was in prison for over a year as part of the corruption investigation called Car Wash, led by judge Sergio Moro. After Lula's arrest, Sergio Moro openly supported Bolsonaro's election in 2018 and became the Justice Minister of his administration. Leaked Telegram conversations later showed that Sergio Moro was releasing insider information to prosecutors and engaging in partial behaviour during the legal process, in a journalistic investigation named #VazaJato or Car Wash Leak [3]. Lula's trial was later claimed invalid, and he was released from prison. In Fig. 10, Bolsonaro claims that Lula should

**Fig. 5.** Shared in a coordinated manner 185 times within cluster 1. In Portuguese: Urgent. Bolsonaro summons commanders of the armed forces after the Brazilian Supreme Electoral Court decisions. President Jair Bolsonaro called an emergency ministerial meeting for this Wednesday, 26, at the Alvorada Palace, with the presence of the commanders of the Army, Freire Gomes; Navy, Almir Garnier Santos; and Aeronautics, Carlos de Almeida Baptista Junior.

**Fig. 6.** Shared in a coordinated manner 95 times within cluster 1. In Portuguese: #ElectoralCrime. Urgent: the Brazilian Supreme Electoral Court exonerates the employee responsible for insertions of electoral propaganda.

**Fig. 7.** Shared in a coordinated manner 94 times within cluster 1. In Portuguese: Both auditing firms have extensive experience and credibility in the market, serving renowned multinationals and even public organisations. Both will release official notes tomorrow morning that will shock Brazil. Just a tip to those who are trying to disqualify the evidence and auditing companies: do not rush, as Alexandre de Moraes did. There's a lot more tomorrow. And the numbers are impressive!

be in prison and criticises the United Nations for saying that Lula should have been able to run for the presidency in 2018 (when he was in prison).

The most prevalent content within cluster 2 includes campaigning images associated with Lula's campaign. These include images criticising Bolsonaro, such as in Figs. 11 and 12. The first one highlights a corruption investigation that involves Bolsonaro. The second one, mentions a case during a political debate on TV that the presenter (William Bonner) received the right to reply to accusations made by Bolsonaro. Usually, only political candidates have the right to reply to each other when a candidate accuses or lies about another, but in this case Bonner responded to Bolsonaro's accusation that the presenter was the only one to absolve Lula from his charges. There were also images promoting Lula and his campaign events (see Fig. 13). These images either promoted Lula's ideas or invited social media users to participate in social media lives and other events.

Some content within cluster 2 also focused on debunking accusations against Lula, including misinformation. A major recurring misinformation narrative pushed by Bolsonaro's supporters during the campaign was that Lula worships the Devil and does not believe in God. Some also said that Lula was planning to shut down churches around the country. Brazil is a majorly Christian country, so this narrative had the potential to hurt Lula's chances in the election. Figures 14–16 shows how CITSB was used to debunk misinformation targeting Lula. Different from cluster 1, there were no misinformation pieces among the most shared content within cluster 2.

**Fig. 8.** Shared in a coordinated manner 111 times within cluster 1. In Portuguese: Everybody knows that in areas dominated by traffic, only those who are friends with the bandits enter in peace. By claiming that he visited a community controlled by one of the biggest factions without any protection, something that not even the police can do, Lula shows once again that he is the candidate of the crime.

**Fig. 9.** Shared in a coordinated manner 109 times within cluster 1. In Portuguese: Bolsonaro visits the Basilic Church of Our Lady of Aparecida and appears on another occasion wearing a Federal Highway Police cap. Lula visits "Red Commando headquarters" in Alemao, RJ, and wears a cap that means *cupinxa* (partner) of crime".

**Fig. 10.** Shared in a coordinated manner 98 times within cluster 1. In Portuguese: Lula was investigated and he was arrested and convicted in three instances of corruption and $$$ laundry. He won nothing, he received a hand to be released and restart the processes. The crimes existed! And about that "victory" in the United Nations, it's as real as democracy in Nicaragua.

**Fig. 11.** Shared in a coordinated manner 254 times within cluster 2. In Portuguese: Urgent. Federal Police bust Bolsolao and arrest people linked to Bolsonaro's secret budget.

**Fig. 12.** Shared in a coordinated manner 119 times within cluster 2. In Portuguese: Bolsonaro lies so much that even Bonner had the right to reply.

**Fig. 13.** Shared in a coordinated manner 93 times within cluster 2. In Portuguese: Today, 19:00. Live with Lula on Janone's Facebook.

**Fig. 14.** Shared in a coordinated manner 60 times within cluster 2. In Portuguese: Stop lying, Bolsonaro! The Superior Electoral Tribunal orders Facebook and Twitter to delete 31 Bolsonarist's posts lying that Lula persecutes Christians and supports the invasion of churches.

**Fig. 15.** Shared in a coordinated manner 50 times within cluster 2. In Portuguese: Fake News. Lula and the Devil. 1 Lula believes in God and is a Christian. 2 Lula has no pact nor has he ever talked to the Devil. 3 Lula believes that a president should take care of those who are hungry. 4 With Lula in the presidency, Brazil lived a moment of prosperity and the country became the 6th largest economy in the world. 5 With Lula, the salary was enough to buy food, gas, pay the rent and even have a barbecue.

**Fig. 16.** Shared in a coordinated manner 31 times within cluster 2. In Portuguese: "The story that Lula is going to close churches is a lie, but that Bolsonaro is practically closing universities, federal schools and kindergartens, this is indeed true. Today, the government saw fit to broaden the cuts.".

Finally, cluster 3 included content from both sides of the political divide. Nevertheless, there was a higher prevalence of pro-Bolsonaro content promoted by CITSB. This content was mostly similar to what was shared within cluster 1 in terms of campaigning. CITSB was used within cluster 3 to criticise Lula and the Workers' Party (see Fig. 17) and to promote Bolsonaro (see Figs. 18 and 19). When promoting Bolsonaro, images also contained his number (22), which is used on election day in Brazil to vote for a candidate.

Pro-Lula content shared within cluster 3 was also similar in terms of campaigning. CITSB was mostly used to promote Lula. In Fig. 20, Lula is with Simone Tebet and Ciro Gomes, presidential candidates who finished third and fourth in the first round and decided to support Lula in the run-off election. This image also includes Lula's number (13). Figures 21 and 22 are examples of posts sharing results from polls that showed that Lula would likely win the election.

The most prevalent content shared within cluster 3 indicates that supporters of both candidates were engaging in CITSB to convince undecided voters to vote for their candidates. This is likely due to the characteristics of cluster 3, as it included mostly Facebook groups for buying and selling products in specific locations (therefore, not intrinsically partisan groups). To convince undecided voters, pro-Bolsonaro content criticised Lula and highlighted Bolsonaro's number. Pro-Lula content highlighted the support he received from other presidential candidates who did not go to the run-off election and electoral polls showing Lula's advantage.

In response to RQ3, both clusters 1 and 2 mostly focused on partisan content aligned with their side of the political divide. Cluster 1 engaged in CITSB to promote Bolsonaro, but also to spread conspiracy theories and misinformation. Cluster 2 engaged in CITSB to promote Lula and debunk false narratives about him. Finally, cluster 3 contained content from both sides of the political divide, with the campaigns seemingly having used CITSB to convince undecided voters.

**Fig. 17.** Shared in a coordinated manner 37 times within cluster 3. In Portuguese: "Lula says he will develop Brazil". Really? The Workers' Party stayed in power for 14 years, created the biggest corruption scandal in history and left 13 million unemployed.

**Fig. 18.** Shared in a coordinated manner 32 times within cluster 3. In Portuguese: Now is 22.

**Fig. 19.** Shared in a coordinated manner 24 times within cluster 3.

**Fig. 20.** Shared in a coordinated manner 28 times within cluster 3. In Portuguese: We are in the second round with Lula.

**Fig. 21.** Shared in a coordinated manner 24 times within cluster 3. In Portuguese: Leader Lula. Datafolha poll points out Lula to be the next Brazilian president.

**Fig. 22.** Shared in a coordinated manner 18 times within cluster 3. In Portuguese: Lula goes ahead and increases the difference. The Quaest poll that was contracted by Genial bank shows Lula with 54% of the valid votes. Bolsonaro has only 46%.

## 4 Discussion

This research shows how CITSB was a strategy used by both sides of the political divide in Brazil. This finding is similar to previous research on elections in the United Kingdom [14] and discussions about unproven drugs for Covid-19 in the United States [8]. Facebook accounts engaging in coordinated behaviour on Facebook might contribute to fuelling polarisation during the election, since partisan content shared in a coordinated manner gains more prevalence in public discussions [6]. This is particularly problematic in Brazil, given the country's history of polarisation, partisanship, and misinformation spread seen in the previous election in 2018 [18]. Nevertheless, this analysis also showed that coordination can be used to debunk misinformation.

Both sides used CITSB to share content associated with Bolsonaro's (for the right-wing accounts within cluster 1) and Lula's (for the left-wing accounts within cluster 2) campaigns. They had similar strategies to promote their candidate, sharing information about events and social media live streams, and criticising their opponent. Interestingly, promotional content was not locked into clusters of their supporters. This research has found evidence of CITSB in local buy-and-sell Facebook groups (within cluster 3). These were spaces of dispute, where content from both sides of the political divide was shared in a coordinated manner. This was likely used to convince undecided voters. This finding shows that CITSB is not restricted to ideological "echo chambers", but crosses ideological borders to convince others and gather votes for either Bolsonaro or Lula in the studied case. This is different from what has been seen in previous research, where coordination was mostly happening within partisan clusters [6–8, 14]. Future research can expand on this study's findings to further explore how coordination is used on social media beyond ideological silos.

While both sides engaged in CITSB to spread promotional content about their campaigns, there were major differences in terms of misinformation and conspiracy theories. Similar to previous research, the spread of misinformation and conspiracy theories in a coordinated manner was strongly associated with right-wing accounts [7, 8, 25]. Two main narratives were shared in a coordinated manner by conservative accounts: the recurring claim that electronic ballots are unreliable and an instrument for election fraud, and the narrative trying to link Lula with criminal factions. Left-leaning accounts, on the other hand, engaged in CITSB to debunk false claims about Lula, such as the narratives that he would shut down churches if elected or that he had a pact with the Devil. Therefore, while there is a higher prevalence of coordinated behaviour being associated with negative outcomes, coordination is not intrinsically negative and can also be used to debunk misinformation. Future studies can further explore how coordinated behaviour might be used for good, such as by sharing fact-checked information.

Although there was evidence of CITSB being used to spread conspiracy theories and misinformation, only one of the most shared images was flagged by Facebook. Additionally, most of the content shared in a coordinated manner was still available on the platform as of March 2023, almost five months after the election. This finding is different from previous research, which identified that much of the content shared in a coordinated manner was later removed or excluded from social media [8, 25]. There are two potential explanations for why most of the content was still available after the election. While previous research focused on coordinated link sharing behaviour, this study focused on image text. Therefore, the first potential explanation is that content moderation of images might be more challenging than monitoring external links. For example, a previous study on Brazilian Instagram found that most posts containing misinformation continued to be available on the platform, and very few were flagged as false [20]. More studies are necessary to explore how Facebook and other social media platforms' content moderation deal with visual misinformation.

Previous research has also found that most links containing Covid-related misinformation shared in Portuguese in a coordinated manner by Brazilian accounts continued to be available on Facebook [8]. Therefore, a second potential explanation for most of the content shared by accounts that engaged in CITSB continue to be available on Facebook is that the platform is not as effective in monitoring non-English content in countries like Brazil. Future studies can also further explore how Facebook and other social media platforms' content moderation might be less effective when dealing with non-English content.

As with any empirical research, this study has limitations that motivate future research and further development in the study of coordinated behaviour on social media. CITSB has limitations since it focuses on the text, not the image. Although visual misinformation often relies on text to spread misleading claims [20], CITSB does not cover manipulated images without text or other types of media such as deepfakes. Future research can explore other ways to analyse how these media are shared in coordinated campaigns. CITSB also relies on a specific time frame to define coordination (in the case of this research, posts shared within 60 s of each other). Some of the accounts in the network might have shared the same image as others without planning or coordination. Nevertheless, even if some of these accounts were not involved in coordinated behaviour, the analysed network indicates that they were part of highly partisan campaigns by sharing political content and, in some cases, conspiracy theories and misinformation.

## 5   Conclusion

This study explored how Facebook accounts engaged in CITSB during the 2022 Brazilian election. Findings include that both sides of the political divide engaged in coordinated behaviour. Both Bolsonaro's and Lula's supporters used CITSB to share promotional campaign-related content on Facebook, such as criticising their opponents, promoting lives on Facebook, and highlighting politicians who were supporting the candidates. This research has also found evidence that CITSB was used beyond their ideological silos, since there was evidence of CITSB in local and buy-and-sell Facebook groups without a particular political ideology. This was likely a strategy to convince undecided voters. In terms of differences, pro-Bolsonaro accounts engaged in CITSB to spread misinformation and conspiracy theories. Pro-Lula accounts, on the other hand, engaged in CITSB to debunk false claims against Lula.

While this study included a mostly exploratory analysis, it identified paths for future research. First, pro-Bolsonaro and pro-Lula clusters engaged in CITSB for similar goals (sharing campaign content), but also for different purposes (spreading misinformation vs. debunking it). Future studies can further explore these different strategies in other political contexts. Additionally, these results show that coordination can also be used to fight misinformation, and future research can focus on how coordination might be used for good. Findings also included that content moderation might be failing to tackle visual misinformation and non-English content, which encourages future studies in these areas. Finally, this study identified how coordination was used beyond political silos, likely to target undecided voters. Future research can focus on coordination during political campaigns with a particular focus on strategies used to target undecided voters.

## References

1. Bastian, M., et al.: Gephi: an open source software for exploring and manipulating networks. ICWSM. **3**(1), 361–362 (2009). https://doi.org/10.1609/icwsm.v3i1.13937
2. Casas, A., Williams, N.W.: Images that Matter: online protests and the mobilizing role of pictures. Polit. Res. Q. **72**(2), 360–375 (2019). https://doi.org/10.1177/1065912918786805
3. Fishman, A., et al.: Breach of Ethics: Exclusive: leaked chats between brazilian judge and prosecutor who imprisoned lula reveal prohibited collaboration and doubts over evidence (2019). https://theintercept.com/2019/06/09/brazil-lula-operation-car-wash-sergio-moro/
4. Giglietto, F.: Coordinated image text sharing behaviour (2022). https://github.com/fabiogiglietto/CooRnet_ImgTxt
5. Giglietto, F., et al.: CooRnet: detect coordinated link sharing behavior on social media (2020). https://github.com/fabiogiglietto/CooRnet
6. Giglietto, F., et al.: It takes a village to manipulate the media: coordinated link sharing behavior during 2018 and 2019 Italian elections. Inf. Commun. Soc. **23**(6), 867–891 (2020). https://doi.org/10.1080/1369118X.2020.1739732
7. Graham, T., et al.: Like a virus the coordinated spread of coronavirus disinformation. Queensland University of Technology (2020)

8. Gruzd, A., et al.: How coordinated link sharing behavior and partisans' narrative framing fan the spread of COVID-19 misinformation and conspiracy theories. Soc. Net. Anal. Min. **12**(1), 118 (2022). https://doi.org/10.1007/s13278-022-00948-y
9. Hameleers, M., et al.: A Picture Paints a Thousand Lies? The effects and mechanisms of multimodal disinformation and rebuttals disseminated via social media. Polit. Commun. **37**(2), 281–301 (2020). https://doi.org/10.1080/10584609.2019.1674979
10. Keller, F.B., et al.: Political Astroturfing on Twitter: how to coordinate a disinformation campaign. Polit. Commun. **37**(2), 256–280 (2020). https://doi.org/10.1080/10584609.2019.1661888
11. Machado, C., et al.: A study of misinformation in WhatsApp groups with a focus on the brazilian presidential elections. In: Companion Proceedings of The 2019 World Wide Web Conference, pp. 1013–1019 Association for Computing Machinery, New York, NY, USA (2019). https://doi.org/10.1145/3308560.3316738
12. Newman, N., et al.: Reuters Institute Digital News Report 2022. University of Oxford, Oxford (2022)
13. Nicas, J., et al.: How Bolsonaro built the myth of stolen elections in Brazil (2022). https://www.nytimes.com/interactive/2022/10/25/world/americas/brazil-bolsonaro-misinformation.html
14. Nizzoli, L., et al.: Coordinated behavior on social media in 2019 UK general election. In: Proceedings of the International AAAI Conference on Web and Social Media, pp. 443–454. AAAI (2021)
15. Powell, T.E., et al.: A Clearer Picture: the contribution of visuals and text to framing effects. J. Commun. **65**(6), 997–1017 (2015). https://doi.org/10.1111/jcom.12184
16. Recuero, R., et al.: Bolsonaro and the Far Right: how disinformation about COVID-19 circulates on Facebook in Brazil. Int. J. Commun. **16**, 148–171 (2022)
17. Recuero, R., et al.: Discursive strategies for disinformation on WhatsApp and Twitter during the 2018 Brazilian presidential election. First Monday. **26**(1) (2021). https://doi.org/10.5210/fm.v26i1.10551
18. Recuero, R., et al.: Hyperpartisanship, disinformation and political conversations on Twitter: the brazilian presidential election of 2018. In: Proceedings of the International AAAI Conference on Web and Social Media, pp. 569–578 (2020)
19. Ricard, J., Medeiros, J.: Using misinformation as a political weapon: COVID-19 and Bolsonaro in Brazil. Harvard Kennedy Sch. Misinformation Rev. **1**(3) (2020). https://doi.org/10.37016/mr-2020-013
20. Soares, F.B., et al.: Infodemia e Instagram: como a plataforma é apropriada para a produção de desinformação sobre a hidroxicloroquina? Fronteiras - Estudos Midiáticos **23**, 2 (2021). https://doi.org/10.4013/fem.2021.232.07
21. Soares, F.B., et al.: Research note: Bolsonaro's firehose: how Covid-19 disinformation on WhatsApp was used to fight a government political crisis in Brazil. Harvard Kennedy Sch. (HKS) Misinformation Rev. **2**(1) (2021). https://doi.org/10.37016/mr-2020-54
22. Soares, F.B., Recuero, R.: Hashtag Wars: political disinformation and discursive struggles on twitter conversations during the 2018 brazilian presidential campaign. Soc. Media + Soc. **7**(2), 20563051211009070 (2021). https://doi.org/10.1177/20563051211009073
23. Weber, D., Neumann, F.: Amplifying influence through coordinated behaviour in social networks. Soc. Netw. Anal. Min. **11**(1), 1–42 (2021). https://doi.org/10.1007/s13278-021-00815-2
24. Yang, Y., Davis, T., Hindman, M.: Visual misinformation on Facebook. J. Commun. **73**(4), 316–328 (2023). https://doi.org/10.1093/joc/jqac051
25. Yu, W.E.S.: A framework for studying coordinated behaviour applied to the 2019 Philippine midterm elections. In: Proceedings of the 6th International Congress on Information and Communication Technology (ICICT 2021), pp. 721–731 Springer (2021). https://doi.org/10.1007/978-981-16-2380-6_63

# The Information Disorder Level (IDL) Index: A Human-Based Metric to Assess the Factuality of Machine-Generated Content

Laurence Dierickx⬚, Carl-Gustav Lindén⬚, and Andreas L. Opdahl[(✉)]⬚

University of Bergen, Bergen, Norway
{l.dierickx,carl-gustav.linden,andreas.opdahl}@uib.no

**Abstract.** Large language models have enabled the rapid production of misleading or fake narratives, presenting a challenge for direct detection methods. Considering that generative artificial intelligence tools are likely to be used either to inform or to disinform, evaluating the (non)human nature of machine-generated content is questioned, especially regarding the 'hallucination' phenomenon, which relates to generated content that does not correspond to real-world input. In this study, we argue that assessing machine-generated content is most reliable when done by humans because doing so involves critical consideration of the meaning of the information and its informative, misinformative or disinformative value, which is related to the accuracy and reliability of the news. To explore human-based judgement methods, we developed the Information Disorder Level (IDL) index, a language-independent metric to evaluate the factuality of machine-generated content. It has been tested on a corpus of forty made-up and actual news stories generated with ChatGPT. For newsrooms using generative AI, results suggest that every piece of machine-generated content should be vetted and post-edited by humans before being published. From a digital media literacy perspective, the IDL index is a valuable tool to understand the limits of generative AI and trigger a reflection on what constitutes the factuality of a reported event.

**Keywords:** Generative AI · natural language processing · social science

## 1 Introduction

Through large language models (LLMs), such as ChatGPT (Generative Pre-trained Transformer), generative artificial intelligence (GenAI) has become a cheap and quick method to generate misleading or fake stories, mimicking human

This research was funded by EU CEF Grant No. 2394203.

D. Ceolin et al. (Eds.): MISDOOM 2023, LNCS 14397, pp. 60–71, 2023.
https://doi.org/10.1007/978-3-031-47896-3_5

writing with coherence and fluidity [1,2]. This new means for creating and disseminating information disorder contributes to the computational amplification phenomenon because of the ability to produce and disseminate content on a large scale [3]. The potential consequences of these activities include causing harm to online communities and manipulating public opinions by spreading disinformation or conspiracy theories [2].

Among the numerous ethical and practical challenges related to the use of GenAI systems, the ability to detect machine-generated text accurately is a crucial issue [4,5]. Hence, the primary approach to encountering machine-generated misinformation or disinformation involves using detection systems. Research in this field has started to grow, and most of the studies are available on arXiv, meaning that they have not yet been peer-reviewed or will be published in the next coming weeks or months, making it difficult to establish a well-defined standard. However, some of the available results demonstrated the limitations of current detection systems. First, they cannot be considered accurate and reliable tools as they do not differentiate between human and machine writing effectively [6]. Second, they still suffer several limitations, the majority of which stem from their binary classification problems and dependence on the English language, rendering them ineffective in many cases [7]. Even the classifier developed by Open AI, the company behind ChatGPT, was unreliable, as it generated more false positives than true positives, leading to the shutdown of the online service [8].

Machine-generated texts have become so sophisticated that they are increasingly difficult to distinguish from human writing, even for experts [2,9,10]. This capacity to generate compelling pieces extends far beyond its (mis)use in creating and disseminating information disorders. For instance, journalists and news publishers also employ GenAI systems to provide information to their audiences. According to a survey published by the World Association of News Publishers (WAN-IFRA) [11], half of the newsrooms worldwide is already using GenAI technologies.

Generating misleading or inaccurate content is not always intentional, as the system is likely to produce wrong or inaccurate outcomes without being prompted [12]. This phenomenon is called 'artificial hallucination', which is described as generating realistic experiences that do not correspond to any real-world input [13]. It occurs when the generated content relies on the internal logic or patterns of the system [14]. It can be explained by the fact that the system was trained on large amounts of unsupervised data [5]. The black-box nature of the system also explains its malfunctions [14]. Furthermore, research pinpointed that the process followed by LLMs is error-prone, starting with biased training data, which poses a threat not only to the accuracy and reliability of the machine-generated content but also to its ability to generate harmful content [15,16].

Because LLMs are just as likely to be used to inform as to misinform or disinform [13], the ability to detect the human or non-human nature of a text cannot guarantee that a given piece of content has been intentionally manipulated. From this perspective, the relevance of direct detection systems is questioned in the context of news information [17,18]. Also, distinguishing truthful text from misinformation has become particularly challenging as they present similar writing styles to machine-generated texts with true content [19], while research primarily focused on detecting AI-generated text without focusing on this specific context [20].

On the other hand, there is a need to develop more comprehensive approaches that consider the broader ecosystem of dis- and misinformation dissemination. This requires a nuanced perspective, acknowledging that transparency about the nature of a text's authorship is insufficient to address the multifaceted challenges posed by misleading content. Although research has stressed the importance of semantic detection and fact-verification in preventing and detecting the misuse of machine-generated content [21, 22], these computational approaches remain limited [23]. This is mainly because verification or automated fact-checking requires socio-technical considerations upstream and downstream of the process, not only because humans use these automated tools at the end but also because verification and fact-checking still require a human touch, especially from the perspective of developing a critical and nuanced approach, which are difficult to automate in news verification and fact-checking [24–26]. At the same time, research also demonstrated the added value of human expertise to evaluate and mitigate artificial hallucinations [27, 28].

Building upon these considerations, this study participates in the paradigm shift from classifying a news piece as human or non-human to focusing on the content quality by evaluating the presence of manipulated or fake content. Therefore, it explores the potential of leveraging human-based judgement methods from the field of natural language processing (NLP) to assess the characteristics of machine-generated content [29, 30]. Specifically, it outlines the potential applications of the Information Disorder Level (IDL) index, a human-based judgement metric designed to evaluate the factual accuracy of machine-generated content. It demonstrates that the assessment of machine-generated content is most reliable when done by humans because it involves critical thought about the meaning of the information and its informative value, which is related to the accuracy and reliability of the news.

## 2    Method

In NLP, human-based evaluations involve judges (experts) who are asked to rate a corpus of generated texts and human-written texts by humans by assigning a score on a rating scale. In Lester and Porter's experiment, for instance, which was one of the first in this field, eight experts were asked to assign a rating to 15 texts according to different criteria (quality, consistency, writing style, content, organisation and accuracy) [31]. Such an approach is intrinsic, i.e., related to the content's quality according to several criteria. In contrast, an extrinsic approach includes measuring the impact of the generated texts on task performance, the quantity or level of post-edition of generated texts or the speed at which people read generated texts [32].

Assessments based on human judgement must ensure that subjects/judges are independent, impartial and familiar with the application domain, considering that the opinions of human experts are likely to vary [33,34]. Although they are long and expensive to implement, their benefits are to assess the quality of the system and its properties, to demonstrate progress in the field and understand the current state of the field [30].

Human-based judgement methods were used in journalism studies to assess the audiences' perception of automatically generated content that derived from a data-to-text approach and to question the human or non-human nature of the author [35–38]. They also used rating scales to assess the intrinsic quality of generated texts, such as coherence, descriptive value, usability, writing quality, informativeness, clarity, pleasantness, interest, boredom, preciseness, trustworthiness and objectivity [39]; or intelligence, education, reliability, bias, accuracy, completeness, factuality, quality and honesty [40]. Hence, one of the main advantages of the method is that the quality indicators are established according to the research objective. In the context of text generated from large language models, such as ChatGPT, they can be valuable to assess both the accuracy of an event report and to what extent the system generates "artificial hallucinations" from a perspective grounded in fact detection and verification.

The development of the Information Disorder Level index is grounded in these considerations. It is derived from human analysis of a corpus of forty news articles generated using ChatGPT (see Fig. 1). Our primary objective, in this experiment, was to test the model's ability to create fake news articles in different styles. First, we asked ChatGPT to generate twenty fake news on three topics (a Russian nuclear threat to Brussels, the Chinese invasion of Taiwan, and a car accident in Norway) using five different editorial styles (factual, sensationalist, high-quality newspaper, pro-Russian, and columnist).

**SAMPLE:**
**THE WAGNER GROUP AND**
**THE RUSSIAN MILITARY**

PROMPT (FACTS)

- Tensions have escalated between the Wagner Group and the Russian military.
- Russia claimed that Ukraine suffered over 3,700 casualties during a Ukrainian offensive in the Donetsk region.
- Ukrainian military had no information about a major attack in the region and called the claims "fake."
- Kyiv officials admitted to offensive actions commencing around the city of Bakhmut.
- Prigozhin's forces withdrew from Bakhmut, transferring control to the Russian army.

Write a neutral factual news article based on these 5 facts

In recent developments, escalating tensions have been observed between the Russian military and the controversial private military company known as the Wagner Group. As both sides engage in a war of words, conflicting reports have emerged regarding casualties during a Ukrainian offensive in the Donetsk region. (...)

In a significant turn of events, it has been reported that forces affiliated with Yevgeny Prigozhin, the Russian businessman linked to the Wagner Group, have withdrawn from Bakhmut. Control of the city has been transferred to the Russian army. The reasons behind this decision and the implications it may have on the overall situation remain unclear at this time. (...)

As the situation continues to unfold, it is crucial for accurate and verified information to be disseminated to ensure an objective understanding of the events and their implications. Both sides should prioritize open communication and a commitment to resolving their differences through peaceful means, in line with international norms and agreements.

The international community remains watchful of the evolving situation in the Donetsk region and hopes for a peaceful resolution that safeguards the well-being of all parties involved and minimizes the impact on the civilian population.

**Fig. 1.** Sample text: Tensions between the Wagner Group and the Russian military (based on real events, factual style).

As we observed that ChatGPT had difficulty sticking to the facts in its writing, we asked the system to generate twenty more news stories, but this time based on real-world events (a Ukrainian invasion of Russia, the death of a famous American spy, the destruction of a dam in Ukraine, and tensions between the Wagner Group and Ukrainian forces in Donetsk). While acknowledging that the system's knowledge does not extend beyond 2021, we sought to evaluate Chat-GPT's ability to generate news articles with real-world insights using prompts based on real-world events.

The content generated by ChatGPT effectively replicated journalistic writing, which can be defined by the use of relatively short sentences and adherence to the inverted pyramid structure. This characteristic feature of journalism implies that the narrative progresses from general information to specific details [41]. [42]. However, strict adherence to the facts seemed to be the most challenging for the system. ChatGPT also tended to add comments or opinions that had nothing to do with factual journalism. We hypothesised that this was due to the nature of the prompts, where the system was also being asked to generate editorials.

To define the Information Disorder Level (IDL) index, we considered that each sentence of a text contains short pieces of information ranging from 'True' to 'False'. However, assessing the factuality of a sentence can be more nuanced than such a binary approach. Hence, we introduced the 'Mostly true' and 'Mostly false' scales. We defined these different levels as follows:

– True: Completely true or accurate and reliable (informative).
– Mostly True: Predominantly true with some elements of falsehood.
– Cannot Say: Difficult to determine accuracy.
– Mostly False: Predominantly false with some elements of truth.
– False: Completely false or incorrect (mis- or dis-informative).

Considering the total number of assessed sentences (the 'Cannot say' answer is not included in the formula, based on the assumption that, as a joker, it does not provide meaningful input to the evaluation process), the IDL index consists of the sum of the cumulative scores for 'Mostly true' (1 point attributed to each sentence), 'Mostly false' (2 points attributed to each sentence), and 'False' (3 points attributed to each sentence), divided by the total number of sentences assessed multiplied by 3 (the maximum possible score). The index is then normalised on a scale ranging from 0 to 10.

The formula for the IDL index can be expressed as:

$$\text{IDL index} = \left( \frac{(\text{MT} \times 1) + (\text{MF} \times 2) + (\text{F} \times 3)}{(\text{MT} + \text{MF} + \text{F}) \times 3} \right) \times 10$$

where:

$\text{MT}$ = number of sentences classified as 'Mostly True'

$\text{MF}$ = number of sentences classified as 'Mostly False'

$\text{F}$ = number of sentences classified as 'False'

At the operational level, we have developed an interface in JavaScript that allows a user to evaluate a text generated by a machine using the metric. The tool consists of a three-stage process. Two fields are displayed on the first screen: the first for pasting the machine-generated text and the second to paste the prompt used (see Fig. 2). The second stage consists of the actual assessment after the sentence tokenisation or segmentation of the text, which is based on the sentences' boundaries, such as dots, question marks or exclamation marks, or ellipsis [43,44]. The evaluator can always refer to the prompt used to generate the text to check if all elements are present and if there are additional elements (see Fig. 3). In other words, the evaluator proceeds by comparisons between the prompt used (source) and the generated text (target). In this prototype version, we did not include the omission of facts, which could be integrated into further developments.

Considering that current information is also characterized by the distinction between facts and comments [45,46], we introduced the Opinion/Comments (OC) rate into the prototype. Also, the human judge has the possibility of marking the sentence as an opinion or a comment, which is computed into the Opinions/Comments (OC) rate that corresponds to the percentage of sentences marked as such. It is considered a complementary indicator of the informational quality of the machine-generated content, although it is not the central element to assess the factuality of a report event. In the third step of the evaluation process, a final screen provides the results (see Fig. 4).

## 3   Results

Each text in the corpus was evaluated using the assessment tool, and the scores for the Information Disorder Level (IDL) index and the Opinion/Comments (OC) rate were recorded in a spreadsheet. Descriptive statistics were computed to evaluate the IDL index and the OC rate. The IDL index ranged from 0 (in only two cases) to 8.2. The average is 3.9, and the median is 3.3. Around 32.5% of the machine-generated texts get a score of 5 or above. In 80% of the cases, ChatGPT added made-up content, regardless of subject or style, and in 35% of the cases, it reached alarming proportions, as measured by an IDL index of 5 or higher.

As explained previously, separating facts from opinions and comments is an ethical prerequisite in journalism. Here also, ChatGPT performed poorly when contributing thoughts or observations in 100% of the cases. No text in the corpus was exempt from such additions, with a minimum Opinions/Comments (OC) rate of 2.31, reaching up to 9.5, an average of 5.65 and a median of 5.75 (see Fig. 5). To mitigate biases in these results, we excluded sensationalist, pro-Russian, and columnist writing styles to examine the OC rate for factual and high-quality newspaper styles (see Fig. 6). The 14 pieces of text retained for this analysis show an average OC rate (which was normalised on a scale of 10) of 3.72, with a minimum of 2.31 and a maximum of 5,45.

# The Information Disorder Level index (IDL index)

The assessment of automatically generated content is most reliable when done humanely. It involves critical thinking about the meaning of the information and its informative or disinformative value, which is related to the accuracy and reliability of the news. The IDL index is a human-based judgement metric. It is language-independent and was developed to evaluate content generated by large language model systems in the context of academic research.

## Paste the generated AI text

> In a devastating incident that unfolded on a quiet street in Norway, four individuals tragically lost their lives as a result of a collision involving a car and a bus. The incident, which took place on [insert street name], has left the local community in shock and mourning.
>
> According to eyewitness accounts, the victims, whose identities have not yet been released pending notification of their families, were crossing the street when a car struck them. The force of the impact was so severe that it drew the attention of nearby witnesses, who immediately dialed emergency

**+ Add prompt (optional)**

Reference: add the prompt used to generate the text

> Facts
> 4 peoples died
> They were crossing the street
> A car hurt them
> Then a bus collided the car
> 911 was called
> Rescuers cannot do nothing
> It happened somewhere in Norway
> Write a factual news article on this

Submit

**Fig. 2.** First step: paste the machine-generated text and the prompt used (optional).

1. In a devastating incident that unfolded on a quiet street in Norway, four individuals tragically lost their lives as a result of a collision involving a car and a bus.

Make a choice

☐ Check if this sentence is an opinion or a comment

Make a choice / True / Mostly True / Cannot say / Mostly False / False

...h took place on [insert street name], has left the local community in shock and mourning.

...ce is an opinion or a comment

...witness accounts, the victims, whose identities have not yet been released pending notification of ...crossing the street when a car struck them.

Make a choice

☐ Check if this sentence is an opinion or a comment

**Reference: the prompt used to generate the text**

Facts 4 peoples died They were crossing the street A car hurt them Then a bus collided the car 911 was called Rescuers cannot do nothing It happened somewhere in Norway Write a factual news article on this

**Fig. 3.** Second step: assessing the content after sentence tokenisation.

There are 3 sentences marked as 'True', 3 marked as 'Mostly true', 3 marked as 'Mostly false', and 11 marked as 'False' out of a total of 20 sentences assessed. You marked 3 sentences as opinion or comment (15% of the total amount of sentences).

**The IDL index for this news is 7**

|7

0
TRUE
INFORMATIVE

10
FALSE
DIS-MIS-MAL-INFORMATIVE

**Fig. 4.** Third and final step: showing the results.

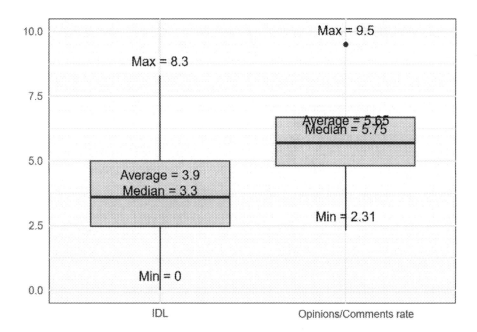

**Fig. 5.** Descriptive statistics of the corpus.

**SAMPLE:**
**A CAR ACCIDENT**
**IN NORWAY**

**PROMPT (FACTS)**

4 peoples died
They were crossing the street
A car hurt them
Then, a bus collided the car
911 was called
Rescuers cannot do anything
It happened somewhere in
Norway
Write a factual news article
on these facts

(...)

The victims, who were attempting to cross the road, were struck by a car and subsequently involved in a collision with a bus, resulting in their untimely demise. The incident has left the local community in a state of shock and mourning.

Authorities have initiated a thorough investigation into the circumstances surrounding the accident. Preliminary findings indicate that the four individuals, whose identities have not been released pending notification of their families, were pedestrians crossing the street when a car collided with them.

Eyewitnesses present at the scene reported a scene of chaos and confusion, as passersby and concerned citizens rushed to aid the victims before the arrival of emergency services.

The community in Norway is coming together to support one another during this difficult time, with grief counseling services being made available to those affected by the loss.

Our thoughts and prayers go out to the families and loved ones of the victims during this challenging period of grief and sorrow.

**Fig. 6.** Sample text: Car accident in Norway (factual style).

A correlation analysis was performed to examine the possible relationship between the IDL index and the OC rate. The correlation coefficient of 0.05 suggested a lack of meaningfulness positive correlation between these two variables, which can be due to the difficulty in assessing the factuality or truthfulness of a comment or an opinion [47]. The results obtained for the t-value (-1.58) and the p-value (0.20) indicate that there is no statistically significant difference between the means of the two variables. Additionally, a linear regression model was fitted to explore the relationship between the IDL index and the OC rate. However, the model did not yield statistically significant results. The low multiple R-squared (0.003) and adjusted R-squared (-0.023) values suggest that the model does not fit the data well. Therefore, based on the analysis, there is no strong evidence to suggest that the IDL index has a significant influence or relationship with the OC rate.

## 4   Conclusion

The limits of this experiment are related to the relatively small size of the corpus (with only forty samples) as well as to a human evaluation carried out by a single judge. Given the subjective nature of any analysis or evaluation activity, a corpus should ideally be submitted to at least two human evaluators to better frame and weigh the results. Nevertheless, the results presented in this paper illustrate the potential of using the IDL index and the OC rate as quality indicators to assess content generated by LLMs.

As ChatGPT added opinions or comments to all the samples related to the factual and high-quality news styles, it is possible to hypothesise that this mixture of genres is a clue to determining that it consists of a machine-generated non-journalistic piece. However, some media outlets and blogs fail to distinguish between facts, opinions, and comments. In addition, the sample included writing styles that, by their very nature, contained opinions or comments. Hence, further investigation is needed in this area.

The invented content by ChatGPT is part of the story's logic and is more akin to fictionalising than to what is commonly called artificial hallucination. While ChatGPT may not fully understand its writing, it can be considered a simulation or extrapolation of content generation. Therefore, we suggest that the invented parts in the generated texts should be understood as a product of pattern-matching abilities rather than manifesting artificial hallucination.

For newsrooms using generative AI, these results suggest that every piece of machine-generated content should be verified and post-edited by a human before being published. From a digital literacy perspective, the IDL index can be considered a useful tool to understand the limits of generative AI and encourage critical thinking about what makes a report event factual. The tool developed for this experiment is available on GitHub: https://laurence001.github.io/idl/. The corpus used and the source code of the web application are also available on GitHub: https://github.com/laurence001/idl/tree/main.

# References

1. Giansiracusa, N.: How algorithms create and prevent fake news: Exploring the impacts of social media, deepfakes, GPT-3, and more. APress (2021)
2. Ferrara, E.: Social bot detection in the age of ChatGPT: Challenges and opportunities. First Monday (2023)
3. Wardle, C., Derakhshan, H.: Information disorder: toward an interdisciplinary framework for research and policymaking. Council of Europe Strasbourg (2017)
4. De Angelis, L., et al.: ChatGPT and the rise of large language models: the new AI-driven infodemic threat in public health. Front. Public Health **11**, 1166120 (2023)
5. Ray, P.: ChatGPT: a comprehensive review on background, applications, key challenges, bias, ethics, limitations and future scope. Internet of Things and Cyber-Physical Systems (2023)
6. Weber-Wulff, D., et al.: Testing of detection tools for AI-generated text. ArXiv [cs.CL]. (2023). http://arxiv.org/abs/2306.15666
7. Crothers, E., Japkowicz, N., Viktor, H.: Machine generated text: A comprehensive survey of threat models and detection methods. ArXiv [cs.CL] (2022). http://arxiv.org/abs/2210.07321
8. Kirchner, J., Ahmad, L., Aaronson, S., Leike, J.: New AI classifier for indicating AI-written text. OpenAI (2023)
9. Gehrmann, S., Strobelt, H., Rush, A.: GLTR: Statistical detection and visualization of generated text. ArXiv [cs.CL]. (2019). http://arxiv.org/abs/1906.04043
10. Gao, C., et al.: Comparing scientific abstracts generated by ChatGPT to real abstracts with detectors and blinded human reviewers. NPJ Digital Med. **6**, 75 (2023)
11. Henriksson, T.: New survey finds half of newsrooms use Generative AI tools; only 20% have guidelines in place - WAN-IFRA. World Association Of News Publishers (2023). https://wan-ifra.org/2023/05/new-genai-survey/
12. Dwivedi, Y., Kshetri, N., Hughes, L., Slade, E., Jeyaraj, A., Kar, A.: So what if ChatGPT wrote it?" Multidisciplinary perspectives on opportunities, challenges and implications of generative conversational AI for research, practice and policy. Int. J. Inf. Manage. **71**, 102642 (2023)
13. Hanley, H., Durumeric, Z.: Machine-made media: monitoring the mobilization of machine-generated articles on misinformation and mainstream news websites. ArXiv [cs.CY] (2023). http://arxiv.org/abs/2305.09820
14. Li, Z.: The dark side of ChatGPT: legal and ethical challenges from stochastic parrots and hallucination. ArXiv [cs.CY] (2023). http://arxiv.org/abs/2304.1434
15. Ferrara, E. Should ChatGPT be biased? Challenges and risks of bias in large language models. ArXiv [cs.CY] (2023). http://arxiv.org/abs/2304.03738
16. Rozado, D.: The political biases of ChatGPT. Soc. Sci. **12**, 148 (2023)
17. Tang, R., Chuang, Y., Hu, X.: The science of detecting LLM-generated texts. ArXiv [cs.CL] (2023). http://arxiv.org/abs/2303.07205
18. Zellers, R., et al.: Defending a. ArXiv [cs.CL] (2019). http://arxiv.org/abs/1905.12616
19. Schuster, T., Schuster, R., Shah, D., Barzilay, R.: The limitations of stylometry for detecting machine-generated fake news. Comput. Linguist. **46**, 499–510 (2020). https://doi.org/10.1162/coli_a_00380
20. Kumarage, T., et al.: phJ-Guard: Journalism Guided Adversarially Robust Detection of AI-generated News. arXiv preprint arXiv:2309.03164 (2023)

21. Pu, J., et al.: Deepfake text detection: Limitations and opportunities. ArXiv [cs.CR] (2022). http://arxiv.org/abs/2210.09421
22. Guo, B., et al.: How close is ChatGPT to human experts? Comparison corpus, evaluation, and detection. ArXiv [cs.CL] (2023). http://arxiv.org/abs/2301.07597
23. Lazarski, E., Al-Khassaweneh, M., Howard, C.: Using NLP for fact checking: a survey. Designs **5**, 42 (2021). https://doi.org/10.3390/designs5030042
24. Dierickx, L., Lindén, C., Opdahl, A.L.: Automated fact-checking to support professional practices: systematic literature review and meta-analysis. Int. J. Commun. **17**, 21 (2023)
25. Graves, D.: Understanding the promise and limits of automated fact-checking. Reuters Institute for the Study of Journalism (2018)
26. Schlichtkrull, M., Ousidhoum, N., Vlachos, A.: The intended uses of automated fact-checking artefacts: Why, how and who. ArXiv [cs.CL] (2023). http://arxiv.org/abs/2304.14238
27. Alkaissi, H., McFarlane, S.: Artificial hallucinations in ChatGPT: implications in scientific writing. Cureus. **15**, 1–5 (2023)
28. Buholayka, M., Zouabi, R., Tadinada, A.: Is ChatGPT ready to write scientific case reports independently? A comparative evaluation between human and artificial intelligence. Cureus. **15**, 1–6 (2023). https://doi.org/10.7759252Fcureus.39386
29. Thomson, C., Reiter, E.: A gold standard methodology for evaluating accuracy in data-to-text systems. ArXiv [cs.CL] (2020). http://arxiv.org/abs/2011.03992
30. van der Lee, C., Gatt, A., Miltenburg, E., Krahmer, E.: Human evaluation of automatically generated text: current trends and best practice guidelines. Comput. Speech Lang. **67**, 101151 (2021)
31. Lester, B.: Developing and empirically evaluating robust explanation generators: The KNIGHT experiments. Comput. Linguist. **23**, 65–101 (1997)
32. Belz, A., Reiter, E.: Comparing automatic and human evaluation of NLG systems. In: 11th Conference of the European Chapter of the Association For Computational Linguistics, pp. 313–320 (2006)
33. Belz, A., Reiter, E.: An investigation into the validity of some metrics for automatically evaluating natural language generation systems. Comput. Linguist. **35**, 529–558 (2009)
34. Dale, R., White, M.: Shared tasks and comparative evaluation in natural language generation. In: Proceedings of the Workshop on Shared Tasks and Comparative Evaluation in Natural Language Generation, pp. 1–6 (2007)
35. Graefe, A., Haim, M., Haarmann, B., Brosius, H.: Perception of automated computer-generated news: credibility, expertise, and readability. 11th Dubrovnik Media Days, Dubrovnik (2015)
36. Haim, M., Graefe, A.: Automated news: better than expected? Digit. J. **5**, 1044–1059 (2017)
37. Wölker, A., Powell, T.: Algorithms in the newsroom? News readers' perceived credibility and selection of automated journalism. Journalism (London, England). **22**, 86–103 (2021). https://doi.org/10.1177/1464884918757072
38. Melin, M., Back, A., Sodergard, C., Munezero, M., Leppanen, L., Toivonen, H.: No landslide for the human journalist - an empirical study of computer-generated election news in Finland. IEEE Access Pract. Innov. Open Solut. **6**, 43356–43367 (2018). https://doi.org/10.1109/access.2018.2861987
39. Clerwall, C.: Enter the robot journalist: users' perceptions of automated content. J. Pract. **8**, 519–531 (2014). https://doi.org/10.1080/17512786.2014.883116

40. Van Der Kaa, H., Krahmer, E.: Journalist versus news consumer: the perceived credibility of machine-written news. In: Proceedings of the Computation+Journalism Conference. (2014)
41. Johnston, J., Graham, C.: The new, old journalism: narrative writing in contemporary newspapers. J. Stud. **13**, 517–533 (2012). https://doi.org/10.1080/1461670x.2011.629803
42. Tandoc Jr, E., Thomas, R., Bishop, L.: What is (fake) news? Analyzing news values (and more) in fake stories. Med. Commun. **9**, 110–119 (2021). https://doi.org/10.17645252Fmac.v9i1.3331
43. Jurish, B., Würzner, K.: Word and sentence tokenization with hidden Markov models. J. Lang. Technol. Comput. Linguist. **28**, 61–83 (2013). https://doi.org/10.21248252Fjlcl.28.2013.176
44. Matusov, E., Leusch, G., Bender, O., Ney, H.: Evaluating machine translation output with automatic sentence segmentation. In: Proceedings of the Second International Workshop on Spoken Language Translation (2005)
45. Hanitzsch, T. Deconstructing journalism culture: toward a universal theory. Communication Theory. **17**, 367–385 (2007). https://doi.org/10.1111252Fj.1468-2885.2007.00303.x
46. Ward, S.: Truth and Objectivity. The Routledge Handbook of Mass Media Ethics, pp. 101–114 (2020). https://doi.org/10.4324252F9781315545929-8
47. Walter, N., Salovich, N.: Unchecked vs. uncheckable: how opinion-based claims can impede corrections of misinformation. Mass Commun. Soc. **24**, 500–526 (2021). https://doi.org/10.1080252F15205436.2020.1864406

# Lost in Transformation: Rediscovering LLM-Generated Campaigns in Social Media

Britta Grimme[1], Janina Pohl[2], Hendrik Winkelmann[3], Lucas Stampe[2], and Christian Grimme[2(✉)]

[1] Department of Computer Science, TU Dortmund University, Dortmund, Germany
britta.grimme@tu-dortmund.de
[2] Computational Social Science and Systems Analysis, University of Münster, Münster, Germany
{janina.pohl,lucas.stampe,christian.grimme}@uni-muenster.de
[3] Practical Computer Science, University of Münster, Münster, Germany
hendrik.winkelmann@uni-muenster.de

**Abstract.** This paper addresses new challenges of detecting campaigns in social media, which emerged with the rise of Large Language Models (LLMs). LLMs particularly challenge algorithms focused on the temporal analysis of topical clusters. Simple similarity measures can no longer capture and map campaigns that were previously broadly similar in content. Herein, we analyze whether the classification of messages over time can be profitably used to rediscover poorly detectable campaigns at the content level. Thus, we evaluate classical classifiers and a new method based on siamese neural networks. Our results show that campaigns can be detected despite the limited reliability of the classifiers as long as they are based on a large amount of simultaneously spread artificial content.

**Keywords:** Social Media · Campaign Detection · Large Language Models · Siamese Neural Networks

## 1 Introduction

The automation of content generation through new developments in the field of Large Language Models (LLMs) has reached a new level of quality – at the latest since the release of ChatGPT as a commercial tool and its perception and public use. The extensively trained models can generate diverse styles of texts in different contexts. Distinguishing human- and machine-generated texts is increasingly difficult for human readers. In the context of social media and automation of agents (also known as social bots), artificial intelligence and LLMs played

The authors acknowledge support by the European Research Center in Information Systems (ERCIS) and by the project HybriD (FKZ: 16KIS1531K) funded by the German Federal Ministry of Education and Research.

D. Ceolin et al. (Eds.): MISDOOM 2023, LNCS 14397, pp. 72–87, 2023.
https://doi.org/10.1007/978-3-031-47896-3_6

only a minor role [5] until recent breakthroughs: Since the rise of transformer models [14,39] the use of these technologies developed into a severe threat: As Grimme and colleagues [23] predicted under the term of *new automation* even before ChatGPT was published, automated content generation may become one of the significant challenges for the medium of text-based (and in the future also multimodal content-based) social networks [19]. This particularly impacts previous detection approaches for automatically distributed social media content development and applicability. While detection mechanisms of individual automated agents (e.g. [13]) were already discarded in 2017 due to several vulnerabilities [21,34], several approaches focused on the detection of coordinated content distribution shortly thereafter [11,22]. In those approaches, automation detection was considered a byproduct of campaign detection [3]. However, these content-level or behavioral-level detection methods rely heavily on detecting similarities in textual content [4] or behavior [11]. These methods screen data or activity streams instead of investigating individual accounts or actors.

Pohl and colleagues [32] have shown that sufficiently large variance in the content of campaign patterns can be generated using LLMs such that the detection at the content level becomes unreliable, even impossible with the current state-of-the-art. For their experiments, they recorded campaign patterns and replaced the original, often very similar content, with LLM-generated content on the same topic. This content was produced using a tweet-trained and topic-primed model based on the GPT3 architecture. The stream mining techniques used for topic discovery were subsequently unable to detect the original campaign patterns.

This paper picks up this thread of research [32] and evaluates to what extent detection of artificially created content can contribute to the "rediscovery" of these campaign patterns. Therefore, we use the same benchmarking setting to determine whether LLM-generated texts can sufficiently be discriminated from human-generated ones to bring previously undiscovered campaigns to the foreground. This information is included in the time-series approach used for topic detection as an additional indicator in campaign detection. As we focus on the case of micro-blogging text messages (like tweets), the detectors have to handle the difficulty of classifying short texts. Methodologically, we train different standard machine learning (ML) approaches and additionally propose a transformer-based Siamese neural network (SNN) as classifiers. While the standard procedures are off-the-shelf available and straightforward to realize, the combination of the transformer architecture's language modeling capabilities and the Siamese network's ability to compare and measure text similarity make transformer-based Siamese neural networks a compelling approach for classifying human-generated and LLM-generated text.

This work is structured as follows: After introducing relevant background on campaign detection and LLM content detection in Sect. 2, we provide details on applied approaches in Sect. 3. In Sect. 4, we specify the experimental parameters and present our results in Sect. 5 before concluding in Sect. 6.

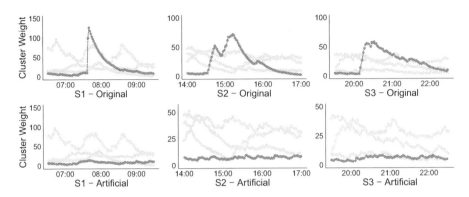

**Fig. 1.** Detection capabilities of `textClust` in the experiments of Pohl et al. [32]. Above, the original campaigns are displayed while their recreated counterparts are below. Few artificial tweets are clustered into the original cluster, resulting in the vanished peak.

## 2    Background

### 2.1    Campaign Detection

In contrast to previous approaches that primarily concentrated on identifying individual accounts for campaign detection [13], recent research has shifted towards detecting coordinated activities. Most approaches focus on accounts, i.e., analyzing various features associated with the accounts [7,41], or investigating the activities of the accounts themselves [10,16,29]. In contrast, Pohl et al. [32] focused on the content of messages shared by coordinated accounts. They developed a framework that enables the creation of artificial benchmarks for coordination detection in an adversarial manner. This framework entails a multi-step process where a researcher can select and analyze any social media platform and its associated campaigns. The insights gained from this analysis are then utilized to create an artificial campaign, which is subsequently incorporated into a real dataset collected from the social media platform. This approach facilitates the creation of an adjustable artificial setting that caters to the specific requirements of the researcher, allowing for the testing of various campaign detection algorithms.

In their work, they collected Twitter data and clustered it using the stream clustering algorithm `textClust` [6]. `textClust` is a one-pass algorithm that utilizes TF-IDF vectors and cosine similarity to form clusters of similar tweets. Each tweet assigned to a cluster increases the corresponding cluster weight, while an exponential fading function gradually decreases the weight over time, allowing less essential topics to be forgotten. By visualizing the clusters over time, human observers can detect unusual patterns, including sudden bursts in cluster weight, which deviate from the expected natural emergence of clusters on social media platforms. Pohl et al. [32] identified three distinctive patterns (or "stereotypes") in their Twitter data, as shown in the upper row of Fig. 1. These patterns comprise accounts tweeting synchronously and creating a single peak in activity (stereotype S1), repeating this behavior multiple times (stereotype S2), and sustaining their initial burst in activity over an extended period (stereotype S3).

Following the identification of these three stereotypes, Pohl et al. [32] proceeded to construct an adversarial artificial campaign by replacing the original campaign tweets with artificially generated ones using a fine-tuned GPT-Neo model. This approach simulates a scenario where an attacker applies an LLM to generate tweets automatically. Then, they re-applied the `textClust` algorithm to assess its campaign detection capabilities. However, as depicted in the bottom row of Fig. 1, the algorithm failed to replicate the distinctive patterns observed previously. Instead, the more diverse tweets generated by GPT-Neo (while still conveying the same message) were dispersed across other clusters, causing the initially visible peaks to disappear. This outcome demonstrated that by employing an LLM, campaign creators can potentially evade detection, posing a significant threat. This work strives to evaluate possibilities to rediscover stereotype patterns that are lost due to LLM usage.

## 2.2 LLM-Generated Content Detection

The detection of automatically generated short texts has emerged as a research topic, particularly following the publication of the initial GPT model [33] and the subsequent realization that humans struggle to classify texts generated by LLMs reliably [25]. Even OpenAI acknowledged the challenge of reliably detecting texts generated by their model [27].

Following the paradigm to fight fire with fire, most approaches focus on using Transformers like RoBERTa to classify artificially generated from non-artificially generated texts [2,17,31]. Others also use the benefits of the transformer architecture by training a classifier on model features [30,40]. Nevertheless, not only sophisticated transformer architectures are used for differentiating human- from LLM-generated texts but also simple ML models. Alamleh et al. [1] tested many classifiers, with Logistic Regression being the most straightforward and a BERT model the most complex approach. Their dataset comprises short student and ChatGPT-answers to computer science problems. Especially a Random Forrest and a Support Vector Machine performed well in distinguishing these two groups.

Finally, researchers also try to demonstrate observable differences between human and machine-generated texts. In the works of Guo et al. [24], and Kumerage et al. [28], the authors not only trained their detector but also focused on examining linguistic features specific to ChatGPT-generated texts in contrast to human-authored texts. Both groups found independently that, in general, ChatGPT exhibits a more formal writing style and displays fewer emotions.

For a more extensive overview on distinguishing artificial from human-generated texts, consider the works of Crothers et al. [12], Singh [37], and Tang et al. [38]. Although we acknowledge that the feasibility of this classification task has been the subject of intense debate [9,35], we follow a different path: we strive to include and evaluate possibly unreliable classifiers (at the individual level) into a higher level indicator for rediscovering bursts of unauthentic content.

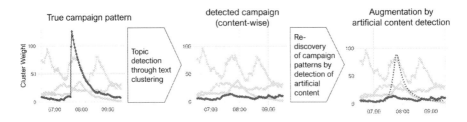

**Fig. 2.** Depiction of the principle idea of rediscovering campaigning patterns by integrating LLM content detection techniques.

# 3    Detection of Artificial Content in Social Media Campaigns

The artificial content detection approach proposed here is not a standalone application that only discriminates "real" or "artificial" social media content. Instead, it is about augmenting the approach proposed by Pohl et al. [32] with an auxiliary indicator. As shown in Fig. 2, a classifier is used to rediscover conspicuous patterns of variable content (produced by using LLMs). As described in Sect. 2, these patterns can be lost to stream clustering-based topic detection due to precisely the diversity introduced by LLMs.

For the purpose of rediscovery, different classifiers are trained and applied to all content in the data stream. Subsequently, the positive (i.e., as artificial) classified content is added to a virtual cluster over time - analogously to the procedure of `textClust` in discovering topics. Also analogous to the method in `textClust`, the weight of the cluster is increased as content is added and decreased when no insertions were made for a while.

The investigation aims to check how well different classifiers contribute to the designed indicator. On the one hand, standard classifiers are used. On the other hand, a method is proposed that embeds a transformer-based encoding into a Siamese neural network. The Siamese network takes on the task of independently learning a distance metric for distinguishing original and artificially generated content. In the following, the methods used for classification are presented.

## 3.1    Transformer-Based Siamese Neural Network Approach

We employ a Siamese neural network (SNN) [8] that integrates Transformer encoder models as its submodels to differentiate between machine-generated and human-generated tweets. SNNs are specialized models designed to extract essential discriminative features from input data and generate a similarity metric based on these features. As schematically shown in Fig. 3, these networks consist of identical neural subnetworks that are jointly trained and behave like siamese twins, sharing the same weights and architectures. In our case, each subnetwork processes a separate input tweet and produces an embedding vector that represents the crucial characteristics of the tweet.

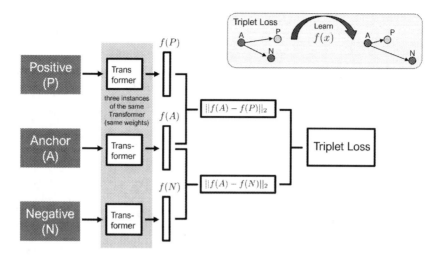

**Fig. 3.** Depiction of the used SNN architecture. The upper right sketch describes the fundamental idea of the triple loss objective function: $f(x)$ is the learned distance function for discriminating human and LLM-generated content.

Similar data points are placed close in the learned embedding space, while dissimilar points are further apart. To optimize this space, we utilize the triplet loss [36] as a specialized loss function, which considers three data points: the anchor (e.g., a human-generated tweet), a positive (e.g., another human-generated tweet), and a negative (e.g., a machine-generated tweet). The objective is to minimize the distance between the anchor and the positive while maximizing the distance between the anchor and the negative. The loss function can be described using the Euclidean distance function, cf. Eqn. 1.

$$L(A, P, N) = max(\|f(A) - f(P)\|_2 - \|f(A) - f(N)\|_2 + m, 0) \qquad (1)$$

In Eq. 1, $m$ is a so-called margin term used to "stretch" the distance differences between similar and dissimilar pairs in the triplet. $f(A)$, $f(P)$, and $f(N)$ represent the embeddings for the anchor, positive, and negative tweet, respectively. Herein, $m$ is set to 2, meaning that the loss value is 0, if the distance between $A$ and $N$ is at least larger by 2 compared to the distance between $A$ and $P$. Unlike comparing only two tweets, the triplet loss allows $f(A)$ and $f(P)$ to lie on a manifold rather than just a single point. The selection of appropriate triplets is crucial for the performance of SNNs. Too simple triplets are ineffective for optimization, while overly challenging triplets can cause the model to converge prematurely. To address this issue, we employ a technique called "online triplet mining" [36]: a large number of triplets are randomly generated, and then a targeted selection of semi-hard triplets is made from this set. In semi-hard triplets, the distance between anchor and positive is smaller than between anchor and negative, but the difference between both distances does not exceed the margin value $m$. We randomly generate $1,500$ triplets from the training dataset, from which 200 semi-hard triplets are selected for model training. If there are fewer than 200 semi-hard triplets in the initial selection, random additional triplets are added to maintain a constant batch size of 200. We utilize the Adam optimizer for optimization, with a learning rate of 0.000006. In our specific scenario, we integrated Transformer models as submodels into the SNNs to differentiate between machine-generated and human-generated tweets.

### 3.2 Traditional ML Models

To compare the SNN with more traditional approaches, we focused our attention on three algorithms: Support Vector Machines (SVMs), Logistic Regression (LR), and Random Forests (RFs) [26]. LR, as a simple baseline model, allows for a comparative analysis with the SVMs and the RFs. SVMs are particularly suitable for text-based classification because their training mechanism explicitly addresses overfitting. RFs, known as an ensemble model that combines multiple decision trees using bagging, possess the advantage of performing remarkably well on a diverse range of practical problems without requiring extensive fine-tuning, despite the "No Free Lunch Theorem" [18]. Additionally, RF and LR are transparent approaches to identifying critical discriminative features in artificial and original social media posts. All three models performed well in other experiments conducting the same task [1]. Furthermore, we use these models individually, harness their collective predictive power, and enhance classification performance by using them as an ensemble classifier.

## 4 Experimental Setup

### 4.1 Data Collection

For training and testing the LLM-detectors, we used the same 3.6 million tweets provided by Pohl et al. [32], collected from October to November 2021. The artificial tweets were created by training a GPT-Neo model that did not receive any social media data during pre-training [20]. GPT-Neo is a scaled-down (thus, slightly worse performing) and freely available version of GPT-3 created by EleutherAI [15]. During fine-tuning, the model received both the tweet content and associated username (<USER> <TWEET>) as input, enabling it to produce tweets similar to those from the original users. We selected a subset of the original dataset combined with artificial tweets to train the LLM detectors. Specifically, we focused on the primary time of the first day of the COP26 climate conference (2021-10-31, 10 a.m. to 4 p.m.). To create a roughly balanced dataset, we created an artificial tweet for every user's original tweet in our dataset but deleted the ones that were either exact duplicates or too long to be valid. As GPT-Neo's output is influenced by the probability distribution of generated tokens, these variations in the model's output are expected. Ultimately, our training dataset comprised 52 % original tweets and 48 % artificial tweets.

## 4.2   Siamese Neural Network Setup

*Preprocessing of input data:* Before training the model, we preprocess the data using the GPT-2 tokenizer. For training purposes, we only keep tweets with a minimum of 30 tokens, ensuring an adequate length for meaningful context. Longer tweets are cut off at 150 tokens to control the input size. To ensure uniform input dimensions, we pad the sequences with zeros, extending them to a fixed length. Additionally, we created a padding mask to differentiate real tokens from padded tokens during the training process.

*Transformer Encoder Architecture.* The transformer encoder architecture comprises two main components: self-attention and a fully connected feed-forward neural network (FFNN). These components are stacked together to form a layer in the encoder. In our specific implementation, the encoder consists of four layers. We employ four attention heads within each attention layer, enabling the model to capture different relationships and dependencies in the input data. The model utilizes positional encoding to account for the positional information of words in the input. Positional encoding assigns sinusoidal and cosine functions to each word in the input, encoding its relative position within the sequence. This positional encoding is added to the input data before passing through the attention layer, providing the model with positional information. The model dimension, also called the embedding size, is set to 128. The inner dimension of the FFNN is set to 512. We apply a dropout rate of 0.1 during training to prevent overfitting and improve the model's generalization ability. To further stabilize the learning process and preserve the representation information across layers, layer normalization is employed after the self-attention and FFNN sublayers. In addition to the encoder layers, the Transformer model includes a dense layer and a final layer. The dense layer, with an output size of 50257 (corresponding to the size of the input vocabulary), is responsible for transforming the encoded representations. The final layer applies L2 normalization to the output embeddings, ensuring they reside on a $d$-dimensional hypersphere. We trained our Transformer model for 600 epochs, continuously optimizing it until it no longer showed improvements in the evaluation data.

*Neural Network Model.* To transform the embedded data of shape (150,128) into predictions, the embedding is put into a neural network model consisting of sequential layers. The architecture of the model involves Long Short-Term Memory (LSTM) units, dropout regularization, batch normalization, and dense layers. The model starts with an LSTM layer consisting of 64 LSTM units. A dropout regularization technique with a rate of 0.1 is applied after the LSTM layer. Following the dropout layer, a dense layer with 32 units and a rectified linear activation function (ReLU) is added. To further regularize the model and prevent overfitting, another dropout layer with a rate of 0.1 is applied after the dense layer. Finally, the model concludes with a dense layer with 2 units and a softmax activation function. The softmax activation function produces probability distributions over the two classes: machine-generated and human-generated tweets. It allows the model to assign a likelihood to each class based on the learned patterns and make a prediction. For optimization, the model is compiled using the Adam optimizer. The loss function chosen for this binary classification task is binary cross-entropy. Additionally, the model's performance is evaluated using accuracy as the metric.

### 4.3   ML Models Setup

In contrast to the preprocessing steps for the SNN, we used 4-character $n$-grams for creating TF-IDF vectors to keep the model simple and approximate a token length. Additionally, to address potential overfitting, we imposed a maximum limit on the number of features considered during vectorization. This restriction allowed for selecting the most frequently occurring $n$-grams, resulting in a variable range of 8000, 9000, 10000, or 11000 features. We opted for a non-dual formulation for the SVM and LR to address convergence issues and long computation times. We furthermore used a linear kernel for the SVM. For RF, we use a majority vote to reduce variance between the decision trees. We use a training-test split to assess the RF model's generalization error. RF model selection is made using out-of-bag (OOB) samples and Gini impurity as the tree split criterion. We tune two parameters: the number of samples that trigger an additional split in each tree (8, 32, or 128) and the percentage of features considered when searching for the best split. The options for the latter parameter include the square root of the total number of features, 2 %, 4 %, or 6 % of the overall feature number. We employ an incremental training scheme, adding trees in batches until no noteworthy improvement in the OOB score is observed. Conversely, for LR and SVM lacking built-in model evaluation metrics, we perform hyperparameter selection using a predefined grid from which we sample 40 configurations randomly and evaluate via using 5-fold cross-validation. In the case of LR, we perform parameter tuning on two factors: the choice between L1 or L2 norm penalty and the regularization strength $C$. The possible values for $C$ are 6.0, 2.0, 1.0, 0.95, 0.9, or 0.8, providing control over the regularization. For SVM, the tuning parameter is also $C$, using the same set of values as LR.

## 5   Results

### 5.1   Detection Quality of the SNN

After undergoing the described preprocessing, the validation data of the training dataset is processed through the Siamese network and, subsequently, the neural network, resulting in a probability value ranging from 0 to 1. A threshold to classify the test data as human-generated or machine-generated tweets must be determined on the training data. As the test dataset primarily consists of human-generated tweets (as expected in real-world data), with only a small proportion of machine-generated tweets, minimizing the False Positive Rate (FPR) is crucial. By analyzing the Receiver Operating Characteristic (ROC) curve, presented in Fig. 4, we selected FPRs of 0.01 and 0.05 to compute the corresponding threshold

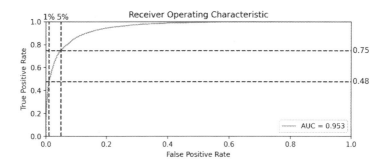

**Fig. 4.** ROC curve for the validation data of the training dataset shows an Area Under the Curve (AUC) value of 0.953. At a fixed FPR of 0.01, the TPR is at 0.48, while an FPR of 0.05 corresponds to a TPR of 0.75. Each FPR/TPR combination represents a specific threshold value used to classify tweets as either machine-generated or not. These thresholds will be applied for classifying the test data.

**Table 1.** Quality metrics for the test datasets on stereotypes S1, S2, and S3. The table includes the AUC values, FPR, and TPR for two threshold values: "01" refers to the threshold associated with a 0.01 FPR, while "05" corresponds to the threshold associated with a 5 % FPR in the training dataset.

| Dataset | AUC | FPR05 | TPR05 | FPR01 | TPR01 |
|---------|-------|-------|-------|-------|-------|
| S1 | 0.879 | 0.130 | 0.732 | 0.041 | 0.405 |
| S2 | 0.875 | 0.122 | 0.562 | 0.035 | 0.320 |
| S3 | 0.910 | 0.129 | 0.776 | 0.039 | 0.456 |

values for identifying machine-generated output. For a FPR of 0.01, the threshold value is determined as 0.9999958, resulting in a True Positive Rate (TPR) of 0.48 on the well-balanced training dataset. The corresponding accuracy is 0.742, and the precision value is 0.978. A false positive rate of 0.05 corresponds to a threshold value of 0.99968, a TPR of 0.75, an accuracy of 0.852, and a precision of 0.933, respectively.

The preprocessing for the test datasets follows a similar approach to the training data, with one key difference: all tweets, including those that have fewer than the minimum of 30 tokens required for training, are included. Applying the transformer-based Siamese neural net and the subsequent LSTM net to the test data produces the quality measures presented in Table 1.

## 5.2 Detection Quality of the Standard Approaches

Similar to the classification process for the SNN, we determined a threshold based on the FPRs of 0.01 and 0.05 for all ML models independently. For both rates during training, all models demonstrated strong performance, considering the problem's complexity. The performance of all three models on the training dataset can be seen in Table 2, while the results of applying these models to the test data are presented in Table 3. The FPR is significantly higher than the SNN

**Table 2.** Quality metrics of the ML models for the training data. The table includes the AUC values, FPR, and TPR for two threshold values for 1 % and 5 % FPR, respectively.

| Model | AUC | Threshold05 | TPR05 | Prec05 | Acc05 | Threshold01 | TPR01 | Prec01 | Acc01 |
|---|---|---|---|---|---|---|---|---|---|
| LR | 0.94 | 0.7839 | 0.71 | 0.93 | 0.83 | 0.9351 | 0.44 | 0.98 | 0.73 |
| SVM | 0.94 | 0.2932 | 0.71 | 0.93 | 0.84 | 0.7093 | 0.45 | 0.98 | 0.73 |
| RF | 0.99 | 0.3075 | 0.99 | 0.95 | 0.97 | 0.3944 | 0.99 | 0.99 | 0.99 |

**Table 3.** Quality metrics of the ML models for the test datasets on stereotypes S1, S2, and S3, including the performance of an ensemble approach. The table includes the AUC values, FPR, and TPR for two threshold values for 1 % and 5 % FPR, respectively.

| Dataset | LR | | | SVM | | | RF | | | Ensemble | |
|---|---|---|---|---|---|---|---|---|---|---|---|
| | AUC | FPR05 | TPR05 | AUC | FPR05 | TPR05 | AUC | FPR05 | TPR05 | FPR05 | TPR05 |
| S1 | 0.78 | 0.20 | 0.54 | 0.78 | 0.21 | 0.56 | 0.77 | 0.73 | 0.97 | 0.08 | 0.33 |
| S2 | 0.88 | 0.17 | 0.76 | 0.87 | 0.18 | 0.77 | 0.87 | 0.69 | 1.00 | 0.06 | 0.37 |
| S3 | 0.84 | 0.21 | 0.72 | 0.84 | 0.21 | 0.73 | 0.80 | 0.70 | 0.95 | 0.08 | 0.45 |
| | | FPR01 | TPR01 | | FPR01 | TPR01 | | FPR01 | TPR01 | FPR01 | TPR01 |
| S1 | | 0.08 | 0.34 | | 0.08 | 0.35 | | 0.58 | 0.97 | 0.20 | 0.54 |
| S2 | | 0.06 | 0.37 | | 0.07 | 0.38 | | 0.56 | 0.97 | 0.16 | 0.74 |
| S3 | | 0.08 | 0.46 | | 0.09 | 0.46 | | 0.58 | 0.94 | 0.20 | 0.70 |

results, especially for the RF. Consequently, the last column of Table 3 reflects the performance of the models as an ensemble, where a record is labeled positive only if all models agree.

Further, we analyzed the feature weights of the LR and RF models to determine their importance. Notably, both models highlighted the significance of 4-grams that include the correct usage of punctuation (like an apostrophe) are essential in accurately discerning the authenticity of tweets.

## 5.3 Pattern Rediscovery Capabilities

To test the detection mechanisms as augmenting indicators for rediscovery of campaigning patterns, we applied them to all three benchmarking stereotypes S1, S2, and S3. The resulting time-series of the weight of our virtual cluster for artificial content are shown in Fig. 5. On the left-hand side, we show the original campaign pattern. The second and third columns show the corresponding patterns that emerge from applying the SNN-based detector with 1 % and 5 % FPR w.r.t. training data, respectively. The rightmost column shows the pattern produced by an ensemble of the standard approaches with 1 % FPR.

We observe that our overall approach can clearly rediscover the strong peak pattern of stereotype S1, while it cannot produce a relevant pattern for stereotypes S2 and S3. We can also observe that the standard approaches had the most significant errors for all conditions due to false positive classification. Especially in conditions S2 and S3, this leads to detecting a "new" but misleading pattern.

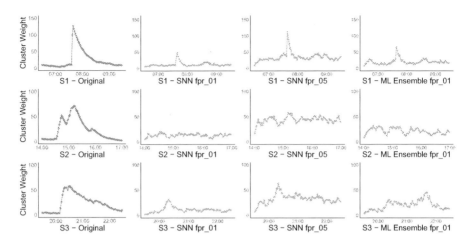

**Fig. 5.** Detection capabilities of the SNN and the ML ensemble. For the first stereotype, a peak can be identified, while for the other ones, the peaks are not distinguishable.

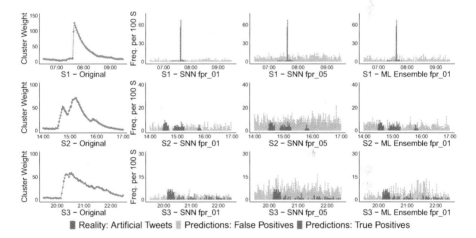

**Fig. 6.** Frequencies of texts classified as artificial by the detection models, fragmented into false positives (green) and true positives (gold); artificial tweets are shown in blue. (Color figure online)

For the SNN-based classifiers, the selected FPRs of 0.01 and 0.05 are still too high to reliably rediscover the campaigning patterns.

Figure 6 details the frequency of true positive results (yellow) in comparison to false positive results (green) and the frequency of real artificial content (blue). While the detected true positives align with the appearance of artificial tweets across all models, the false positive items contribute too much weight to the clustering over time for S2 and S3. Only for S1, where all artificial content appears at almost the same time, the contrast between true and false positives is sufficiently large for producing the corresponding campaign pattern over time.

## 6   Discussion and Conclusion

In this work, we proposed the augmentation of stream-clustering-based campaign detection by identifying LLM-generated content. Instead of classifying single artifacts, we integrated the classification results into the time-series-based interpretation of the topic-based campaign detection mechanism. From our results, we can conclude that the overall approach of including LLM content detection in text-based clustering for topic detection is capable of rediscovering bursts of artificial content. However, the burst of artificial content has to be large enough to ensure that the detection quality is sufficient to exceed the false positive rate produced by the approaches. At the same time, these results show that no perfect detection of artificial content is necessary to rediscover artificial patterns in principle. Since we focus on pattern re-identification, the quality of classification of a single message plays a minor role. Of crucial importance is the accumulation of artificial content. Since our approach for detecting LLM-driven campaigns does not consider the content of posts, simultaneously executed LLM-driven campaigns with varying content will be aggregated into a common cluster resulting in a very strong pattern (certainly, often a pronounced peak). In such cases, it is necessary to apply a post-processing clustering method based on campaign content (this method does not necessarily have to be real-time) to retrospectively identify individual campaigning themes.

The results also show that our proposed SNN-based classifiers can deliver reasonable results in the context of our new indicator, while standard approaches expose a very large false positive rate that may lead to misleading interpretations. Future work will focus on the improvement of the proposed technique and its integration into the campaign detection mechanism.

## References

1. Alamleh, H., Al Qahtani, A., ElSaid, A.: Distinguishing human-written and ChatGPT-generated text using machine learning. In: Systems and Information Engineering Design Symposium, pp. 154–158. IEEE, Charlottesville, USA (2023)
2. Antoun, W., Mouilleron, V., Sagot, B., Seddah, D.: Towards a Robust Detection of Language Model Generated Text. arXiv 2306.05871 (2023)
3. Assenmacher, D., Adam, L., Trautmann, H., Grimme, C.: Towards real-time and unsupervised campaign detection in social media. In: Proceedings of the Florida Artificial Intelligence Research Society Conference. AAAI Press, Florida, USA (2020)
4. Assenmacher, D., Clever, L., Pohl, J.S., Trautmann, H., Grimme, C.: A two-phase framework for detecting manipulation campaigns in social media. In: Meiselwitz, G. (ed.) HCII 2020. LNCS, vol. 12194, pp. 201–214. Springer, Cham (2020). https://doi.org/10.1007/978-3-030-49570-1_14

5. Assenmacher, D., et al.: Demystifying social bots: on the intelligence of automated social media actors. Soc. Med. Soc. **6**(3), 1–14 (2020)

6. Assenmacher, D., Trautmann, H.: Textual one-pass stream clustering with automated distance threshold adaption. In: Nguyen, N.T., Tran, T.K., Tukayev, U., Hong, TP., Trawiń,ski B., Szczerbicki, E. (eds.) Intelligent Information and Database Systems. ACIIDS 2022. LNCS, vol. 13757, pp. 3–16. Springer, Cham (2022). https://doi.org/10.1007/978-3-031-21743-2_1

7. Bellutta, D., Carley, K.M.: Investigating coordinated account creation using burst detection and network analysis. J. Big Data **10**(1), 1–17 (2023)

8. Bromley, J., Guyon, I., LeCun, Y., Säckinger, E., Shah, R.: Signature verification using a siamese time delay neural network. In: Cowan, J.D., Tesauro, G., Alspector, J. (eds.) Advances in Neural Information Processing Systems, vol. 6, NIPS, pp. 737–744. Morgan Kaufmann (1993)

9. Chakraborty, S., Bedi, A.S., Zhu, S., An, B., Manocha, D., Huang, F.: On the Possibilities of AI-Generated Text Detection (2023). arXiv:2304.04736

10. Cinelli, M., Cresci, S., Quattrociocchi, W., Tesconi, M., Zola, P.: Coordinated inauthentic behavior and information spreading on Twitter. Decis. Support Syst. **160**, 1–28 (2022). https://doi.org/10.1016/j.dss.2022.113819

11. Cresci, S., Di Pietro, R., Petrocchi, M., Spognardi, A., Tesconi, M.: DNA-inspired online behavioral modeling and its application to spambot detection. IEEE Intell. Syst. **31**(5), 58–64 (2016)

12. Crothers, E., Japkowicz, N., Viktor, H.: Machine Generated Text: A Comprehensive Survey of Threat Models and Detection Methods (2023). arXiv:2210.07321

13. Davis, C.A., Varol, O., Ferrara, E., Flammini, A., Menczer, F.: BotOrNot: a system to evaluate social bots. In: Proceedings of the 25th International Conference Companion on World Wide Web, pp. 273–274 (2016)

14. Devlin, J., Chang, M.W., Lee, K., Toutanova, K.: BERT: pre-training of deep bidirectional transformers for language understanding (2018). arXiv:1810.04805

15. EleutherAI: GPT Neo - An Implementation of Model & Data Parallel GPT3-Like Models Using the Mesh-Tensorflow Library (2022). https://github.com/EleutherAI/gpt-neo. Accessed 02 July 2023

16. Erhardt, K., Albassam, D.: Detecting the hidden dynamics of networked actors using temporal correlations. In: Companion Proceedings of the ACM Web Conference 2023, pp. 1214–1217. WWW 2023 Companion, ACM, Austin, TX, USA (2023)

17. Fagni, T., Falchi, F., Gambini, M., Martella, A., Tesconi, M.: TweepFake: about detecting deepfake Tweets. PLOS ONE. **16**(5), e0251415 (2021)

18. Fernández-Delgado, M., Cernadas, E., Barro, S., Amorim, D.: Do we need hundreds of classifiers to solve real world classification problems? J. Mach. Learn. Res. **15**(1), 3133–3181 (2014)

19. Ferrara, E.: Social bot detection in the age of ChatGPT: challenges and opportunities. First Monday. **28**(6), 1–30 (2023). https://doi.org/10.5210/fm.v28i6.13185

20. Gao, L., et al.: The Pile: An 800 GB Dataset of Diverse Text for Language Modeling (2020). arXiv:2101.00027

21. Grimme, C., Preuss, M., Adam, L., Trautmann, H.: Social bots: human-like by means of human control? Big Data **5**(4), 279–293 (2017)

22. Grimme, C., Assenmacher, D., Adam, L.: Changing perspectives: is it sufficient to detect social bots? In: Proceedings of the International Conference on Human-Computer Interaction. Las Vegas, United States of America (2018)

23. Grimme, C., Pohl, J., Cresci, S., Lüling, R., Preuss, M.: New automation for social bots: from trivial behavior to AI-powered communication. In: Spezzano, F., Amaral, A., Ceolin, D., Fazio, L., Serra, E. (eds.) Disinformation in Open Online Media. MISDOOM 2022. LNCS, vol. 13545, pp. 79–99. Springer, Cham (2022). https://doi.org/10.1007/978-3-031-18253-2_6

24. Guo, B., et al.: How Close is ChatGPT to Human Experts? Comparison Corpus, Evaluation, and Detection (2023). arXiv:2301.07597

25. Ippolito, D., Duckworth, D., Callison-Burch, C., Eck, D.: Automatic detection of generated text is easiest when humans are fooled. In: Proceedings of the 58th Annual Meeting of the ACL, pp. 1808–1822. ACL, Online (2020)

26. James, G., Witten, D., Hastie, T., Tibshirani, R.: An Introduction to Statistical Learning, 2nd edn. Springer, New York (2021). https://doi.org/10.1007/978-1-4614-7138-7

27. Kirchner, J.H., Ahmad, L., Aaronson, S., Leike, J.: New AI classifier for indicating AI-written text. https://openai.com/blog/new-ai-classifier-for-indicating-ai-written-text (2022). Accessed 30 June 2023

28. Kumarage, T., Garland, J., Bhattacharjee, A., Trapeznikov, K., Ruston, S., Liu, H.: Stylometric Detection of AI-Generated Text in Twitter Timelines (2023). arXiv:2303.03697

29. Michail, D., Kanakaris, N., Varlamis, I.: Detection of fake news campaigns using graph convolutional networks. Int. J. Inf. Manage. Data Insights **2**(2), 100104 (2022)

30. Mitchell, E., Lee, Y., Khazatsky, A., Manning, C.D., Finn, C.: DetectGPT: Zero-Shot Machine-Generated Text Detection using Probability Curvature (2023). arXiv:2301.11305

31. Mitrović, S., Andreoletti, D., Ayoub, O.: ChatGPT or Human? Detect and Explain. Explaining Decisions of Machine Learning Model for Detecting Short ChatGPT-generated Text (2023). arXiv:2301.13852

32. Pohl, J., Assenmacher, D., Seiler, M., Trautmann, H., Grimme, C.: Artificial social media campaign creation for benchmarking and challenging detection approaches. In: Workshop Proceedings of the $16^{th}$ International Conference on Web and Social Media. AAAI Press, Atlanta, GA, USA (2022)

33. Radford, A., Narasimhan, K., Salimans, T., Sutskever, I.: Improving Language Understanding by Generative Pre-Training. Technical report, OpenAI (2018)

34. Rauchfleisch, A., Kaiser, J.: The false positive problem of automatic bot detection in social science research. PLoS ONE **15**(10), e0241045 (2020)

35. Sadasivan, V.S., Kumar, A., Balasubramanian, S., Wang, W., Feizi, S.: Can AI-Generated Text be Reliably Detected? (2023). arXiv:2303.11156

36. Schroff, F., Kalenichenko, D., Philbin, J.: FaceNet: a unified embedding for face recognition and clustering. In: 2015 IEEE Conference on Computer Vision and Pattern Recognition (CVPR), pp. 815–823 (2015)

37. Singh, A.: A comparison study on AI language detector. In: 2023 IEEE 13th Annual Computing and Communication Workshop and Conference (CCWC), pp. 489–493. IEEE, Las Vegas, NV, USA (2023)

38. Tang, R., Chuang, Y.N., Hu, X.: The Science of Detecting LLM-Generated Texts (2023). arXiv:2303.07205

39. Vaswani, A., et al.: Attention is all you need. In: Guyon, I., et al. (eds.) Advances in Neural Information Processing Systems. vol. 30. Curran Associates, Inc. (2017)

40. Verma, V., Fleisig, E., Tomlin, N., Klein, D.: Ghostbuster: Detecting Text Ghost-written by Large Language Models (2023). arXiv:2305.15047
41. Weber, D., Neumann, F.: Amplifying influence through coordinated behaviour in social networks. Soc. Netw. Anal. Min. **11**(1), 1–42 (2021). https://doi.org/10.1007/s13278-021-00815-2

# The Effect of Misinformation Intervention: Evidence from Trump's Tweets and the 2020 Election

Zhuofang Li[1(✉)], Jian Cao[2], Nicholas Adams-Cohen[3], and R. Michael Alvarez[1]

[1] California Institution of Technology, Pasadena, USA
zhuofang@caltech.edu
[2] Trinity College of Dublin, Dublin, Ireland
[3] Adobe, Inc., San Jose, USA

**Abstract.** In this study, we examine the effect of actions of misinformation mitigation. We use three datasets that contain a wide range of misinformation stories during the 2020 election, and we use synthetic controls to examine the causal effect of Twitter's restrictions on Trump's tweets in the 2020 presidential election on the spread of misinformation. We find a nuanced set of results. While it is not always the case that Twitter's actions reduced the subsequent flow of misinformation about the election, we find that in a number of instances content moderation reduced the flow of social media misinformation. We estimate that Twitter's actions, on the universe of tweets we study in our paper, reduced the flow of misinformation on Twitter by approximately 15%.

**Keywords:** Social media · misinformation · platform intervention · public opinion · Twitter · Election

## 1 Introduction

Research shows that people use social media platforms like Twitter, Facebook, and YouTube to spread misinformation and conspiracy theories about many different subjects [7]. Recognizing this problem, these platforms have engaged in different approaches to protect their users from misinformation and platform manipulation, for example Twitter's Platform Manipulation efforts.[1] However, recently some states like Florida and Texas have developed policies to block social media platforms from moderating conversations online, especially those that might involve constitutionally-protected political speech.

Much of the concern about the role of social media platforms in the rapid and viral spread of misinformation and conspiratorial ideas has roots in the 2016 American presidential election, with allegations of foreign interference on social media [22]. Other studies showed that the spread and consumption of fake news on social media was widespread among Americans in the 2016 election cycle

---

[1] See https://transparency.twitter.com/en/reports/platform-manipulation.html.

© The Author(s) 2023
D. Ceolin et al. (Eds.): MISDOOM 2023, LNCS 14397, pp. 88–102, 2023.
https://doi.org/10.1007/978-3-031-47896-3_7

[6]. Social media platforms developed monitoring and intervention policies in the aftermath of the 2016 election, often with limited public transparency and unknown efficacy.

Detecting misinformation and other undesirable behavior on social media in real-time is difficult, in particular when well-resourced and strategic agents are conducting the behavior [20]. They engage in many strategies to avoid detection, and have strong incentives to hide their activities and identities. In response, social media platforms use many approaches to detect, mitigate, and prevent the spread of false and misleading information. However, research is mixed about whether the strategies used by social media platforms are effective at preventing the spread of misinformation [9, 10, 15, 17, 19, 21, 23].

In this paper, we use a unique set of natural experiments that occurred during the 2020 presidential election, employing three unique datasets described below in the Data section. In 2020 (as we discuss in the next section), Twitter used various tools to prevent the spread of information in a series of tweets that President Donald Trump posted. These tweets were deemed to violate Twitter's policies about spreading electoral misinformation. We use a synthetic control methodology to develop counterfactuals that allow us to test the efficacy of Twitter's actions on Trump's tweets, allowing us to make causal inferences from the real-world observational data from the 2020 election. Research demonstrates that the synthetic control methodology is a powerful tool for causal inference [1–3]. This is one of the important contributions of our work – showing how synthetic control can help researchers make causal inferences about interventions in social media.

Using this methodology we produce important causal estimates that allow us to study whether Twitter's content moderation actions in the 2020 presidential election were effective. Our results indicate that for the Trump tweets we studied, Twitter's actions can reduce their dissemination. This is not universally the case, as there are situations where misinformation continues to flow after Twitter's content moderation efforts — and where there seems to be little change (one way or the other) after the platform used restrictions or warnings to slow the spread of misinformation. Our results have implications for the current debates about social media platform content moderation which we consider in the paper's Discussion.

## 2   Twitter's Moderation of Trump's Tweets in 2020

In October 2020, Twitter applied a "Civic Integrity Policy"[2] to prevent use of their platform for electoral or civic interference. Policy violations included misleading information about how to participate in the election, voter suppression or intimidation, and false details about electoral outcomes. Depending on the severity of the violation, Twitter could engage in several actions, including labeling the tweet as misinformation, deleting the message entirely, or locking or permanently suspending the offending account.

---

[2] https://help.twitter.com/en/rules-and-policies/election-integrity-policy.

One of the most prominent uses of the Civic Integrity Policy in 2020 was for Twitter to use warnings or restrictions on then-President Trump's tweets, as he was disputing the integrity of the election and disseminating misinformation about election fraud. During the period of time we focus on in this study, Twitter mainly applied two types of treatments to Trump's tweets that were determined as violations of the "Civic Integrity Policy":

- Disputed (restricted): Content could be hidden or deleted; the user's ability to reply, retweet, and like the tweet could be turned off; or a label/warning message could be applied to the tweet before it was shared or liked. This treatment was applied frequently between November 4th, 2020 to November 7th, 2020.
- Disputed (not restricted): Content was visible, and users can reply, retweet, or like the tweet; and a warning message was applied to the tweet. This treatment appears throughout the study period.

On January 8, 2021, Twitter suspended @realDonaldTrump, at which time the account had approximately 88.7 million followers.

(a)                                        (b)

**Fig. 1.** Examples of Twitter-labeled Trump tweets. Source https://factba.se/topic/deleted-tweets

In Fig. 1 we provide two examples of Trump's tweets, one for each measure. The example in Panel 1a regards allegations being made regarding the election tabulation and post-election auditing in Georgia from November 18, 2020. The example in Panel 1b shows an example of restricted tweet, which was posted on November 4th, 2020.

Twitter's decision to censor and label Trump's tweets in an attempt to prevent the spread of misinformation was highly controversial. Many people, particularly those within the Republican party, launched a backlash against Twitter following their decision to label Trump's tweets as misinformation. Crucially, it remains uncertain whether Twitter's actions worked as intended: did censoring and labeling these tweets in the 2020 election prevent the subsequent spread of election misinformation on Twitter?

We are interested in the effects of Twitter's actions. Labeling Trump's tweets could have two different consequences: it could have operated as (we assume) Twitter desired: suppressing the further spread of misleading information. Or, given the backlash towards Twitter's policy, it could have amplified the spread of misleading information.

In this paper, we use three novel datasets to study the question. The first one is a unique dataset of over 15 million tweets about the election, a real-time collection that started before the November 2020 general election and ended after Twitter suspended Trump's account. The second one is the $ElectionMisinfo2020$ dataset which consists of tweets directly linked to confirmed misinformation stories in the 2020 election. The third one is from Trump's tweet archive, which collected Trump's tweets and showed whether Twitter took action regarding each of those tweets.

Our main findings are nuanced. There is evidence that for some of Trump's tweets, Twitter's actions reduced misinformation. We find that this is in particular the case for a set of tweets that Twitter placed restrictions on early in election 2020. But we also show that the content moderation efforts generally worked in many cases, but did not work in others. In the set of social media conversations about election fraud in the 2020 election that form the basis of our study, we find that Twitter's actions reduced the subsequent flow of election misinformation by approximately 15%.

In the next section of the paper, we connect our research to the theory about how the public receives and processes information, and what happens when attempts are made to suppress the dissemination of political information. These theories guide and shape our hypotheses. Following this, we delve into our data sources, detailing both the collection and preprocessing of tweets, and then outline the methodologies employed to test our hypotheses. We then present our results and conclude by discussing the implications and limitations of our analysis.

## 3   Does Labelling and Limiting Misinformation Work?

We use public opinion and censorship theory to guide our research. Public opinion theory regards how the public receives, accepts, and processes political information. Assuming that the public acts in a rational manner, they will use information short-cuts to reduce information costs [11]. Rational citizens will not obtain and process all available information, as argued in the theory of public opinion [24], and applied to the reception and processing of social media information. We assume that citizens will follow and process incoming social media information following the "receive-accept-sample" (or RAS) model [4,5,24].

In the RAS model, the citizen receives information (usually from elites), accepts the information (usually filtering it ideologically or by partisanship), and then samples from recently received information when needed (say answering a survey or voting on a ballot measure). The RAS model provides a theoretical framework in which citizens will be selective about information; partisan citizens will receive and accept information from elites with whom they share partisan affiliations. Partisanship is an important heuristic or information shortcut used by citizens [13,14,16].

However, on social media platforms like Twitter, information is not necessarily passed from a partisan elite to a partisan citizen directly – the platform uses algorithms that can alter the flow of information. Furthermore, as was made clear with many of Trump's tweets concerning the 2020 election, the platform can intervene directly by blocking or impeding the ability of an elite to tweet, labeling the elite's messages as misinformation, or making it difficult or impossible for those who view the elite's post to redistribute the message. While Twitter, and similar social media platforms, are private companies, like governments they can control the flow of information on their platforms.

Next, we draw upon the theory of censorship [18]. That theory argues that three mechanisms can be used to censor information online: fear, friction, and flooding. Censoring information through fear means using tools like financial sanctions or the threat of imprisonment to coerce citizens and elites to not disseminate information. Friction regards efforts to slow or make more difficult the dissemination of information. Flooding involves disseminating large quantities of competing information, which serves to make it more difficult and costly to find the information that the government aims to censor.

As [18] points out, introducing friction works in situations where "the cost added by censorship to the information is enough to offset the benefits of consuming or disseminating information" (p. 72). Recall that the RAS model notes that citizens use heuristics like partisanship to determine which elites they follow and whether they receive information from those elites. In situations where Twitter imposes no friction on Trump's tweets, the RAS model should apply: Republicans should be more likely to receive and accept Trump's tweets, most likely in the form of additional conversation about the topics of Trump's tweets online.

This theoretical foundation allows us to formulate the following two hypotheses:

- Hypothesis 1: Trump's tweets steer the direction of conversation, resulting in a higher volume of tweets concerning the topics that Trump discusses.
- Hypothesis 2: Actions taken by Twitter (restrictions, warnings) lessen the influence of Trump's tweets. Intervening on Trump's tweets will reduce the subsequent discussions, mitigating the effect of our first hypothesis. Consequently, these measures decrease the number of election fraud tweets by Republicans relative to unrestricted tweets.

In the next section we describe our data and methods, as well as how we test these hypotheses.

# 4  Data

We used three datasets in this study: Trump's tweets obtained from the Trump Twitter Archive[3] and Factba.se[4]; 2020 general election tweets that we collected using the Twitter API; and election misinformation tweets dataset *ElectionMisinfo2020* [12].[5]

Since Twitter suspended Trump's account, we could not directly obtain his tweets from the Twitter API. Therefore, we used the Trump Twitter Archive to obtain all tweets posted by Trump from September 1, 2020, to December 15, 2020. This dataset contains tweet ids, times, retweet counts, and texts. Additionally, we used Factba.se to identify the tweets that were labeled. Since Factba.se does not differentiate between restricted and warned tweets (documenting both types as "flagged" tweets), we marked "flagged" tweets with zero retweet counts as restricted tweets, and the remaining "flagged" tweets as warned tweets.

We collected the 2020 general election tweets dataset using the Twitter API from June 2020 to January 2021. We utilized the long-term Twitter monitor developed by [8] and keywords related to election fraud, remote voting, polling places, and other election topics. We used this dataset to study how Twitter's restrictions influenced the retweeting of Trump's tweets.

The election misinformation tweets dataset [12] is at the core of this study. It comprises tweets identified in 456 distinct misinformation stories from September through December 2020. For each tweet, the dataset displays the misinformation story it is part of, its identification number[6], the identification numbers of the tweets it retweeted/quoted/replied to, and its partisan lean (left, right, unknown). We used this dataset to construct time series of misinformation counts and study how Trump's tweets and Twitter's labeling impacted these time series.

We find 576 tweets of Trump directly appear in the dataset. Among the 576 tweets, there are 10 restricted tweets, 108 warned tweets, and 458 unrestricted/unwarned tweets. Fifty-nine tweets are directly labeled as misinformation and the summary of the 59 tweets can be found in Table 1.

# 5  Effects of Trump's Tweets

The first question we are interested in is the effects of Trump's tweets on the spread of misinformation. Our hypothesis is that Trump's tweets would directly lead to an increasing spread of the corresponding misinformation. To investigate this, we take each of Trump's tweets that appear in the ElectionMisinfo2020 dataset, plot the volumes of the corresponding misinformation story around the posting time of Trump, and look at the direct effect of Trump's posting on the

---

[3] https://www.thetrumparchive.com.

[4] https://factba.se/topic/flagged-tweets.

[5] The data and code used in this paper is available at https://github.com/jian-frank-cao/Disinformation-Intervention.

[6] The tweet ID can uniquely identify a message on Twitter, including tweet, reply, quote, and retweet.

**Table 1.** Summary of Trump's Tweets in the ElecMisinfo2020 Dataset

| Story Number | Description | Count | Hard | Soft | Unrestricted | Retweet |
|---|---|---|---|---|---|---|
| Story 1 | ballot harvesting: Ilhan Omar Project Veritas Video | 3 | 0 | 0 | 3 | 1 |
| Story 2 | tech: dominion | 34 | 0 | 23 | 11 | 12 |
| Story 3 | Late:Extended Ballots | 1 | 0 | 0 | 1 | 0 |
| Story 4 | dead voters: general ticket | 5 | 0 | 5 | 0 | 1 |
| Story 5 | Digital dumps: Michigan 128000 votes | 2 | 2 | 0 | 0 | 0 |
| Story 6 | partisan vcr: Nevada whistleblower | 1 | 0 | 1 | 0 | 1 |
| Story 7 | Physical Mail Mistakes: Deceased and Inactive CA | 1 | 0 | 0 | 1 | 1 |
| Story 8 | Physical Mail Mistakes:MI Misprints for Troops | 2 | 0 | 0 | 2 | 2 |
| Story 9 | poll watchers: Philly no entry list | 1 | 0 | 1 | 0 | 0 |
| Story 10 | Physical Mail Fraud: Democratic TX Mayor | 1 | 0 | 0 | 1 | 0 |
| Story 11 | Other: Stop The Steal Pushed | 1 | 0 | 0 | 1 | 0 |
| Story 12 | Other: Candidate Fraud Biden Fraud Quote | 2 | 0 | 0 | 2 | 0 |
| Story 13 | protests:stop the steal rallies | 1 | 0 | 1 | 0 | 1 |
| Story 14 | Physical Mail Fraud: PA Misprinted Corrections | 2 | 0 | 0 | 2 | 0 |
| Story 15 | Statistics: Math Video | 1 | 0 | 0 | 1 | 0 |
| Story 16 | Physical Mail Mistakes:NYPost Ballot Typo | 1 | 0 | 0 | 1 | 0 |

time series.[7] Note that we take all of Trump's tweets, regardless of Twitter's actions, which could bias the result downward. Therefore, the effect we discuss here might be a lower bound.

We find very similar patterns among almost all the 120-min windows around Trump's posting time: the tweet volume rises sharply, and then gradually decreases, eventually equilibrating at a stable volume that is higher than the level before the posting event. To estimate the average effect, we first normalize each 120-min window by applying the following transformation to each time window.

$$\hat{Y}_i = \frac{Y_i - min(Y)}{max(Y) - min(Y)}$$

Fig. 2a shows the average time series and the confidence interval among all the time windows. We also independently count retweets of Trump's tweets. The normalized average time series and the confidence interval among all windows are shown in Fig. 2b. Additional, we also plot the average normalized volume for left-lean and right-lean tweets separately in Fig. 2c and Fig. 2d. This shows that the overall effect on volume is much larger for right-leaning tweets, which is consistent with hypothesis 1.

---

[7] Out of all Trump's tweets, there are two that were posted close enough in time that their active periods overlap. In this specific instance, we study the combined effect of these tweets, using the timestamp of the first tweet as the reference point for our analysis.

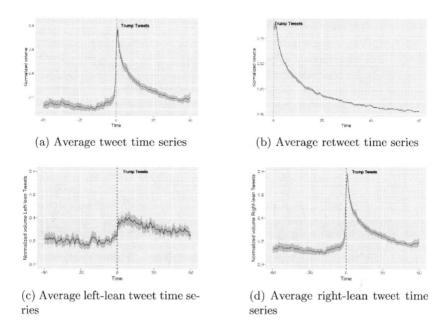

(a) Average tweet time series

(b) Average retweet time series

(c) Average left-lean tweet time series

(d) Average right-lean tweet time series

**Fig. 2.** Average normalized time series among all 120-min time intervals affected by Trump's tweet

To quantify the effect of Trump's tweets and the heterogeneity across different topics, we perform a t-test for each story on the average column in three time periods. Period 1 spans 30 minutes before Trump's tweet ($T = -30$ to $T = -1$). Period 2 spans 30 minutes after Trump's tweet ($T = 0$ to $T = 29$). Lastly, Period 3 is 30 minutes to 60 minutes after Trump's tweet ($T = 30$ to $T = 59$).

We compare the data from Periods 1 and 2 to see the immediate effect of the tweet, and from Periods 1 and 3 for the longer-term impact. The volume per minute comparisons before and after each tweet, along with the t-test results, are displayed in Fig. 3. The graph indicates that Trump's tweet has a heterogeneous effect across different topics. We can observe that for most of the topics, there is an increase in volume either immediately or after 30 minutes. The volume does not immediately increase for some topics with Twitter's intervention like "Dead voters", "Nevada Whistleblower", and "Poll Watcher", which provides evidence in support of hypothesis 2.

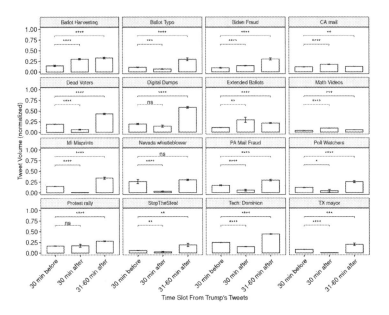

**Fig. 3.** Effect of Trump's tweets By Topic and Time. Note: ns: $p > 0.05$; *: $p \leq 0.05$; **: $p \leq 0.01$; ***: $p \leq 0.001$; ****: $p \leq 0.0001$

## 6   Effects of Twitter's Actions

To study the effects of labeling, we first estimate the time Twitter applied the label. We then derive time series of misinformation related to Trump's tweets. We compare the time series of messages where a label was applied against counterfactuals derived from messages that were not subject to any restriction. Using this data, we estimate the effects of labeling.

To study the effects of labeling, it is necessary to know when the labeling became effective, i.e., the treatment time. However, Twitter has not disclosed the exact timing of the labels, only stating that they applied labels between 5 to 30 minutes after Trump posted the tweets.[8] Fortunately, our 2020 general election data contains real-time retweets of 7 out of 26 of Trump's restricted tweets. Each retweet contains a retweet status object that points to Trump's original tweet and shows its latest retweet count by the time the retweet was collected by our Twitter monitor. The time series of cumulative retweets are shown in Fig. 4. We can see that the time series stopped around 20 to 240 minutes after Trump tweeted because Twitter restricted users' ability to retweet, and no more new retweets were collected. The stopping points (red) are our estimates of labeling time. Notice that labeling took around 1.5 to 4 h in September, while it only took around 30 minutes in November. Twitter expedited its labeling, likely because election misinformation was spreading fast and the potential damage to society was great. Since we cannot directly estimate the labeling time of warned tweets

---

[8] https://www.youtube.com/watch?v=ONYuLP7sHFQ&t=4701s.

as retweeting was not restricted, we assume it is similar to that of the restricted tweets.

Next, we derive the time series of misinformation tweets related to Trump's tweets. For each of Trump's tweets included in the misinformation data set, we find that tweet's corresponding story.[9] We then compute the number of tweets posted per minute, across the entire misinformation dataset, from the associated misinformation story. We focus on the time series from $T$ to $T + 120$, where $T$ is the timestamp of Trump's tweet. Thus, each of Trump's tweets produces a misinformation time series. When the Trump tweet that produces this time series is "labeled" by Twitter, we refer to this as a "labeled misinformation time series", and if the Trump tweet is "unlabeled", an "unlabeled misinformation time series."[10].

We use synthetic control to construct counterfactuals of the labeled time series. For each labeled misinformation time series, if there are more than five unlabeled misinformation time series in the same story, we use them to estimate the synthetic control. Otherwise, we disregard the stories and use all unlabeled time series. Based on the estimates of labeling time in Fig. 4, assuming most labeling was imposed after $T + 20$, we estimate the synthetic control using the $T$ to $T + 19$ sub-series to ensure that it closely resembles the labeled time series in the first 20 minutes.

We show synthetic controls for all of Trump's restricted tweets in Fig. 5a and 15 out of 201 warned tweets in Fig. 5b. The synthetic control, i.e., the estimated tweets if there was no restriction, is shown in red, and the observed tweets are shown in blue. The area between the red and blue curves are the estimated effects of labeling. If the red curve is above the blue curve, then the effect of labeling is negative, which means labeling reduces the spreading of misinformation. For example, those where there is solid evidence from the synthetic control methodology that Twitter's content moderation reduced misinformation are Trump's that Twitter restricted on Nov 04 15:37:40, Nov 04 21:56:11, and Nov 05 16:22:46. Additionally the synthetic control methodology indicates that Twitter's content moderation reduced misinformation in the instances where they placed warnings on Trump's tweets about the election on Nov 04 21:56:10, Nov 09 00:23:26, and Nov 12 15:16:02. On the other hand, if the blue curve is above the red curve, this indicates positive treatment effects, in which Twitter's labeling stimulates more discussion about misinformation. For example, the synthetic control method indicates positive treatment effects when Twitter restricted Trump's tweets on

---

[9] In some cases, the Trump tweet is not directly in the misinformation dataset, but we do find the tweet's associated retweets, quotes, and replies. In all cases where we find more than ten examples of retweets, quotes, or replies with a story in the misinformation dataset, we define the Trump tweet's misinformation story as the most common across this set of retweets, quotes, and replies. If we find fewer than ten examples, we drop this Trump tweet from our analysis.

[10] If any Trump tweet did not lead to significant corresponding misinformation time series from T to $T + 120$, i.e. less than 100 tweets per minute on average, we dropped it from our analysis.

Nov 05 15:09:19 and when Twitter placed warning labels on his election-related tweets on Nov 19 17:34:26, Nov 30 00:34:38, and Dec 14 14:38:38.

Overall, the synthetic control results shown for the thirty examples in Fig. 5a and Fig. 5b provide a nuanced perspective on Twitter's attempts in 2020 to slow or stop the spread of election misinformation by restricting or placing warning labels on Trump's tweets. Among the restricted tweets (Fig. 5a) we see relatively clear evidence in 8 of the 15 instances for restriction reducing the subsequent spread of misinformation. Similarly, among the Trump tweets where warning labels were used, 6 of the 15 examples show that the subsequent spread of misinformation was slowed.

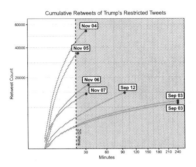

**Fig. 4.** How Fast Did Twitter Apply the Restriction?

With these synthetic controls, we quantify the labeling effect using ratios of average tweets in the second hour:

$$\phi_i = \frac{\frac{\sum_{t=61}^{120}(Observed)_{i,t}}{60}}{\frac{\sum_{t=61}^{120}(Estimated\ No\ Restriction)_{i,t}}{60}} \tag{1}$$

The ratio is less than one if the average observed tweets from $T+61$ to $T+120$ is smaller than the average estimated tweets if there was no restriction, i.e., the blue curve is above the red curve, and it is larger than one otherwise. Since this study is interested in analyzing how Twitter's labeling reduces the spreading of misinformation, we focus on Trump's tweets that are associated with a large number of misinformation tweets and exclude time series that have on average fewer than 100 tweets per minute.

The ratios are shown in Fig. 6 and Table 2. We use shapes to distinguish Trump's restricted and warned tweets and use colors to show stories. We see that the majority of the ratios are less than one, i.e., in the green area, as 55 of the tweets in this analysis are in the green area. Importantly we note that of the six tweets in this sample that were restricted, five of the restricted instances were ones where the subsequent flow of misinformation were reduced, and in only one of those instances was the subsequent flow of misinformation

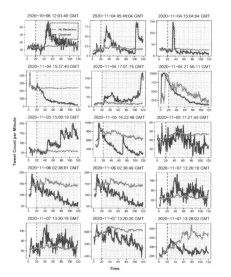

(a) Estimated No Restriction Tweets vs. Observed Tweets (Restricted)

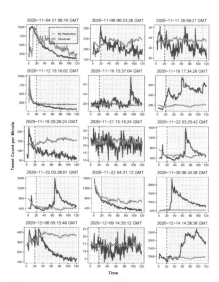

(b) Estimated No Restriction Tweets vs. Observed Tweets (Warned) (Sample)

**Fig. 5.** Effects of Restriction

not reduced by the restriction of Trump's tweets. It is also important to note that these six restricted tweets were in the immediate aftermath of the 2020 presidential election, at a time when mitigating the spread of misinformation might have been most influential. We also must note, however, that 30 of the tweets in this analysis (the vast majority of which were those with warning labels) show positive treatment effects, meaning that misinformation increased after the warning labels were used. Some of the tweets with warning labels have sizable increases in post-moderation spread, one of the tweets with a warning label in early December 2020 saw a 1600% increase in post-treatment misinformation spread.

Finally, for interested readers, we also show the distribution of $\phi_i$ in Table 2. A t-test of $log(\phi_i)$ yields a t-value of $-2.4737$ and a p-value of $0.0149$, which means labeling significantly ($P < 0.05$) reduces the volume of misinformation tweets in the testing period $[T+61, T+120]$. The mean of the log effect $\overline{log(\phi_i)} = -0.1673$ indicates that, on average, Twitter's labeling reduces $1 - e^{-0.1673} = 15.41\%$ of misinformation tweets.

## 7   Discussion

Existing literature presents conflicting findings on the ability of social media platforms to mitigate the spread of misinformation effectively. Our study, however,

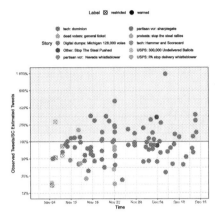

**Fig. 6.** Quantification of the Estimated Treatment Effect

**Table 2.** Tweets in Estimated Ratio Ranges

|                  | Restricted   | Warned      |
|------------------|--------------|-------------|
| (12.5%, 25%]     | 1(16.67%)    | 4(3.92%)    |
| (25%, 50%]       | 0(0%)        | 17(16.67%)  |
| (50%, 100%]      | 4(66.67%)    | 45(44.12%)  |
| (100%, 200%]     | 0(0%)        | 25(24.51%)  |
| (200%, 400%]     | 1(16.67%)    | 9(8.82%)    |
| (400%, 800%]     | 0(0%)        | 1(0.98%)    |
| (800%, 1600%]    | 0(0%)        | 1(0.98%)    |
| **Total**        | 6            | 102         |

takes a more targeted approach, examining a particular facet of platform moderation. We utilize a unique dataset and adopt a sophisticated causal inference methodology to increase the validity of our conclusions. Our findings suggest that actions taken by social media platforms can mitigate the subsequent spread of misinformation. We call for further research to better understand the conditions under which moderation is possible and which interventions are the most effective.

In particular, the next stage of research needs to tackle the conditions when content moderation has the desired treatment effect. Is restriction more effective than labeling (we see intriguing evidence that the answer may be yes in Fig. 6)? Does it matter when a platform applies restrictions or labels? Does the speed at which moderation is carried out affect its effectiveness? Is the wording of the warning label important for restricting subsequent spread? There are many additional questions that researchers and social media companies should tackle.

It is important to view our conclusions in through lens of the current moment, wherein some social media channels opt for less moderation, ostensibly to champion free speech. Discussions surrounding the policies being implemented by states such as Florida and Texas, in conjunction with legal debates about the moderation of certain social media dialogues, highlight potential restrictions on content moderation. While Constitutionally-protected political speech might be an area where content moderation is problematic, that should not imply that social media platforms should stop efforts to prevent the spread of child pornography, voting disenfranchisement, sexual and racial harassment, or the use of their platforms by terrorists organizations. The research community needs to step up our involvement in these debates, and provide research that can help social media platforms develop appropriate content moderation policies that protect rights while preventing illegal behavior and social harm.

# References

1. Abadie, A., Diamond, A., Hainmueller, J.: Synthetic control methods for comparative case studies: Estimating the effect of California's tobacco control program. J. Am. Stat. Assoc. **105**(490), 493–505 (2010)
2. Abadie, A.: Using synthetic controls: feasibility, data requirements, and methodological aspects. J. Econ. Lit. **59**(2), 391–425 (2021)
3. Abadie, A., Gardeazabal, J.: The economic costs of conflict: a case study of the Basque country. Am. Econ. Rev. **93**, 113–32 (2003)
4. Adams-Cohen, N.: New Perspectives in Political Communication. Ph.D. thesis (2019), California Institute of Technology. https://doi.org/10.7907/7TDG-4R42
5. Adams-Cohen, N.: Policy change and public opinion: measuring shifting political sentiment with social media data. Am. Politics Res. **48**(5), 612–621 (2020)
6. Allcott, H., Gentzkow, M.: Social media and fake news in the 2016 election. J. Econ. Perspect. **31**, 211–236 (2017). https://doi.org/10.1257/JEP.31.2.211
7. Allington, D., Duffy, B., Wessely, S., Dhavan, N., Rubin, J.: Health-protective behaviour, social media usage and conspiracy belief during the COVID-19 public health emergency. Psychol. Med. **51**(10), 1763–1769 (2021). https://doi.org/10.1017/S003329172000224X
8. Cao, J., Adams-Cohen, N., Alvarez, R.M.: Reliable and efficient long-term social media monitoring. J. Comput. Commun. **09**(10), 97–109 (2021)
9. Carey, J.M., et al.: The ephemeral effects of fact-checks on COVID-19 misperceptions in the united states, great Britain and Canada. Nat. Human Behav. **6**, 236–243 (2022). https://doi.org/10.1038/s41562-021-01278-3
10. Clayton, K., et al.: Real solutions for fake news? Measuring the effectiveness of general warnings and fact-check tags in reducing belief in false stories on social media. Polit. Behav. **42**, 1073–1095 (2020). https://doi.org/10.1007/S11109-019-09533-0
11. Downs, A.: An economic theory of democracy (1957)
12. Kennedy, I., et al.: Repeat spreaders and election delegitimization: a comprehensive dataset of misinformation tweets from the 2020 US election. J. Quant. Descrip. Digital Med. **2**, 1–49 (2022)
13. Lupia, A.: Busy voters, agenda control, and the power of information. Am. Polit. Sci. Rev. **86**(2), 390–403 (1992)
14. Lupia, A.: Shortcuts versus encyclopedias: information and voting behavior in California insurance reform elections. Am. Polit. Sci. Rev. **88**(1), 63–76 (1994)

15. Pennycook, G., Rand, D.G.: Fighting misinformation on social media using crowd-sourced judgments of news source quality. Proc. Natl. Acad. Sci. U.S.A. **116**, 2521–2526 (2019). https://doi.org/10.1073/PNAS.1806781116
16. Popkin, S.L.: The Reasoning Voter: Communication and Persuasion in Presidential Campaigns. University of Chicago Press (1991)
17. Porter, E., Wood, T.J.: The global effectiveness of fact-checking: evidence from simultaneous experiments in Argentina, Nigeria, South Africa, and the United Kingdom. Proc. Natl. Acad. Sci. U.S.A. **118**, e2104235118 (2021). https://doi.org/10.1073/PNAS.2104235118/SUPPL_FILE/PNAS.2104235118.SAPP.PDF, https://www.pnas.org/doi/abs/10.1073/pnas.2104235118
18. Roberts, M.E.: Censored. Princeton University Press, Princeton (2018)
19. Sanderson, Z., Brown, M.A., Bonneau, R., Nagler, J., Tucker, J.A.: Twitter flagged Donald Trump's tweets with election misinformation: They continued to spread both on and off the platform. Harvard Kennedy School Misinformation Review 2 (2021)
20. Srikanth, M., Liu, A., Adams-Cohen, N., Cao, J., Alvarez, R.M., Anandkumar, A.: Dynamic social media monitoring for fast-evolving online discussions. In: Proceedings of the 27th ACM SIGKDD Conference on Knowledge Discovery & Data Mining, pp. 3576–3584. KDD 2021, Association for Computing Machinery, New York, NY, USA (2021). https://doi.org/10.1145/3447548.3467171, https://doi.org/10.1145/3447548.3467171
21. Thèro, H., Vincent, E.M.: Investigating Facebook's interventions against accounts that repeatedly share misinformation. Inf. Process. Manage. **59**, 102804 (2022). https://doi.org/10.1016/j.ipm.2021.102804
22. U.S. Senate Select Committee on Intelligence: Russian active measures campaigns and interference in the the 2016 U.S. election, volume 2: Russia's use of social media. U.S. Senate Select Committee on Intelligence Report 116-XX (2020). https://www.intelligence.senate.gov/sites/default/files/documents/Report_Volume2.pdf
23. Vosoughi, S., Roy, D., Aral, S.: The spread of true and false news online. Science **359**, 1146–1151 (2018). https://doi.org/10.1126/SCIENCE.AAP9559
24. Zaller, J.R.: The Nature and Origins of Mass Opinion. Cambridge University Press, Cambridge (1992)

# Coordinated Information Campaigns on Social Media: A Multifaceted Framework for Detection and Analysis

Kin Wai Ng[1(✉)] [iD] and Adriana Iamnitchi[2] [iD]

1 University of South Florida, Tampa 33620, USA
`kinwaing@usf.edu`
2 Maastricht University, Maastricht, The Netherlands
`a.iamnitchi@maastrichtuniversity.nl`

**Abstract.** The prevalence of coordinated information campaigns in social media platforms has significant negative consequences across various domains, including social, political, and economic processes. This paper proposes a multifaceted framework for detecting and analyzing coordinated message promotion on social media. By simultaneously considering features related to content, time, and network dimensions, our framework can capture the diverse nature of coordinated activity and identify anomalous user accounts who likely engaged in suspicious behavior. Unlike existing solutions that rely on specific constraints, our approach is more flexible as it employs specialized components to extract the significant structures within a network and to detect the most unusual interactions. We apply our framework to two Twitter datasets, the Russian Internet Research Agency (IRA), and long-term discussions on Data Science topics. The results demonstrate our framework's ability to isolate unusual activity from expected normal behavior and provide valuable insights for further qualitative investigation.

**Keywords:** Coordinated Campaigns · Information Operations · Social Media

## 1 Introduction

Social media platforms have been under scrutiny for allowing nefarious processes on their sites. Information coordination campaigns are such processes that can inflict significant damage on the society. Implemented as disinformation campaigns [19,26], elections [14], or digital currency manipulation [21] to name a few, they appear as organic, spontaneous conversations among unrelated user accounts who post different messages in support of the same agenda within a short time interval. Such accounts are not necessarily bot accounts, but very often verified and even influencer accounts[1], escaping thus bot detection tools.

---

[1] https://www.vice.com/en/article/akewea/a-pr-firm-is-paying-tiktok-influencers-to-promote-liberal-causes-and-hype-democrats-middling-accomplishments.

D. Ceolin et al. (Eds.): MISDOOM 2023, LNCS 14397, pp. 103–118, 2023.
https://doi.org/10.1007/978-3-031-47896-3_8

The messaging promoted is not always in bad faith, as it can be part of health promotion campaigns or legitimate political campaigns. However, recognizing such coordinated campaigns and distinguishing them from organic social media interactions and message sharing is important both for understanding the media landscape and for limiting manipulation.

Coordinated message promotion is characterized by locality in content and time, and similarity in the activities of the user accounts involved. Therefore, attempts to detect such campaigns focus on identifying unusual patterns related to time, content, and user activity. For example, some solutions assumed pre-defined thresholds on time [4,19,23] or on content similarity [11,20] to separate organic from potentially suspicious actions. Moreover, many of the previous solutions functioned as a pipeline in which the time, content and user actions (often modeled as network anomalies) were detected in a sequential order. However, predefined thresholds are somewhat artificial and easy to bypass.

We propose a methodology that avoids fixed time or similarity thresholds and can generalize to different social media platforms. Our solution starts by building a network of user accounts connected by weighted edges that quantify similar interest in content posted. We then reduce this very dense network to its backbone, a procedure which maintains only the edges that represent the higher information similarity. Information similarity, in our case, is measured as vocabulary overlap of sets of posted messages. On the resulting backbone network we run a community detection algorithm to identify clusters of user accounts with stronger connections. In each cluster, we identify the pairs of accounts that deviate the most from the pair-wise activity of the other accounts in the cluster in terms of timing as measured by inter-arrival time between actions, content similarity as measured by the cosine similarity between text embeddings, and network similarity as measured by the cosine similarity of node embeddings. It is this subset of anomalous user accounts that we believe should be studied via qualitative methods to reliably identify coordinated campaigns. Our solution, like [3], looks simultaneously at all the three dimensions necessary for a coordinated information campaign: time synchronicity, content locality and coordinated user activity. However, we define a different network than their follower-followee network in an attempt to provide a platform-independent solution. Our solution could augment previous solutions tailored for particular platforms.

## 2    Related Work

Previous studies have proposed different frameworks to identify coordination among actors by examining platform-specific features such as co-retweet or co-tweet networks [9], or the retweet network [8]. Similar to our work, other studies have identified coordination via shared pieces of content, such as topics, narratives, hashtags, or URLs. Giglietto et al. [4] identified groups of coordinated accounts based on co-shared URLs. Pacheco et al. [23] proposed a generalized, qualitative approach for detecting coordinated behavior by exploiting behavioral traces (e.g., temporal patterns of activity) or common actions (e.g., sharing the same content or URLs). More recently, Magelinski et al. [16] focused on constructing a multi-view network using common interactions to uncover synchronized actions within narrow time windows. A limitation of these frameworks is that they rely on discrete time windows or predefined short time thresholds to detect coordinated instances, which may result in missing instances of coordination in more intricate and adaptive campaigns.

Only a few studies have focused on developing frameworks that specifically target the identification of coordinated campaigns by considering several dimensions such as network, time, and content. Kriel et al. [10] studied the IRA dataset using network analysis to investigate the temporal evolution of network content pushed by Twitter bots and accounts related to online influence campaigns. The framework proposed by Francois et al. [3] shares some similarities with our proposed methodology as it also focuses on identifying coordinated activities through the analysis of network, temporal and semantic dimensions. However, their approach relies on constructing networks based on follower-followee interactions, which are specific to some platforms only, and can be challenging or very expensive to obtain.

In this work, we proposed a framework that also investigates coordinated activity through the analysis of three different axes: content, timing and network structures. Unlike previous work, our approach leverages techniques to extract the key structural components of the network and employs an unsupervised machine-learning model for effective anomaly detection. The objective of our framework is to isolate unusual activity from what is considered normal behavior in a particular context.

## 3 Methodology

Our approach to identifying potentially coordinated information operations is based on the following intuition: in order for a message to reach a large number of people, it has to be repeated within a short interval of time by multiple apparently unrelated user accounts. Thus, a coordinated information operation requires content and time locality, where content locality means possibly distinct messages in support of a shared objective.

Our solution is based on the following observations from forensic studies of information campaigns [1,3,23,25,26]. First, accounts involved in a coordinated campaign will exhibit persistent behavior: the same account will post repeatedly on the same topic to promote a message. Second, multiple accounts will participate in promoting the same narrative for a successful (and thus, worth identifying) campaign. Third, we assume that users who are engaged in a coordinated information operation are likely to have similar tasks to perform, which might translate into similar network structures or connection patterns. Fourth, we implicitly assume that normal behavior is more common than coordinated behavior. This observation typically holds true even in datasets directly associated with an information campaign. For example, in the IRA dataset, accounts identified as part of the campaign frequently shared banal content, including sports or local news, along with trending hashtags to inject themselves into popular discussions and gain followers [10].

We propose a methodology that consists of five stages, namely *network construction, backbone extraction, community detection, feature extraction*, and *anomaly detection*. Briefly, we first construct a network of user accounts connected by posts with similar content. In order to provide a platform-independent solution, we ignore resharing activities (typical of Twitter and LinkedIn, but not typical of YouTube or Reddit, for example) and only consider the original posting activities (e.g., posts in Reddit, tweets in Twitter, etc.). From this potentially large and quite dense network, we extract its backbone to ignore the user connections that are less active or less similar in the content promoted. We then detect network clusters that, due to the network construction methodology, will map onto shared topics in the promoted content. We extract features that capture content, time, and network similarity among user connections in each cluster. Finally, we identify anomalies from "typical" user behavior based on the observed features. Each component is described below.

## 3.1   Co-Sharing Network Construction

The objective of this component is to identify shared interests among users based on the topics/information they post. We construct networks among social media user accounts based on the co-occurrence of similar pieces of information. We can define similarity of information in different ways, from identical URLs or hashtags to content-based analysis revealing the same topics or narratives. In this study, we focus on hashtags.

The co-sharing network is defined as a bipartite graph, $B = (U, V, E)$, where the nodes $u \in U$ represent social media accounts, and nodes $v \in V$ represent pieces of information. An edge $e \in E$ between $u$ and $v$ refers to the number of times a social media user shared a particular information entity. We project this bipartite graph onto the social media user nodes to obtain an undirected graph consisting of user co-occurrence connections. The edge weight between two users refers to the minimum number of times that both users were observed sharing the same pieces of information. As an attempt to reduce false positive connections (i.e., user co-shares happening by chance), we filter out those edges with an edge weight of 1. This includes user pairs who are only seen sharing a piece of information once over the entire period.

## 3.2   Network Backbone Extraction

The goal of this component is to identify and extract the most relevant accounts and their connections from the original network, aiming to eliminate accounts that do not often contribute on shared topics. Projections of bipartite networks lead to very dense structures where many of the edges are possibly affected by infrequent ties between the different node types in the original network, which in our context may be seen as noise (e.g., spontaneous reactions to particular news or real-world events). To address this challenge, previous work has adopted global threshold approaches where edges with weights higher than some threshold are kept while all others are removed [11,23]. This approach is not ideal for networks with skewed weight distributions, as it is often the case for social media networks. Instead, a better strategy is to focus on locality, where the salient core network structure is decided at the node level.

We apply the Noise-Corrected (NC) backbone strategy proposed by Coscia et al. [2]. While other backbone approaches have been proposed [6,24], the NC backbone method is considered a more robust approach as it can reduce the occurrence of spurious correlations by comparing edge weights at the level of node pairs rather than at the level of individual nodes. The NC backbone uses a null-model based on the assumption that edge weights in the network are drawn from a binomial distribution. An edge is kept in the backbone if and only if its observed weight is higher than $\delta\sqrt{V[L_{ij}]}$, where $V[L_{ij}]$ is the estimation of the expected variance for the observed edge weight $L_{ij}$ between node $i$ and $j$, and $\delta$ is a parameter for the tolerance of noise in a particular network. We set $\delta$ to 2.32 which approximates p-values at a significance level of 0.01, as suggested by the authors.

### 3.3 Community Detection

The objective of this component is to enable the selection of groups of users that exhibit overlapping content-based interests. Specifically, this component involves identifying the communities of users within the backbone of the co-share network. We employ the Louvain algorithm for community detection, which is frequently used in prior related research [17,18,22]. The Louvain algorithm works by optimizing a modularity score. It measures the strength of the communities detected by comparing the density of connections among nodes in a given network with that in a random network. We accounted for edge weights in the Louvain algorithm, which enables the identification of communities based on the strength of links between users instead of just their presence.

### 3.4 Edge Feature Extraction

We focus on extracting edge features related to content, time, and network dimensions. These dimensions have been highlighted in prior research as critical factors for detecting coordination phenomena in social media platforms [1,3]. Content features capture the similarity of content being shared between users, while temporal features capture the timing of their interactions. Network features capture the structural role of users within the network. Our assumption is that users who engaged in coordinated operations are likely to perform similar tasks, which might translate into similar connections patterns or network structures.

**Edge Weight** measures the propensity of two users to share similar pieces of information. Specifically, the edge weight is computed by considering the total frequency of co-occurrence of shared elements (e.g., hashtags) by two users. It is computed as follows:

$$W_{ij} = \sum_{n=1}^{N} \min[\sigma(i,n), \sigma(j,n)] \tag{1}$$

where $\sigma(i,n)$ denotes the number of messages posted by user $i$ that contain a given element $n$.

**Content Similarity** measures the degree of similarity in the content posted by two users. In this study, we focus on measuring content similarity between users' posts with the same hashtags. We use the cosine similarity measure to compute the similarity between the semantic embeddings of posts by two users under the same hashtags. We take the average of the cosine similarity values over the hashtags that both users have in common. The formula is as follows:

$$C_{ij} = \frac{\sum_{n=1}^{N} cosineSimilarity[\sigma(i,n), \sigma(j,n)]}{N} \tag{2}$$

where $\sigma(i,n)$ denotes the average embedding vector of tweets posted by user $i$ under hashtag $n$. The embeddings are extracted using a pre-trained sentence transformer model available in Hugging Face[2], which maps text in multiple languages to a 768 dimensional vector representation. We chose this model because it was fine-tuned for sentence similarity tasks; thus, its vector representations are better for capturing semantic textual similarity. While there are language models trained on Twitter data, they are primarily designed for tasks other than sentence similarity, and few of them incorporate multilingual data.

**Temporal Signature** measures the timing between the posts of two users under the same hashtag. Specifically, we compute the shortest $\delta$ interarrival times, where $\delta$ is the number of co-shares between two users for a given hashtag. The resulting distribution of interarrival times is summarized by taking the median interarrival time as the final value to represent timing for the particular user pair. Unlike the mean, which is very sensitive to outliers, the median offers a more robust estimate of central tendency.

**Node Similarity** captures the similarity between two users in terms of their respective network position or structural role. This feature is measured through computing the cosine similarity between the node2vec [7] embeddings of two users. Node2vec is a graph representation learning algorithm that maps nodes in a network to a low-dimensional embedding vector that captures their structural properties. The choice of node2vec is motivated by the assumption that users who are engaged in coordinated activity are likely to have similar network structures or connection patterns.

### 3.5   Anomaly Detection

The objective of this component is to isolate organic from inorganic behavior, with the assumption that organic behavior is more common and inorganic

---

[2] https://huggingface.co/sentence-transformers/paraphrase-multilingual-mpnet-base-v2.

behavior (reflected by coordinated operations) will stand out. In this study, we employ Isolation Forests (iForest) [13] for anomaly detection in the context of coordinated behavior in social media. The algorithm consists of multiple binary decision trees trained with different subsamples drawn from the original data. During training, each decision tree decomposes the data space into two subtrees using the arbitrary values of randomly selected features. iForests measure the degree of anomaly of a particular data instance by computing its average path length from the root of the tree. The idea is that anomalous samples should require less effort to separate from the rest of the samples, which results in shorter path lengths across the trees. We trained an iForest for each identified cluster from the community detection stage by considering their respective edge characteristics as input features.

The anomalous data instances identified by the iForests consist of edges with significantly different characteristics from the normal distribution of edges in each cluster. This approach allows an understanding of what is considered normal and abnormal in a given distribution, thus providing important insights into coordinated behavior. The results from the iForests can be combined with explainable methods such as SHAP [15] to understand what features contribute the most to these anomalies.

## 4    Datasets

Our analysis focuses on two datasets collected from Twitter. The first is related to social media manipulation operations, and the second covers general topics of discussion related to technology trends. We selected these datasets to cover a span of known coordinated information operations to likely only organic discussions. For each dataset, we report basic summary statistics and information related to data collection and pre-processing. We focus only on original tweets containing at least one hashtag.

**Russian Internet Research Agency (IRA).** This dataset consists of a subset of accounts that Twitter has identified as being linked to the Russian Internet Research Agency. The corpus of tweets and corresponding metadata, posted between 2009 and 2018 by these accounts, has been publicly released as part of the Twitter Election Integrity dataset[3]. We narrow our focus on the period between July 7th 2014 to November 31st 2016 since it contains several real-world events, such as the 2016 U.S. presidential election or the downing of the Malaysian airplane flight in Ukraine, which have been shown to be subject of significant intervention from the IRA in online discussions [5,14]. In total, the dataset contains 1,577,082 tweets on 18,826 unique hashtags from 3,594 users. For each hashtag, the number of tweets ranged from 2 to 236,322 with an average of 111 tweets per hashtag. The number of unique users per hashtag ranged from 2 to 1,143 with an average of 11.5 users per hashtag.

---

[3] https://transparency.twitter.com/en/reports/moderation-research.html.

**Data Science Tweets (DS).** This dataset is a collection of tweets related to the trends and advancements in the field of data science over the past decade. It includes tweets that mention data science, data visualization, or data analysis. The dataset is publicly available on Kaggle[4]. We focus on tweets over the period of January 1st 2016 to June 19th 2021. In total, there are 142,282 tweets from 5,730 users and with 7,521 unique hashtags. To allow for a better comparison in coordinated behavior within different contexts, we subsample the user accounts in the DS dataset to match the number of users in the IRA. We ensure that the distribution of activities of the subsampled users approximates the distribution of user activity rates in the IRA dataset. The resulting sampled user accounts are more representative of the activity levels of users in the IRA, and thus more comparable across the two datasets. Overall, the sampled dataset contains 136,429 tweets on 7,192 unique hashtags from 3,594 users.

Each dataset includes the following fields: a unique identifier for the author of the tweet, a unique identifier for the tweet, the timestamp indicating when the tweet was posted, the text of the tweet, and a list of hashtags used in the tweet. For each dataset, we removed user accounts with only one tweet over the entire period of the dataset, as they are unlikely to provide useful information for coordinated activity. We cleaned the tweets by removing mentions, URLs, and hashtags from the text to keep only the natural language content that likely reflects the user's opinion. We use the `langdetect`[5] Python library to detect the language of the tweets in each dataset. The proportion of non-English tweets within each dataset was 39.8% in the case of the IRA, and 2.9% in DS. This observation informed our decision to use multilingual pre-trained language models for text embedding extraction.

## 5   Results

In this section, we present the results of our framework as applied to the two datasets in this study. We investigate the impact of the backbone extraction component on reducing the size of the network and highlighting relevant structures. We explore how features related to time, content, and network dimensions contribute in identifying anomalous instances. Finally, we conduct a qualitative analysis of the anomalous clusters identified by our method, aiming to characterize each cluster based on their shared content and edge features.

### 5.1   Extracting the Backbone of Co-Sharing Networks

As mentioned in Sect. 3.1, the co-sharing networks were constructed by connecting user accounts based on shares of the same hashtags. The total number of co-sharing interactions was 1,897,678 for the IRA and 3,199,919 in Data Science. To reduce spurious co-sharing interactions, all edges with weight of 1 were

---

[4] https://www.kaggle.com/datasets/ruchi798/data-science-tweets.
[5] https://pypi.org/project/langdetect/.

removed from the original networks as they do not necessarily indicate coordinated behavior. The proportion of edges removed from the co-sharing networks was 21.5% for the IRA, and 33.4% for the Data Science dataset. We applied the NC backbone strategy to each of these networks. Table 1 presents a comparison between the original networks and their backbones across several graph measures. The backbone strategy reduces significantly the size of edges in the original co-sharing networks, while still preserving important network structures. Particularly, the proportion of edges removed from the original networks was 59% in the IRA and 88% in Data Science. We observed that the original networks exhibit higher density and centralization scores than their respective backbones. The centralization scores of the original networks are 3 and 4.9 times higher than their backbone in IRA and Data Science, respectively. This indicates that the original networks tend to be centralized around a small set of nodes with a high concentration of shared hashtags. The backbone strategy reduces the centralization score by removing some particular connections to hubs, which are considered less important as hubs have a tendency to connect to a large number of nodes in the network. This is also observed in the mean node degree of the backbone networks, which on average decreases by a factor of 5 compared to the original networks.

The backbone networks are capable of highlighting the underlying structures of the original graphs as seen by the increase in modularity scores, and preserving the most relevant interactions as evidenced by the increase in the average edge weight. We ran Louvain community detection on the backbone networks to detect strongly connected clusters of users. The algorithm identified 6 clusters in the IRA ranging from 37 to 937 users, and 5 clusters in Data Science from 135 to 1,661 users.

**Table 1.** Network summary statistics for the original co-sharing networks and their corresponding backbone. Edges with a weight of 1 are omitted.

|  | IRA | | Data Science | |
|---|---|---|---|---|
|  | **Original** | **Backbone** | **Original** | **Backbone** |
| **Nodes (#)** | 3,575 | 3,575 | 3,421 | 3,421 |
| **Edges (#)** | 1,489k | 604k | 2,131k | 249k |
| **Density** | 0.23 | 0.09 | 0.36 | 0.04 |
| **Centralization** | 0.46 | 0.15 | 0.54 | 0.11 |
| **Modularity** | 0.58 | 0.65 | 0.16 | 0.43 |
| **Mean Edge Weight** | $32.7\pm158$ | $62.7\pm239$ | $6.7\pm37$ | $12.1\pm106$ |
| **Mean Node Degree** | $833\pm511$ | $338\pm162$ | $1246\pm888$ | $146\pm95$ |

### 5.2   Anomaly Detection Using Isolation Forest

Isolation forest was applied on the backbone networks to identify anomalous edges/interactions (i.e., those that deviate from the overall distribution of the data). Specifically, an individual isolation forest model with 100 estimators was trained for each cluster in each dataset. The input to the model consisted of four features as described in Sect. 3.4, which are edge weight, content similarity, inter-arrival time (IAT), and node similarity. We used the treeSHAP algorithm to compute the SHAP value of each instance within their respective clusters. The SHAP value measures the contribution of each feature to the overall output of the model, which in this study is the average path length required to reach a data instance. Figure 1 shows the mean absolute SHAP value of each feature across the population of identified anomalies for each dataset. The higher the mean absolute SHAP value of a feature, the more influential the feature is for detecting anomalies. We found that the IAT feature had the highest impact for identifying anomalous instances in the IRA while the edge weight feature contributed more to the output of the model in Data Science.

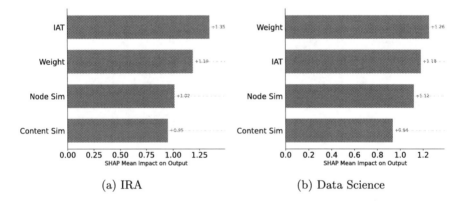

(a) IRA                          (b) Data Science

**Fig. 1.** Contribution score of each feature variable to the anomalous instances identified by the Isolation Forest model, as estimated by SHAP values. The features are ordered from the highest to the lowest contribution. IAT refers to the inter-arrival time feature. Node Sim refers to the network similarity feature.

It is important to note that isolation forest can identify outliers that are present in both tails of the distribution, thus it will classify instances with unusually long inter-arrival times as anomalies. However, coordinated campaigns typically do not exhibit very large gaps of time between actions (e.g., weeks, months, etc.), instead the time difference between actions is shorter but can still be diverse (e.g., seconds, minutes, hours, or even a few days). To narrow our focus on the most suspicious instances, we use the median IAT of the distribution of non-anomalous instances as a threshold to remove anomalies with higher IAT values than the norm. Table 2 shows the median value of the distribution for each edge feature between anomalous and normal interactions in each cluster and dataset. We have several observations related to the identified anomalies in each cluster. First, we found that the clusters of anomalous instances in the IRA exhibit higher content similarity ($0.65 \pm 0.15$) on average than clusters from DS ($0.53 \pm 0.18$). Second, we observed that the IRA clusters exhibit very low IAT values compared to clusters in DS, specifically 4 out of 6 clusters have a median IAT of less than 20 min. The DS clusters, on the other hand, range from a minimum of 5 h to a maximum of more than a month. This observation is consistent with our expectation that topics discussed in this dataset are less likely to be associated with a specific information campaign. Finally, the node similarity feature exhibits relatively higher values in clusters of anomalous interactions in the IRA and two clusters in Data Science. This suggests that the nodes within these particular clusters are more likely to have similar neighborhoods and co-share hashtags more frequently.

**Table 2.** Median value of the distribution of relevant features for anomalous and normal interactions, grouped by previously identified user clusters in each dataset. The inter-arrival time (IAT) is recorded in hours. The content similarity and node similarity is measured using cosine similarity. Anomalous interactions are filtered based on the median IAT of normal interactions.

|  | Cluster | Weight | | Content Sim | | IAT | | Node Sim | |
| --- | --- | --- | --- | --- | --- | --- | --- | --- | --- |
|  |  | **Anom** | **Norm** | **Anom** | **Norm** | **Anom** | **Norm** | **Anom** | **Norm** |
| **IRA** | 1 | 21416 | 3561.5 | 0.35 | 0.33 | 0.15 | 0.43 | 0.45 | 0.26 |
|  | 2 | 537 | 200 | 0.82 | 0.82 | 0.02 | 0.08 | 0.81 | 0.27 |
|  | 3 | 114 | 10 | 0.77 | 0.79 | 0.02 | 0.27 | 0.67 | 0.25 |
|  | 4 | 25 | 5 | 0.70 | 0.63 | 122.82 | 1995 | 0.68 | 0.25 |
|  | 5 | 194 | 13 | 0.59 | 0.46 | 0.33 | 147.4 | 0.62 | 0.26 |
|  | 6 | 408 | 69 | 0.66 | 0.49 | 3.16 | 107.68 | 0.42 | 0.25 |
| **DS** | 1 | 33 | 21 | 0.46 | 0.49 | 440.04 | 1053.38 | 0.53 | 0.30 |
|  | 2 | 2305 | 288 | 0.47 | 0.44 | 5.47 | 69.69 | 0.82 | 0.33 |
|  | 3 | 135 | 69 | 0.47 | 0.46 | 100.08 | 218.48 | 0.63 | 0.30 |
|  | 4 | 9 | 2 | 0.46 | 0.35 | 986.05 | 4988.58 | 0.30 | 0.26 |
|  | 5 | 8 | 3 | 0.46 | 0.38 | 1420.33 | 5528.77 | 0.37 | 0.32 |

## 5.3  Qualitative Analysis of Anomalous Clusters

We examined the content shared by anomalous users within each cluster, as identified by our framework. We use topic modeling to identify the general themes and topics of discussion within each cluster, as well as analyze the most frequently shared hashtags by these users. Our goal is to identify which clusters are likely related to suspicious activity and potential coordination.

In the DS dataset, all clusters exhibited similar behavior and characteristics. The discussions revolve around advancements in data science and its growing importance in various fields. Tweets primarily share information about resources, opportunities, applications and the overall impact of data science. We observed that the inter-arrival times (ranging from a minimum of 5 h to a maximum of 59 days) and content similarity (ranging from a minimum of 0.46 to a maximum of 0.47) across clusters likely indicate no evidence of coordinated behavior. The discussions appear to be organic and align with the behavior we expected for this dataset.

In the IRA dataset, we grouped the identified user clusters into three categories: *News Feed, Pro-Russian Nationalistic Voices*, and *Fear-mongers and Trolls*. Our observations for this dataset align with some of the categories previously identified in the work of Linvil et al. [12], which unlike our framework, heavily relies on several qualitative analyses for cluster identification.

**News Feed (Cluster 1 and 4).** Cluster 1 consists of 13 accounts and a total of 21 edges, indicating a relatively small network. The cluster exhibits a very high level of co-hashtag promotion as evidenced by the edge weight of co-shares (with a median of 21,416). There is a moderate degree of similarity in the users' posts with a median cosine similarity of 0.35. The median inter-arrival time between actions is relatively short (around 9 min). The main topics of discussion were around news related to political events on a global scale. The analysis of the most frequently shared hashtags revealed the presence of hashtags such as #news, #local, #politics, #sports, and #entertainment, which indicates a broad coverage of topics. Cluster 4, consisting of 703 users and 8,892 edges, also engaged in actively sharing news content, but especially related to Russia. The tweets in this cluster exhibit a broad coverage of news from different regions within Russia as seen by the presence of hashtags referring to specific Russian cities such as #UFA, #SPB, #Yaroslavl, and #Voronezh. Contrary to cluster 1, cluster 4 does not exhibit strong indications of synchronized behavior. Its inter-arrival time between actions is long, with a median of around 5 days, which suggest more sporadic engagement compared to other clusters.

**Pro-Russian Nationalistic Voices (Clusters 2 and 3).** Cluster 2 consists of 422 users and 3,213 edges while cluster 3 consists of 346 users and 1,283 edges. Both clusters exhibit high levels of content similarity, with cluster 2 having a median cosine similarity of 0.82 and cluster 3 with 0.77. The inter-arrival time between actions is relatively short for both clusters, with 1 min and 1.5 min for cluster 2 and 3, respectively. There is also high similarity in connections among users as seen by a node similarity of 0.81 for cluster 2 and 0.67 for cluster 3. The content shared within both clusters primarily focuses on the ongoing conflict between Ukraine and Russia, with messages criticizing foreign policies, particularly those of Western countries. Cluster 2 engages in discussions related to the downing of the Malaysian airlines flight in 2014 and makes claims regarding Ukraine's involvement. Both clusters actively promote a sense of national identity in Russia through their tweets. Cluster 2 frequently promotes hashtags such as #RussianSpirit, #KievShotDowntheBoeing, #KievTellTheTruth, while cluster 3 promotes hashtags such as #AmericanPlague, #AgainstSanctions, and #MadeInRussia. The high levels of content similarity, short inter-arrival times, and presence of hashtags with provocative allegations suggest a likely coordinated effort to disseminate specific narratives focused on the Ukraine-Russia conflict.

**Fear-Mongers and Trolls (Cluster 5 and 6).** Cluster 5 consists of 735 users and 6,220 edges and cluster 6 consists of 710 users and 9,234 edges. These clusters present behaviors and characteristics that strongly indicate suspicious and coordinated behavior. In cluster 5, we observed that messages are mostly around the 2016 US presidential elections, with users frequently sharing hashtags such as #WakeUpAmerica, #tcot (Top Conservatives on Twitter), and #pjnet (Patriot Journalist Network). The cluster also targets cultural identity and social issues as seen by the sharing of hashtags such as #BlackLivesMatter, #IslamKills, and #IslamistIsTheProblem. The median content similarity is 0.59, which is a moderate level of similarity, and the median inter-arrival time was 20 min. Cluster 6, on the other hand, engages in pushing fabricated crisis events. Some were related to nuclear incidents as indicated by the frequent sharing of hashtags such as #Fukushima2015 and #ColumbianChecmicals. Another frequently pushed story was related to Koch Farms during the Thanksgiving of 2015. The story alleged that Koch Farms' turkey production was contaminated with salmonella, resulting in severe food poisoning. The content similarity in cluster 6 was 0.66 and with slightly higher inter-arrival times of approximately 3 h. Our observations for cluster 5 and 6 align with the *Trolls* and *Fearmonger* categories identified in [12]. Overall, the content shared in these clusters, which are politically divisive and contain inflammatory messages, along with their particular characteristics suggest a strong presence of coordinated information campaigns.

# 6 Conclusions and Future Work

This study proposes a multifaceted framework to detect user accounts possibly involved in coordinated activity on social media platforms. Our approach involves the analysis of content, timing, and network dimensions to distinguish between organic behavior and suspicious coordinated operations. Our analyses revealed the following observations.

First, we demonstrated the effectiveness of our framework in isolating normal behavior from inorganic behavior across discussions on two Twitter datasets of known coordinated information operations to likely only organic discussions. Second, we showed that our backbone extraction component proved valuable in reducing the search space within the original co-sharing networks, revealing the underlying core structures. Third, our anomaly detection model based on isolation forests effectively identified anomalous instances, and combined with explainable methods like SHAP, it provides additional insights into the contribution and importance of each feature. Finally, we identified and characterized clusters of users who likely engaged in coordinated campaigns based on their shared content and time locality.

However, our framework does have some limitations some by choice others due to the nature of social media data. First, we rely on certain assumptions such as the prevalence of organic behavior outweighing inorganic behavior. As campaigns evolve and become more sophisticated (e.g., mimicking human behavior better), it may become increasingly challenging to detect anomalies. Second, the absence of ground truth data on coordinated behaviors for some of our datasets makes it difficult to claim with certainty the presence of an actual coordinated effort. Our claims are based solely on the observed characteristics and patterns within the data, thus further research is necessary to confirm the extent to which particular accounts are linked to the coordinated campaign. Third, data accessibility is a pressing concern for studies aiming to identify nefarious processes on social media platforms. Recently, some platforms have restricted their APIs or have shifted towards paid models for data access, making it challenging for researchers to obtain valuable data. Fourth, our analysis does not consider reposting behavior (e.g., retweets) or user engagement (e.g., replies) as we only focus on coordinated information promotion. Incorporating this information in our framework can provide insights on the actual scale of the campaign, its reach, and its impact on online discussions. Fifth, while our framework can effectively isolate unusual interactions, it cannot automatically detect if clusters are part of a coordinated inauthentic campaign. Qualitative analysis is still needed to determine the level of inauthenticity in these interactions. In future work, we could create random baselines that disrupt temporal relationships between users. This would help in assessing how much the multivariate distributions of observed coordinated features deviate from chance.

Future work will also focus on augmenting the features used for anomaly detection to make them more adaptable with evolving coordination strategies. Another venue for future work is the detection of coordinated campaigns in multi-platform settings, where accounts on multiple social media platforms promote a shared agenda.

# References

1. Bellutta, D., Carley, K.M.: Investigating coordinated account creation using burst detection and network analysis. J. Big Data **10**(1), 1–17 (2023)
2. Coscia, M., Neffke, F.M.: Network backboning with noisy data. In: 2017 IEEE 33rd International Conference on Data Engineering (ICDE), pp. 425–436. IEEE (2017)
3. Francois, C., Barash, V., Kelly, J.: Measuring coordinated versus spontaneous activity in online social movements. New Med. Soc. **25**(11), 3065–3092 (2021)
4. Giglietto, F., Righetti, N., Marino, G.: Detecting Coordinated Link Sharing Behavior on Facebook during the Italian Coronavirus Outbreak. AoIR Selected Papers of Internet Research (2020)
5. Golovchenko, Y., Hartmann, M., Adler-Nissen, R.: State, media and civil society in the information warfare over Ukraine: citizen curators of digital disinformation. Int. Aff. **94**(5), 975–994 (2018)
6. Grady, D., Thiemann, C., Brockmann, D.: Robust classification of salient links in complex networks. Nat. Commun. **3**(1), 864 (2012)

 7. Grover, A., Leskovec, J.: node2vec: scalable feature learning for networks. In: Proceedings of the 22nd ACM SIGKDD International Conference on Knowledge Discovery and Data Mining, pp. 855–864 (2016)
 8. Gupta, S., Kumaraguru, P., Chakraborty, T.: MalReG: detecting and analyzing malicious ReTweeter groups. In: Proceedings of the ACM India Joint International Conference on Data Science and Management of Data, pp. 61–69 (2019)
 9. Keller, F.B., Schoch, D., Stier, S., Yang, J.: Political astroturfing on Twitter: how to coordinate a disinformation campaign. Polit. Commun. **37**(2), 256–280 (2020)
10. Kriel, C., Pavliuc, A.: Reverse engineering Russian internet research agency tactics through network analysis. Defence Strateg. Commun. **6**, 199–227 (2019)
11. Lee, K., Caverlee, J., Cheng, Z., Sui, D.Z.: Campaign extraction from social media. ACM Trans. Intell. Syst. Technol. (TIST) **5**(1), 1–28 (2014)
12. Linvill, D.L., Warren, P.L.: Troll factories: manufacturing specialized disinformation on twitter. Polit. Commun. **37**(4), 447–467 (2020)
13. Liu, F.T., Ting, K.M., Zhou, Z.H.: Isolation forest. In: 2008 Eighth Ieee International Conference on Data Mining, pp. 413–422. IEEE (2008)
14. Lukito, J.: Coordinating a multi-platform disinformation campaign: internet research agency activity on three US social media platforms, 2015 to 2017. Polit. Commun. **37**(2), 238–255 (2020)
15. Lundberg, S.M., Lee, S.I.: A unified approach to interpreting model predictions. In: Advances in Neural Information Processing Systems, vol. 30 (2017)
16. Magelinski, T., Ng, L., Carley, K.: A synchronized action framework for detection of coordination on social media. J. Online Trust Saf. **1**(2), 1–24 (2022)
17. Morstatter, F., Shao, Y., Galstyan, A., Karunasekera, S.: From alt-right to alt-rechts: Twitter analysis of the 2017 German federal election. In: Companion Proceedings of the The Web Conference 2018, pp. 621–628 (2018)
18. Nasim, M., Nguyen, A., Lothian, N., Cope, R., Mitchell, L.: Real-time detection of content polluters in partially observable Twitter networks. In: Companion Proceedings of the The Web Conference 2018, pp. 1331–1339 (2018)
19. Ng, K.W., Horawalavithana, S., Iamnitchi, A.: Multi-platform information operations: Twitter, Facebook and YouTube against the White Helmets. In: The Workshop Proceedings of the 14th International AAAI Conference on Web and Social Media (ICWSM), Atlanta, USA (2021)
20. Ng, L.H.X., Cruickshank, I.J., Carley, K.M.: Cross-platform information spread during the January 6th capitol riots. Soc. Netw. Anal. Min. **12**(1), 133 (2022)
21. Nghiem, H., Muric, G., Morstatter, F., Ferrara, E.: Detecting cryptocurrency pump-and-dump frauds using market and social signals. Expert Syst. Appl. **182**, 115284 (2021)
22. Nizzoli, L., Tardelli, S., Avvenuti, M., Cresci, S., Tesconi, M.: Coordinated behavior on social media in 2019 UK general election. In: Proceedings of the International AAAI Conference on Web and Social Media, vol. 15, pp. 443–454 (2021)
23. Pacheco, D., Hui, P.M., Torres-Lugo, C., Truong, B.T., Flammini, A., Menczer, F.: Uncovering coordinated networks on social media: methods and case studies. ICWSM **21**, 455–466 (2021)
24. Serrano, M.Á., Boguná, M., Vespignani, A.: Extracting the multiscale backbone of complex weighted networks. Proc. Natl. Acad. Sci. **106**(16), 6483–6488 (2009)

25. Sharma, K., Zhang, Y., Ferrara, E., Liu, Y.: Identifying coordinated accounts on social media through hidden influence and group behaviours. In: Proceedings of the 27th ACM SIGKDD Conference on Knowledge Discovery & Data Mining, pp. 1441–1451. KDD 2021, Association for Computing Machinery (2021)
26. Wilson, T., Starbird, K.: Cross-platform information operations: mobilizing narratives & building resilience through both Big & Alt tech. Proc. ACM Hum. Comput. Interact. 5(CSCW2), 1–32 (2021)

# Unveiling Truth Amidst the Pandemic: Multimodal Detection of COVID-19 Unreliable News

Royal Pathak[✉], Bishal Lakha, Rohan Raut, Hongmin (Steven) Kim, and Francesca Spezzano

Computer Science Department, Boise State University, Boise, ID, USA
{royalpathak,bishallakha,rohanraut,stevenkim}@u.boisestate.edu,
francescaspezzano@boisestate.edu

**Abstract.** The prevalence of social media as a primary news source raises concerns due to the rapid spread of fake news. A significant majority of Twitter users (59%) and Facebook users (54%) rely on these platforms for their day-to-day news consumption, as observed by the PEW Research Center. This reliance extends to other social media platforms like Reddit, YouTube, and TikTok. The increasing dependence on social media for news has significant impacts, particularly in critical areas such as healthcare during the COVID-19 pandemic, election outcomes, emergency management, and public trust in institutions. To combat the detrimental effects of fake news, computational analysis techniques that incorporate multimodal features are crucial for effective detection and countermeasures. This study proposes a multimodal approach utilizing text embeddings from Fine-tuned BERT and image embeddings from CLIP to detect unreliable news. Experimental results on a ReCOVery COVID-19 dataset demonstrate the model's superiority over competitive baselines, particularly in detecting unreliable news. The findings highlight the potential of this approach in identifying and mitigating the spread of fake news. By combining text and image embeddings, this research offers a promising strategy for enhancing fake news detection capabilities and fostering trust in news dissemination on social media platforms.

**Keywords:** Social media · Fake News · Misinformation

## 1 Introduction

Fake news refers to intentionally deceptive or false information that is presented as genuine news with the aim of deceiving people [20]. It can manifest in various ways, such as fabricated user-generated content, manipulated images using tools like Photoshop, satirical or parody content, and clickbait, among others. The rise of social networks like Facebook and Twitter has made them popular sources of information. Still, algorithmic bias (popularity, network-based) in recommendation systems has contributed to the spread of misinformation among users [25].

© The Author(s), under exclusive license to Springer Nature Switzerland AG 2023
D. Ceolin et al. (Eds.): MISDOOM 2023, LNCS 14397, pp. 119–131, 2023.
https://doi.org/10.1007/978-3-031-47896-3_9

The internet's unrestricted nature allows cybercriminals to quickly disseminate fake news, while factors such as age, orientation, social behavior [20], perceived news preferences, and self-perceptions of opinion leadership [6] can influence individuals to become unwitting conduits for spreading falsehoods. Furthermore, people's trust in news articles based on indicators like shares, likes, and views can make them more susceptible to believing sensational or emotionally charged fake news. The visual presentation of news, including audio, images, embedded content, and social media post links, also significantly shapes people's belief in fake news.

The escalation of fake news amplification through social networks has increased substantially, starting from the 2016 U.S. Presidential Election and continuing through the ongoing COVID-19 pandemic [1,2]. These developments have had far-reaching consequences, affecting various aspects such as health, politics, economy, and responses to natural disasters [4,10,22,47]. Therefore, it is imperative to detect and address fake news early, preventing its dissemination and impact on the public. By proactively identifying misinformation and taking necessary measures, we can safeguard the integrity of information and minimize its reach among people.

Verifying the authenticity of every piece of information is often unfeasible, presenting a significant challenge in identifying fake news. Fake news is deliberately crafted using emotional appeals and sensational language to captivate readers. Consequently, relying solely on human intervention to distinguish between fake and genuine news is often insufficient. Researchers have employed various approaches, including machine learning models, graph networks, and deep network techniques, to tackle the problem of fake news. Previous studies have explored different aspects, such as user-news-publisher relations, writing style, propagation patterns, source credibility, content analysis, readability, and emotional features (such as anger, anticipation, and fear), to identify fake news [15,36,49,52]. Our work proposes combining text features extracted from BERT and image features to detect fake news. Through the concatenation of text and image embeddings, this research introduces a compelling method to advance the identification of false information and foster trust in the dissemination of news on social media platforms.

## 2    Related Work

Several studies have investigated various methods for detecting fake news by considering features of news content and social context [9,26]. These studies have examined features extracted from news excerpts, headlines, and associated visual elements, as well as social context features such as demographics, political orientation, network structure, and social emotions [17,18,33,37]. For example, Potthast et al. [26] focused on the analysis of writing style as a feature for identifying fake news, while Horne and Adali [9] considered linguistic and complexity-based features from both the news body and headline to determine the authenticity of news.

Numerous studies have explored different aspects related to detecting and characterizing fake news, as well as the individuals who propagate it on social networks. For instance, researchers have examined the incorporation of images as supplementary cues to augment the identification of fake news, as evidenced by the works of Shrestha et al. [32] and Zhou et al. [51]. Additionally, investigations have been conducted to understand the traits of users who are more likely to spread fake news. Vosoughi et al. [41] discovered that on Twitter, individuals disseminating fake news tended to have fewer followers, follow fewer people, and exhibit lower activity levels. Shu et al. [35] analyzed user profiles to ascertain the characteristics associated with trust or distrust in fake news. Moreover, Guess et al. [6] found that user demographics, such as political orientation, age, and social media usage, were significant predictors of fake news sharing on Facebook. Giachanou et al. [5] employed profile and psycho-linguistic patterns to identify social media users who support and propagate conspiracy theories.

In the realm of combating fake news, in addition to traditional feature engineering methods, researchers have also delved into employing deep learning techniques to incorporate information from news, social context, and propagation patterns, thus enhancing the detection process. One such method for modeling news content is the Hierarchical Attention Neural Network (HAN) framework [45], which adopts a hierarchical structure and attention mechanisms. Another approach, known as text-CNN, utilizes convolutional neural networks to process textual data [14]. SAFE, presented by Zhou et al. [51], extracts textual and visual features from news articles and utilizes their relationship to predict the authenticity of the news. It incorporates self-attention mechanisms and a bidirectional LSTM network to capture important information from both modalities. Xu et al. [42] proposed a model that incorporates claims and pieces of evidence structured as a graph to feed into graph neural networks to enhance fake news detection. Other models such as TCNN-URG [27], CSI [31], dEFEND [34], FinerFact [11], and SureFact [43] incorporate both news contents and user comments for fake news detection. On the other hand, HPA-BLSTM [7] focuses solely on using user comments. Furthermore, graph-based approaches that employ graph neural networks have also been utilized for encoding the propagation of news on social media to detect fake news [3,8,13,19,23,24,29,30]. Ren et al. [29] explore the modeling of news articles and their associated entities, such as news creators and subjects, as a heterogeneous information network. To detect fake news, they propose the application of an Adversarial Active Learning-based Heterogeneous Graph Neural Network. However, a limitation of this approach is the reliance on human input for active learning, which prevents it from being a fully automated method. Nguyen et al. [24] utilize the connections among news, users, and publishers to detect fake news. Their approach, known as FANG, incorporates temporal news representations that consider user engagements over time. Yu et al. [46] applied convolutional neural networks to detect whether an event is misinformation, where a sequence of microblog posts describes an event.

Shu et al. [36] proposed a framework called "TriFN" to model relationships among publishers, news contents, and social engagements for fake news detection.

They conducted an experiment using fake news datasets, which demonstrated the TriFN framework's effectiveness and highlighted the tri-relationship's importance for predicting fake news.

Monti et al. [23] presented a fake news detection model based on geometric deep learning. The researchers trained and tested the model using news stories verified by professional fact-checking organizations. Their investigation revealed that features such as social network structure and propagation played a crucial role in achieving high accuracy in fake news detection. Furthermore, the study emphasized that propagation-based approaches can complement content-based methods in fake news detection.

Zhou et al. [49] presented a theory-driven model for fake news detection. Their study focused on investigating news content by considering different levels categorized according to social and forensic psychology. To detect fake news, the researchers employed a supervised machine-learning framework. By utilizing this framework, they were able to identify and classify fake news effectively.

Yang et al. [44] introduced an approach for investigating fake news using an unsupervised learning framework. The study focused on variables such as the truths of news and the credibility of users. To explore the relationships among these variables, the researchers employed a Bayesian network model, which allowed them to identify the conditional dependencies between the truths of the news, opinions, and credibility of users. To infer the news truths and users' credibility without relying on labeled data, the authors proposed an efficient collapsed Gibbs sampling approach. This approach facilitated the detection of fake news by leveraging unsupervised learning techniques.

As presented in [12], some research employs a bidirectional training approach for fake news detection. The authors propose FakeBert, a BERT-based deep learning method that combines parallel blocks of a single-layer deep Convolutional Neural Network (CNN) with different kernel sizes and filters. The study utilizes a dataset comprising fake and real news articles from the 2016 U.S. General Presidential Election and evaluates the model using metrics such as Accuracy, FPR, FNR, and cross-entropy loss.

Zhang et al. [48] combines textual and visual information using contrastive learning to improve performance. Experimental results on a COVID-19 dataset, ReCOVery, demonstrate its superiority over competitive baselines in detecting unreliable news. The framework shows promise in addressing the challenge of identifying misinformation and unreliable news when the experiment is performed on both randomly shuffled data and chronologically ordered data.

*In this work, we present a methodology that combines multimodal techniques by integrating textual BERT representations with image features extracted from CLIP. Our study's objective is to evaluate this approach's effectiveness, specifically on the ReCOVery COVID-19 dataset. Through rigorous experimentation and in-depth analysis, we unequivocally demonstrate the superiority of our proposed methodology over other competitive baselines, particularly in detecting unreliable news.*

# 3  Dataset

The rationale for utilizing COVID-19-related news in our fake news detection research is rooted in its global relevance and far-reaching implications. The COVID-19 pandemic has caused a significant influx of information, including misinformation and fake news, which can lead to confusion and potential harm. By analyzing COVID-19 news specifically, this research addresses a timely and critical issue, contributing to developing effective detection strategies and fostering a more reliable information ecosystem.

We utilize the ReCOVery dataset [50] to facilitate this research. The ReCOVery dataset was explicitly developed to address the challenges associated with COVID-19 information. It comprises a comprehensive collection of news articles about the coronavirus, gathered from nearly 2,000 news outlets. The dataset includes 2,029 news pieces published between January and May 2020, along with 140,820 associated tweets that reflect the dissemination of these articles on Twitter. To ensure a diverse range of sources, 60 news outlets with varying credibility levels, 22 for reliable news and 38 for unreliable news were selected [50]. The dataset provides various types of information, such as textual content, visual elements, temporal data, and network details. After data cleaning and eliminating posts with unavailable image links, we obtained a final dataset comprising 1,859 news articles. Among these articles, 1,297 are categorized as 'Reliable', while 562 are classified as 'Unreliable'.

Although having multiple datasets with images to validate and compare findings would be ideal, the scarcity of such datasets may limit the options available. Nonetheless, the ReCOVery dataset's inclusion of images provides a valuable opportunity to study the visual aspects of COVID-19 news, contributing to proposed multimodal fake news detection.

# 4  Methodology

We present a comprehensive system that utilizes textual and visual components to detect unreliable news, as illustrated in Fig. 1. Our approach incorporates transformer-based encoders, such as BERT for text and CLIP for images. BERT is employed to extract embeddings from the content and title of the news article, while CLIP generates embeddings from the corresponding images. We create a dataset to train a conventional machine learning classifier by concatenating these text and image embeddings. This process enables the development of a robust fake news detection model.

## 4.1  Fine-Tuned BERT for Text Embedding

We employed fine-tuned BERT (Bidirectional Encoder Representations from Transformers) for text embedding. BERT [40] effectively preserves the semantic meaning of news text by considering both word- and sentence-level semantics. Before fine-tuning BERT, we performed preprocessing steps on the news text of

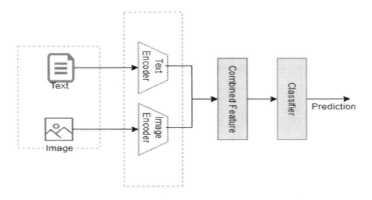

**Fig. 1.** Framework of our proposed model

the ReCOVery [50] dataset, including text cleaning and tokenization. The pre-trained BERT model selected for fine-tuning was BERT-base, which provides a strong baseline with 12 transformer layers, 768 hidden units, and 12 attention heads. BERT-base was chosen based on its compatibility with our task requirements, the availability of computational resources, and its proven performance on various natural language processing tasks. By fine-tuning BERT, we aimed to capture rich contextual information from the news text and generate meaningful fixed-size embeddings that can be used as features for fake news detection.

## 4.2   CLIP for Image Embedding

We utilized CLIP (Contrastive Language-Image Pretraining) to generate image embeddings. To prepare the data for CLIP training, we executed preprocessing techniques that aimed to enhance the quality of the images. These techniques encompass tasks such as standardizing the image resolution and normalizing pixel values. By implementing these steps, we achieved uniformity and improved comparability of the visual features within the dataset, thus facilitating more effective training of the CLIP model [28]. The CLIP model, which integrates vision and language encoders, underwent extensive pretraining on a large-scale dataset comprising image-text pairs [28]. By leveraging CLIP's pretrained architecture, we obtained semantically meaningful image embeddings that capture the intrinsic relationships between images and associated text. Our aim in employing CLIP for image embedding was to acquire comprehensive and context-rich image representations, which could be effectively utilized as another set of features in fake news detection [28].

## 4.3   Classification

After completing the training process on BERT and CLIP, we extracted relevant features for our experiments, including embeddings for both text and images.

These embeddings serve as informative representations of the input data, capturing the semantic meaning of both the text and visual content. We utilized logistic regression as our classification algorithm to detect fake news, leveraging the concatenation of combined textual and image features. Logistic regression **(LR)**[1] allowed us to model the relationship between the extracted features and the binary classification of news articles as reliable or unreliable.

## 5 Experiments

In this section, we present the experiments' settings and analysis of our results to evaluate the efficiency of our methodology.

### 5.1 Experimental Settings

Our classification experiments were conducted on two datasets: randomly shuffled data and chronologically ordered data. In the randomly shuffled data, 80% of the dataset was used for training, while the remaining portion was used for testing. Similarly, we split the dataset based on publication timestamps with an 8:2 ratio in the chronologically ordered data. We repeated each experiment five times and reported a range of evaluation metrics to assess the performance of our classification model in predicting reliable news and unreliable news. These metrics encompassed the macro F1 score [38], precision [21], recall [21], and F1 score [39]. The macro F1 score provided a holistic measure, considering precision and recall across all classes. Precision gauged the accuracy of identifying reliable news by determining the ratio of true positives to the total instances classified as reliable news. On the other hand, recall measured the model's ability to correctly identify reliable news by comparing it to the total number of actual reliable news instances. The same precision and recall metrics were utilized for evaluating the model's performance in identifying unreliable news. The F1 score, which combines precision and recall, presented a balanced measure of the model's classification accuracy for both reliable and unreliable news. By utilizing these evaluation metrics, we gained comprehensive insights into the model's effectiveness in accurately classifying reliable and unreliable news while considering the impact of false positives and false negatives.

We compared our methodology with recent works on fake news detection, such as CNN [14], LSTM [16], SAFE [51], and $BTIC_\alpha$ [48], where $\alpha$ is the weight value in the final loss function.

---

[1] We performed classification using various supervised techniques, including Support Vector Machines (SVM), Logistic Regression, XGBoost, and Random Forest. However, we only reported the results obtained from logistic regression, as it demonstrated superior performance compared to the other classifiers.

**Table 1.** Comparison of our framework with existing approaches on randomly shuffled data. Best results are in bold.

| Method | MacF1. | Reliable News | | | Unreliable News | | |
|---|---|---|---|---|---|---|---|
| | | Pre. | Rec. | F1. | Pre. | Rec. | F1. |
| CNN [14] | 0.736 | 0.813 | 0.928 | 0.866 | 0.766 | 0.508 | 0.606 |
| LSTM [16] | 0.750 | 0.823 | 0.931 | 0.873 | 0.782 | 0.535 | 0.627 |
| SAFE [51] | 0.633 | 0.759 | **0.942** | 0.840 | 0.702 | 0.308 | 0.425 |
| BTIC$_{best}$ [48] | 0.778 | 0.836 | 0.938 | 0.884 | 0.804 | 0.577 | 0.671 |
| LR with Text Embeddings | 0.755 | 0.829 | 0.869 | 0.848 | 0.703 | 0.630 | 0.662 |
| LR with Image Embeddings | 0.839 | 0.903 | 0.882 | 0.892 | 0.770 | 0.805 | 0.786 |
| LR with Text + Images Embeddings | 0.862 | 0.907 | 0.914 | 0.911 | 0.821 | 0.808 | 0.814 |
| LR with Fine-tuned Text Embeddings | 0.830 | 0.872 | 0.920 | 0.895 | 0.820 | 0.720 | 0.764 |
| LR with Fine-tuned Text Embeddings + Images | **0.883** | **0.919** | 0.930 | **0.924** | **0.853** | **0.832** | **0.841** |

**Table 2.** Comparison of our framework with existing approaches on chronologically ordered data. Best results are in bold.

| Method | MacF1. | Reliable News | | | Unreliable News | | |
|---|---|---|---|---|---|---|---|
| | | Pre. | Rec. | F1. | Pre. | Rec. | F1. |
| CNN [14] | 0.666 | 0.807 | 0.834 | 0.809 | 0.653 | 0.512 | 0.523 |
| LSTM [16] | 0.716 | 0.865 | 0.746 | 0.800 | 0.559 | 0.731 | 0.632 |
| SAFE [51] | 0.556 | 0.729 | 0.929 | **0.817** | 0.566 | 0.203 | 0.295 |
| BTIC$_{best}$ [48] | 0.735 | **0.876** | 0.763 | 0.815 | 0.580 | **0.750** | 0.654 |
| LR with Text Embeddings | 0.674 | 0.423 | 0.807 | 0.555 | 0.928 | 0.692 | 0.793 |
| LR with Image Embeddings | 0.559 | 0.200 | 0.941 | 0.330 | 0.992 | 0.653 | 0.788 |
| LR with Text + Images Embeddings | **0.738** | 0.488 | 0.943 | 0.643 | 0.979 | 0.724 | **0.832** |
| LR with Fine-tuned Text Embeddings | 0.569 | 0.209 | 0.971 | 0.344 | 0.996 | 0.661 | 0.795 |
| LR with Fine-tuned Text Embeddings + Images | 0.562 | 0.204 | **0.972** | 0.337 | **0.996** | 0.650 | 0.787 |

## 5.2   Analysis and Discussion

The classification results for randomly shuffled data can be found in Table 1, while the classification results for chronologically ordered data are presented in Table 2.

Based on the results presented in Table 1, it is evident that our proposed model, which integrates logistic regression (LR) with fine-tuned BERT text embeddings and images, exhibits a substantial improvement over the current state-of-the-art including the best variant of BTIC. In the case of randomly shuffled data, BTIC$_{0.1}$ has the best result among its variants. Specifically, our proposed model showcases a remarkable enhancement of 10.5–11.3%

Based on the findings outlined in Table 2, it is evident that our proposed model achieves comparable results to the state-of-the-art baselines when it comes to chronologically ordered data (macro F1 score). Additionally, our model surpasses the baselines for detecting unreliable news, as indicated by the F1 score. In the case of chronologically ordered data, BTIC$_{0.2}$ shows the best results among its variants. Specifically, when compared to other models, the BTIC$_{0.2}$ model demonstrates a remarkable precision score of 0.876 in the classification of reliable news and the highest recall score of 0.750 in the classification of unreliable news. SAFE outperforms other models in terms of the F1 score of 0.817 in the classification of reliable news.

However, our proposed model (LR with Fine-tuned Text Embeddings + Images) surpasses the state-of-the-art in terms of recall in the classification of reliable news with a score of 0.972, and precision in the classification of unreliable news with a score of 0.996. It is surprising that one of our proposed methods (LR with Text + Images Embeddings) outperforms other methodologies, including our fine-tuned proposed variant (LR with Fine-tuned Text Embeddings + Images), in terms of the macro F1 score with a score of 0.738, and the F1 score of 0.832 when classifying unreliable news. We attribute the improved performance of the unfine-tuned model compared to the fine-tuned model in the chronological dataset to its greater resilience to noise.

The results from Table 1 and Table 2 indicate that using BERT embeddings and Image CLIP embeddings alone may not accurately classify chronologically ordered data for all metrics. Despite their effectiveness in capturing semantic information from text and images, these embeddings did not adequately capture the temporal dependencies and sequential patterns present in the data. Our findings suggest that additional consideration should be given to models and approaches that explicitly account for temporal information, such as recurrent neural networks or transformers with positional encodings. Moreover, aligning the features from both modalities according to the chronological order is crucial to ensure accurate representations. Furthermore, the limited availability of labeled data and the selection of optimal hyperparameters remain important factors that can significantly impact the performance of the classification models. Therefore, further research and experimentation are necessary to develop more effective approaches for chronologically ordered data classification tasks.

# 6    Conclusions, Limitations, and Future Work

In conclusion, this work introduces a novel methodology for detecting unreliable news that leverages multimodal features, combining text embeddings from fine-tuned BERT and image embeddings from CLIP. Experimental results on the ReCOVery COVID-19 dataset, collected from various media outlets, demonstrate the effectiveness of the proposed model on randomly shuffled data and chronologically ordered data at detecting unreliable news. In experiments with randomly shuffled data, we obtained a macro F1 score of 0.883 and precision, recall, and F1 scores of 0.919, 0.930, and 0.924, respectively, during the classification of reliable news. Additionally, we achieved precision, recall, and F1 scores of 0.853, 0.832, and 0.841, respectively, during the classification of unreliable news.

Likewise, our proposed model is comparable to state-of-the-art methods for chronologically ordered data (macro F1 of 0.738) and performs better at detecting unreliable news with an F1 score of 0.832. However, limitations are identified when applying the methodology to chronologically ordered data, as the image and text embeddings struggle to capture temporal dependencies and sequential patterns adequately. To address these limitations, our future research will focus on refining the methodology to better capture the temporal aspects of news articles. Similarly, we will also attempt to apply the methods to additional datasets. By doing so, we can develop a more comprehensive and robust approach to detecting unreliable news across different domains.

**Acknowledgements.** This research has been partially supported by the National Science Foundation under award no. 1943370.

# References

1. Barberá, P.: Explaining the spread of misinformation on social media: evidence from the 2016 US presidential election. In: Fake News and the Politics of Misinformation. APSA (2018)
2. Cheng, M., Yin, C., Nazarian, S., Bogdan, P.: Deciphering the laws of social network-transcendent COVID-19 misinformation dynamics and implications for combating misinformation phenomena. Sci. Rep. **11**(1), 1–14 (2021)
3. Dou, Y., Shu, K., Xia, C., Yu, P.S., Sun, L.: User preference-aware fake news detection. In: Proceedings of the 44th International ACM SIGIR Conference on Research and Development in Information Retrieval, pp. 2051–2055 (2021)
4. Furini, M., Mirri, S., Montangero, M., Prandi, C.: Untangling between fake-news and truth in social media to understand the COVID-19 coronavirus. In: 2020 IEEE Symposium on Computers and Communications (ISCC), pp. 1–6. IEEE (2020)
5. Giachanou, A., Ghanem, B., Rosso, P.: Detection of conspiracy propagators using psycho-linguistic characteristics. J. Inf. Sci. **49**(1), 3–17 (2023). https://doi.org/10.1177/0165551520985486
6. Guess, A., Nagler, J., Tucker, J.: Less than you think: prevalence and predictors of fake news dissemination on Facebook. Sci. Adv. **5**(1), eaau4586 (2019)
7. Guo, H., Cao, J., Zhang, Y., Guo, J., Li, J.: Rumor detection with hierarchical social attention network. In: Proceedings of the 27th ACM International Conference on Information and Knowledge Management, pp. 943–951 (2018)
8. Han, Y., Karunasekera, S., Leckie, C.: Graph neural networks with continual learning for fake news detection from social media. CoRR abs/2007.03316 (2020)
9. Horne, B.D., Adali, S.: This just in: fake news packs a lot in title, uses simpler, repetitive content in text body, more similar to satire than real news. In: The 2nd International Workshop on News and Public Opinion at ICWSM (2017)
10. Jin, F., Dougherty, E., Saraf, P., Cao, Y., Ramakrishnan, N.: Epidemiological modeling of news and rumors on Twitter. In: Proceedings of the 7th Workshop on Social Network Mining and Analysis, SNAKDD 2013. Association for Computing Machinery, New York (2013). https://doi.org/10.1145/2501025.2501027
11. Jin, Y., et al.: Towards fine-grained reasoning for fake news detection. In: Proceedings of the AAAI Conference on Artificial Intelligence, vol. 36, pp. 5746–5754 (2022)
12. Kaliyar, R.K., Goswami, A., Narang, P.: FakeBERT: fake news detection in social media with a BERT-based deep learning approach. Multimedia Tools Appl. **80**(8), 11765–11788 (2021)

13. Khoo, L.M.S., Chieu, H.L., Qian, Z., Jiang, J.: Interpretable rumor detection in microblogs by attending to user interactions. In: The Thirty-Fourth AAAI Conference on Artificial Intelligence, AAAI 2020, The Thirty-Second Innovative Applications of Artificial Intelligence Conference, IAAI 2020, The Tenth AAAI Symposium on Educational Advances in Artificial Intelligence, EAAI 2020, New York, NY, USA, 7–12 February 2020, pp. 8783–8790. AAAI Press (2020). https://ojs.aaai.org/index.php/AAAI/article/view/6405

14. Kim, Y.: Convolutional neural networks for sentence classification. In: Proceedings of the 2014 Conference on Empirical Methods in Natural Language Processing (EMNLP), Doha, Qatar, October 2014, pp. 1746–1751. Association for Computational Linguistics (2014). https://doi.org/10.3115/v1/D14-1181. https://aclanthology.org/D14-1181

15. Kumar, S., Shah, N.: False information on web and social media: a survey. arXiv preprint arXiv:1804.08559 (2018)

16. Liu, P., Qiu, X., Chen, X., Wu, S., Huang, X.: Multi-timescale long short-term memory neural network for modelling sentences and documents. In: Proceedings of the 2015 Conference on Empirical Methods in Natural Language Processing, Lisbon, Portugal, September 2015, pp. 2326–2335. Association for Computational Linguistics (2015). https://doi.org/10.18653/v1/D15-1280. https://aclanthology.org/D15-1280

17. Long, Y.: Fake news detection through multi-perspective speaker profiles. Association for Computational Linguistics (2017)

18. Luvembe, A.M., Li, W., Li, S., Liu, F., Xu, G.: Dual emotion based fake news detection: a deep attention-weight update approach. Inf. Process. Manage. **60**(4), 103354 (2023). https://doi.org/10.1016/j.ipm.2023.103354. https://www.sciencedirect.com/science/article/pii/S0306457323000912

19. Ma, J., Gao, W.: Debunking rumors on Twitter with tree transformer. In: Scott, D., Bel, N., Zong, C. (eds.) Proceedings of the 28th International Conference on Computational Linguistics, COLING 2020, Barcelona, Spain (Online), 8–13 December 2020, pp. 5455–5466. International Committee on Computational Linguistics (2020). https://doi.org/10.18653/v1/2020.coling-main.476

20. Ma, L., Lee, C.S., Goh, D.H.L.: Understanding news sharing in social media: an explanation from the diffusion of innovations theory. Online Inf. Rev. **38**(5), 598–615 (2014)

21. Manning, C.D., Raghavan, P., Schütze, H.: Introduction to Information Retrieval. Cambridge University Press (2008)

22. Mendoza, M., Poblete, B., Castillo, C.: Twitter under crisis: can we trust what we RT? In: Proceedings of the First Workshop on Social Media Analytics, SOMA 2010, pp. 71–79. Association for Computing Machinery, New York (2010). https://doi.org/10.1145/1964858.1964869

23. Monti, F., Frasca, F., Eynard, D., Mannion, D., Bronstein, M.M.: Fake news detection on social media using geometric deep learning. arXiv preprint arXiv:1902.06673 (2019)

24. Nguyen, V.H., Sugiyama, K., Nakov, P., Kan, M.Y.: FANG: leveraging social context for fake news detection using graph representation. In: Proceedings of the 29th ACM International Conference on Information & Knowledge Management, pp. 1165–1174 (2020)

25. Pathak, R., Spezzano, F., Pera, M.S.: Understanding the contribution of recommendation algorithms on misinformation recommendation and misinformation dissemination on social networks. ACM Trans. Web (2023). https://doi.org/10.1145/3616088

26. Potthast, M., Kiesel, J., Reinartz, K., Bevendorff, J., Stein, B.: A stylometric inquiry into hyperpartisan and fake news. In: Proceedings of the 56th Annual Meeting of the Association for Computational Linguistics (Volume 1: Long Papers), pp. 231–240 (2018)
27. Qian, F., Gong, C., Sharma, K., Liu, Y.: Neural user response generator: fake news detection with collective user intelligence. In: Proceedings of the Twenty-Seventh International Joint Conference on Artificial Intelligence, IJCAI-18, July 2018, pp. 3834–3840. International Joint Conferences on Artificial Intelligence Organization (2018)
28. Radford, A., et al.: Learning transferable visual models from natural language supervision (2021)
29. Ren, Y., Wang, B., Zhang, J., Chang, Y.: Adversarial active learning based heterogeneous graph neural network for fake news detection. In: 2020 IEEE International Conference on Data Mining (ICDM), pp. 452–461. IEEE (2020)
30. Rosenfeld, N., Szanto, A., Parkes, D.C.: A kernel of truth: determining rumor veracity on Twitter by diffusion pattern alone. In: Huang, Y., King, I., Liu, T., van Steen, M. (eds.) The Web Conference 2020, WWW 2020, Taipei, Taiwan, 20–24 April 2020, pp. 1018–1028. ACM/IW3C2 (2020). https://doi.org/10.1145/3366423.3380180
31. Ruchansky, N., Seo, S., Liu, Y.: CSI: a hybrid deep model for fake news detection. In: Lim, E., et al. (eds.) Proceedings of the 2017 ACM on Conference on Information and Knowledge Management, CIKM 2017, Singapore, 06–10 November 2017, pp. 797–806. ACM (2017)
32. Shrestha, A., Serra, E., Spezzano, F.: Multi-modal social and psycho-linguistic embedding via recurrent neural networks to identify depressed users in online forums. Netw. Model. Anal. Health Inf. Bioinf. **9**(1), 22 (2020). https://doi.org/10.1007/s13721-020-0226-0
33. Shu, K., Bernard, H.R., Liu, H.: Studying fake news via network analysis: detection and mitigation. In: Agarwal, N., Dokoohaki, N., Tokdemir, S. (eds.) Emerging Research Challenges and Opportunities in Computational Social Network Analysis and Mining. LNSN, pp. 43–65. Springer, Cham (2019). https://doi.org/10.1007/978-3-319-94105-9_3
34. Shu, K., Cui, L., Wang, S., Lee, D., Liu, H.: dEFEND: explainable fake news detection. In: Proceedings of the 25th ACM SIGKDD International Conference on Knowledge Discovery & Data Mining, pp. 395–405 (2019)
35. Shu, K., Wang, S., Liu, H.: Understanding user profiles on social media for fake news detection. In: 1st IEEE International Workshop on Fake MultiMedia, FakeMM 2018 (2018)
36. Shu, K., Wang, S., Liu, H.: Beyond news contents: the role of social context for fake news detection. In: Proceedings of the Twelfth ACM International Conference on Web Search and Data Mining, pp. 312–320 (2019)
37. Shu, K., Wang, S., Liu, H.: Beyond news contents: the role of social context for fake news detection. In: Proceedings of the Twelfth ACM International Conference on Web Search and Data Mining, WSDM 2019, pp. 312–320. Association for Computing Machinery, New York (2019)
38. Sokolova, M., Lapalme, G.: A systematic analysis of performance measures for classification tasks. Inf. Process. Manage. **45**(4), 427–437 (2009)
39. Van Rijsbergen, C.J.: Information Retrieval, 2 edn. Butterworth-Heinemann (1979)
40. Vaswani, A., et al.: Attention is all you need. In: Advances in Neural Information Processing Systems, vol. 30 (2017)

41. Vosoughi, S., Roy, D., Aral, S.: The spread of true and false news online. Science **359**(6380), 1146–1151 (2018)

42. Xu, W., Wu, J., Liu, Q., Wu, S., Wang, L.: Evidence-aware fake news detection with graph neural networks. In: Proceedings of the ACM Web Conference 2022, WWW 2022, pp. 2501–2510. Association for Computing Machinery, New York (2022). https://doi.org/10.1145/3485447.3512122

43. Yang, R., Wang, X., Jin, Y., Li, C., Lian, J., Xie, X.: Reinforcement subgraph reasoning for fake news detection. In: Proceedings of the 28th ACM SIGKDD Conference on Knowledge Discovery and Data Mining, pp. 2253–2262 (2022)

44. Yang, S., Shu, K., Wang, S., Gu, R., Wu, F., Liu, H.: Unsupervised fake news detection on social media: a generative approach. In: Proceedings of the AAAI Conference on Artificial Intelligence, vol. 33, pp. 5644–5651 (2019)

45. Yang, Z., Yang, D., Dyer, C., He, X., Smola, A., Hovy, E.: Hierarchical attention networks for document classification. In: Proceedings of the 2016 Conference of the North American Chapter of the Association for Computational Linguistics: Human Language Technologies, San Diego, California, June 2016, pp. 1480–1489. Association for Computational Linguistics (2016)

46. Yu, F., Liu, Q., Wu, S., Wang, L., Tan, T.: A convolutional approach for misinformation identification. In: Sierra, C. (ed.) Proceedings of the Twenty-Sixth International Joint Conference on Artificial Intelligence, IJCAI 2017, Melbourne, Australia, 19–25 August 2017, pp. 3901–3907. ijcai.org (2017). https://doi.org/10.24963/ijcai.2017/545

47. Zhang, H., Alim, M.A., Li, X., Thai, M.T., Nguyen, H.T.: Misinformation in online social networks: detect them all with a limited budget. ACM Trans. Inf. Syst. **34**(3) (2016). https://doi.org/10.1145/2885494

48. Zhang, W., Gui, L., He, Y.: Supervised contrastive learning for multimodal unreliable news detection in COVID-19 pandemic. In: Proceedings of the 30th ACM International Conference on Information & Knowledge Management, CIKM 2021, pp. 3637–3641. Association for Computing Machinery, New York (2021). https://doi.org/10.1145/3459637.3482196

49. Zhou, X., Jain, A., Phoha, V.V., Zafarani, R.: Fake news early detection: a theory-driven model. Digit. Threats Res. Pract. **1**(2), 1–25 (2020)

50. Zhou, X., Mulay, A., Ferrara, E., Zafarani, R.: Recovery: a multimodal repository for COVID-19 news credibility research. In: Proceedings of the 29th ACM International Conference on Information & Knowledge Management, pp. 3205–3212 (2020)

51. Zhou, X., Wu, J., Zafarani, R.: SAFE: similarity-aware multi-modal fake news detection. In: Lauw, H.W., Wong, R.C.-W., Ntoulas, A., Lim, E.-P., Ng, S.-K., Pan, S.J. (eds.) PAKDD 2020. LNCS (LNAI), vol. 12085, pp. 354–367. Springer, Cham (2020). https://doi.org/10.1007/978-3-030-47436-2_27

52. Zhou, X., Zafarani, R.: A survey of fake news: fundamental theories, detection methods, and opportunities. ACM Comput. Surv. (CSUR) **53**(5), 1–40 (2020)

# Holistic Analysis of Organised Misinformation Activity in Social Networks

Anselmo Peñas[1]($\boxtimes$), Jan Deriu[2], Rajesh Sharma[3], Guilhem Valentin[4], and Julio Reyes-Montesinos[1]

[1] NLP & IR Group, UNED, Madrid, Spain
anselmo@lsi.uned.es
[2] CAI, ZHAW, Winterthur, Switzerland
jan.deriu@zhaw.ch
[3] University of Tartu, Tartu, Estonia
rajesh.sharma@ut.ee
[4] Synapse Développement, Toulouse, France
guilhem.valentin@synapse-fr.com

**Abstract.** To tackle the problem of disinformation, society must be aware not only of the existence of intentional misinformation campaigns, but also of the agents that introduce the misleading information, their supporting media, the nodes they use in social networks, the propaganda techniques they employ and their overall narratives and intentions. Disinformation is a challenge that must be addressed holistically: identifying and describing a disinformation campaign requires studying misinformation locally, at the message level, as well as globally, by modelling its propagation process to identify its sources and main players. In this paper, we argue that the integration of these two levels of analysis hinges on studying underlying features such as disinformation's intentionality, and benefited and injured agents. Taking these features into account could make automated decisions more explainable for end users and analysts. Moreover, simultaneously identifying misleading messages, knowing their narratives and hidden intentions, modelling their diffusion in social networks, and monitoring the sources of disinformation will also allow a faster reaction, even anticipation, against the spreading of disinformation.

**Keywords:** Disinformation · Social Networks · News Content Analysis · Intentions and Narratives

## 1 Introduction

Among the different kinds of misinformation, perhaps the most dangerous is the one created with the intention to harm, polarise, destabilise, generate distrust

This work has been supported by the CHIST-ERA HAMiSoN project grant CHIST-ERA-21-OSNEM-002, by AEI PCI2022-135026-2, SNF 20CH21 209672, ANR ANR-22-CHR4-0004 and ETAg.

D. Ceolin et al. (Eds.): MISDOOM 2023, LNCS 14397, pp. 132–143, 2023.
https://doi.org/10.1007/978-3-031-47896-3_10

or destroy reputation by means of spreading false information. In a scenario of organised intentional misinformation campaigns (also called disinformation[1]) current fact-checking strategies are not enough.

Fact Checkers need Artificial Intelligence tools to help them identify the most important claims to check (check-worthiness), detect claims that they have already checked (verified claim retrieval), and be able to check claims as soon as possible. This is important because fake news spreads 6 times faster than true ones [37], and 50% of the fake news propagation occurs in the first 10 min [39]. Disinformation is carefully constructed to behave this way, it has an intention (not always explicit) and a coordinated spreading (opportunistic most of the times).

Given this scenario of organised intentional misinformation campaigns, we need a comprehensive strategy to anticipate and mitigate the spreading of disinformation. We, as a society, must be aware not only about fake news, but also about the agents that introduce false or misleading information, their supporting media, the nodes they use in the social networks, the propaganda techniques they use, the narratives they try to push and their intentions.

Therefore, we must address this challenge in a holistic way, considering the different dimensions involved in the spreading of disinformation and bring them together to really identify and describe the orchestrated disinformation campaigns:

1. Detect misinformation: claim worthiness checking, stance detection, fake news identification and verified claim retrieval;
2. Acknowledging their organised spreading in social networks: models of disinformation propagation and source detection using social network analysis;
3. Identifying its malicious intent: narratives that are wanted to be spread, benefited and harmed agents and final goals;
4. Bring everything together: collect all the evidence and give them to final assessors and users in explainable ways, and use the aggregated information in a loop to recover in a new cycle the data missed in the previous ones.

To clarify the importance of attempting an holistic approach we need to consider the stakeholders of the technology under development. The main recipients would be content analysts that make use of services such as fact-checkers for a further analysis and better understanding of the agents and narratives involved in disinformation campaigns. For example, in electoral processes, independent observers must study disinformation campaigns in an holistic fashion to identify underlying communication intentions with specific narratives aimed to influence the elections outcome.

Tackling the hidden intention behind disinformation campaigns will help us fighting in a more efficient way. Fighting a misleading narrative should be easier than fighting all the single messages spread to promote that narrative. But for this purpose we need to move from just checking single messages or just analysing alterations in the social network to contemplating the whole picture.

---

[1] From here we use misinformation and disinformation interchangeably.

## 2   Previous Work

Previous works have addressed the problem of disinformation from two main different perspectives:

### 2.1   Content Analysis

Researchers have analysed misinformation-related tasks with various NLP-related features. The first task is to identify whether a new incoming content contains one or more claims that are worth to be checked [9,12,21,35]. Strategies to detect disinformation include the study of the correlation between psycholinguistics features and misinformation [2,4,23], usage of state of the art techniques such as knowledge graphs [18], reinforcement learning [20], context-aware misinformation detection [43] or the detection of alterations in original news [29]. Apart from exploring only text-based mechanisms, multimodal co-Attention networks (MCAN) have been used to exploit both textual and visual features for fake news detection [8,38]. Besides, recent works have improved the detection process by including non-textual features related to the user sharing the news, although there is a lack of datasets in this direction [25,28,30].

Proper fact-checking the claims of a content is a task that still requires the intervention of experts, usually journalists or domain experts from the civil society [26]. Hence, this task typically consumes a large amount of resources and time, while fake news tends to spread fast and come back repeatedly, even after having been checked and debunked. Thus, the verified claim retrieval task consists in ranking verified claims that can "help verify the input claim, or a subclaim in it" [24] to avoid a costly repeated task of fact-checking similar claims [36].

There have also been works for detecting suspicious and fake user profiles on online social media platforms often involved in spreading misinformation related news, such as Facebook [11], Twitter [1,27] or Tuenti [3]. These techniques include exploring user information such as immediate connections [1] and other meta-information such as user names [33].

Usually, disinformation is produced using propaganda techniques that help to accelerate its propagation. These techniques include specific rhetorical and psychological techniques, ranging from leveraging of emotions (such as using loaded language, flag waving, appeal to authority, slogans, and cliches) to using logical fallacies such as straw men (misrepresenting someone's opinion), red herring (presenting irrelevant data), black-and-white fallacy (presenting two alternatives as the only possibilities), and *whataboutism* [17]. A shared task was held within the 2019 on the PTC corpus [6] to identify both the specific text fragments where a propaganda technique is used and the type of technique used among 18 types. The best-performing models for both tasks used BERT based contextual representations.

## 2.2   Social Network Analysis

Disinformation campaigns rely nowadays on coordinated efforts to spread messages at scale. Such coordination is achieved by leveraging botnets (groups of fully automated accounts), cyborgs (partially automated) and troll armies (human-driven).

At the social network level, the current research trend is to target groups of accounts as a whole, rather than focusing on individual accounts [27]. The rationale for this choice is that malicious accounts act in coordination to amplify their effect [40]. Coordinated behaviour appears as near-fully connected communities in graphs, dense blocks in adjacency matrices, or peculiar patterns in spectral subspaces [13]. A large cluster of accounts with highly similar behaviour along time series are indications of a disinformation campaign.

The spreading of disinformation has been modelled through epidemic metaphors [7]. A (fake) piece of information, indeed, can be seen as a virus that may potentially infect people. Many SIR-based models have been proposed to model rumour spreading [19], adding forgetting and remembering mechanisms [42], sceptical agents [14], and competition among rumours [34]. [32] simulated the spreading of a hoax and its debunking at the same time taking forgetfulness into account by making a user lose interest in the fake news item with a given probability. The same authors extended their previous work comparing different fact-checking strategies on different network topologies to limit the spreading of fake news [31]. [22] studied the influence of online bots on a network through simulations, in an opinion dynamic setting. [5] studied how the presence of heterogeneous agents affects the competitive spreading of low- and high-quality information.

## 2.3   Multi-modal Analysis

Although there exists within the research community an awareness of the need to integrate content analysis and social network analysis to tackle misinformation [17], hitherto efforts in this direction have been limited. There are currently three approaches to combining signals from different modalities: (i) early-fusion, where features from different modalities are learned, fused, and fed into a single prediction model [8]; (ii) late-fusion, where unimodal decisions are fused via some averaging mechanism, and (iii) hybrid-fusion, where some of the features are early-fused, and other modalities are late-fused [15]. In these fusion strategies, the learning setup can also be divided into unsupervised, semi-supervised, supervised and self-supervised methods.

# 3   Problem Statement

There is a lack of research efforts that jointly consider the content analysis dimension and the network analysis dimension of disinformation [17].

Integrating multi-modal models for misinformation detection with network models of misinformation diffusion to identify large misinformation campaigns and their narratives constitutes a novel, holistic view of misinformation. It poses considerable and exciting challenges both on the conceptual and technical level.

There are two main current technologies to deal with the detection of disinformation. One, related to the needs of fact-checkers, focusing on the processing and analysis of single messages. The other, related to the detection of disinformation campaigns organised to influence a social network, relies on social network analysis: highly similar behaviour of different user accounts along time series are indications of a disinformation campaign.

However, both research lines remain separate research fields, although one gives context to the other. In fact, current AI models for misinformation detection are limited in the ability to represent and consider contextual information. It is still a research frontier we want to address. We must address the integration of different technologies at both message and social network levels into a single system.

A straightforward approach would be to run all involved systems separately and then compare and combine their output. However, they don't leverage each other's signals and, in fact, the current state of the art achieves rather low performance.

Thus, the alternative is what we call an "holistic" approach, where all tasks are considered simultaneously by one integrated system. Our position here is that, in order to integrate these two signal sources we must take advantage of the hidden variable they share: the intentionality of the communication. Following this perspective, many research questions arise and have to be addressed.

This resembles the end-to-end approach with neural networks which has replaced component-based architectures for several NLP tasks. Apart from solving the "whole" task—i.e. detection and description of organised disinformation campaigns—we also see a great potential to improve each single subtask, since they have access to much more data and insights. This hope is motivated by the success of multi-task learning, where additional unrelated subtasks help each other [41]. Messages that would be missed by local analysis could be uncovered at this deeper latent level if they are strongly connected to an identified potential harmful network and, provided with contextual information to better interpret their intention, eventually bring them to the attention of analysts.

## 4   Towards a Holistic Methodology for Disinformation Analysis

Our position is that we need methodologies that gather evidence from the message and social network levels and try to integrate both by inferring the narratives and intentions behind their spreading. In the following subsections we describe in more detail some of the core elements such methodologies must integrate.

## 4.1   Disinformation Detection at the Message Level in Multiple Modalities

Tackling disinformation at the local level of individual messages has been extensively reviewed in literature, specially with respect to the identification of fake news. However, moving beyond twitter that used to provide a network context for the message, and a user profile also as context, the task is still unsolved. There are several reasons for this, such as the combination of images and text, the lack of broader communication contexts, and the pragmatic use of language where implicatures are raised into the receptor by means of humor, irony or misleading reasoning.

The reconstruction of the communicative context justify the need of holistic methodologies but, still, there are some signals to be recovered from single messages both related to the semantic content and to the communication style.

**Stylometric Analysis.** Current systems for disinformation identification, such as fake-news checkers, usually rely on text. Under the assumption that the text content might use specific writing styles focused on convincing readers, we can conduct stylometric analysis of this content.

**Studying the Use of Propaganda Techniques.** While studies about disinformation detection often employ definitions of the term that differ on the conditions of untruthfulness and harmfulness, some widely employed rhetorical and psychological devices are more stably defined and therefore allow more straightforward approaches to disinformation at the message level. For instance, harmful content often makes use of well-defined propaganda techniques [17], which we can leverage to detect common patterns in disinformation writing.

**Multi-modal Content Analysis.** Multi-modal content analysis needs to account for each of the modalities present in the message, as well as for the interactions between these different modalities. Another clear challenge in multi-modal content is that audio and video posts feature spoken language, while current language models have been trained on written language. The use of speech-to-text technology to transcribe audio and video posts requires taking into account those models for misinformation detection that perform well on written text but still have to be adapted to robustly handle the repetitions, stutters, and interjections present in spoken language transcripts.

**Addressing Content in Low-Resource Languages.** Automatic disinformation classifiers at message-level are by nature limited for low-resource languages. Introducing multilingual and cross-lingual language models would be a significant improvement for the verified claim retrieval and message clustering sub tasks, especially for languages with less support in terms of labelled data and limited verified claim knowledge base [16]. Such approach has demonstrated its value as for fact checking [10], but it has not yet been exploited to perform verified claim retrieval.

## 4.2   Disinformation Detection at Social Network Level

**User Profile Features.** It is difficult to verify new information as it spreads quickly through social networks. Thus, we must consider features related to user profile such as followers with the goal of modelling the behaviour of disinformation spreaders. To this end, different ways of combining textual and non-textual features - still an open research question - must be explored.

**Leveraging the Diffusion Network to Model Communities and Echo Chambers.** Social metadata attached to messages often describes a network by listing all the nodes involved in the propagation of a certain message. In combination with the network's structure, this information allows describing the role of different nodes in the disinformation diffusion network in terms of their structural position in such network.

By studying the spread of multiple (clustered) messages we can identify and model communities, determining whether nodes are part of multiple communities or to single ones. The presence of multiple nodes that remain stuck to a single community can be an indication of polarisation and reveal that such community is an echo chamber.

**Sources and Means of Diffusion.** To identify misinformation sources, we can take advantage of the techniques developed in the previous step at message level. Subsequently, network science techniques can be applied to identify the sources of disinformation. Nodes in the network represent the individuals involved in disinformation propagation (edges) by forwarding, retweeting or reposting.

## 4.3   Studying the Context Behind Intentional Spreading of Misleading Information

Disinformation campaigns consist of multiple messages and multiple related claims which spread in a coordinated way through multiple pathways in social networks. We can only can observe the messages and their spreading in the network, but their occurrence is due to some intention or goal which is pushed by means of a set of narratives. Narratives and intentions are the primary communication context we need to infer in order to correctly analyse the content of individual messages.

**Modelling Intentionality.** The integration of evidence coming from the message and network levels can be articulated around the idea of disinformation intentionality: agents that create and introduce disinformation in the social media networks carefully select narratives aimed to have a concrete impact such as influencing the outcome of elections by discrediting political adversaries, influence financial markets, polarise and destabilise society, generate distrust, destroy reputation, etc. This adversarial game has, at the end, benefited and injured agents.

**Modelling Narratives.** Our hypothesis is that, given a scenario (e.g. a political election process), the set of intentions at play will be finite (e.g. destroying an opponent's reputation), and the narratives used to achieve it (e.g. X has money overseas) will be limited and predictable according to some general taxonomies.

Real scenarios of disinformation such as political elections can be seen as event-type instances from which to build these taxonomies of intents and narratives in disinformation.

### 4.4   Holistic Integration and Prediction

The holistic integration is an important stepping stone for modelling and detecting organised misinformation campaigns. We have so far described which steps would be taken at the local (individual message) and global (diffusion network) levels, and how these would be combined at a third level (intentions and narratives). New findings at this third level should improve detection at the former levels, in a virtuous loop. In other words, once the hidden intent is detected, we would come back to the message and network levels, this time bringing the aggregated evidence from all three levels. In this way, we will find new opportunities to capture the items that local approaches missed in the first pass, and new disinformation propagation paths.

The reconstruction of a broader communicative context will also give us the chance to find patterns that enable some kind of prediction power. For example, we could observe that in the scenario of a political election there will be some agents with the goal of delegitimizing the outcome of the process, so we can expect narratives questioning the counting process, so we can predict messages discrediting the agents involved in this process. This prediction power at the narrative level could help us to rise mitigation actions even before the disinformation comes into play.

## 5   Risks and Challenges

A general challenge for computational approaches to disinformation mitigation stems from the lack of agreement on a definition of disinformation. Studies differ on whether they require disinformation to be both untrue and harmful, and some authors propose that these two dimensions are not binary. For instance, information can be true but misleading. Another problem with disinformation's definition is that it is usually done in reactive terms, meaning that by the time of detection, the damage is already done. We pose that focusing on modelling underlying features such as intentionality helps to circumvent these problems.

A significant challenge for the holistic approach arises from the divergent focuses of the technologies involved, namely Natural Language Processing, Social Network Analysis, Epidemic Modelling, and Agent-based Simulation. Leaving aside the ambitious goal of a complete integration of signals from both the message and the network levels, a holistic approach can still advance the current state of the art in various tasks even if only partial integrations can ultimately be realized.

For instance, considering implicit narratives can help us cluster messages and therefore capture those misleading messages that a local approach would miss. This, in turn, will help identify undetected social network nodes involved in the spreading of disinformation. In the opposite direction, clusters of similar misleading messages can help us build language models that identify implicit narratives and hidden intentions. Such an approach would help addressing the issue with mitigation action's reactive definition.

However, there are some risks also related to the interpretation of the scenarios where disinformation campaigns occur. For example, we must be very careful about making explicit intentions or benefited agents of disinformation campaigns due to the subjective nature of their inference. Although we could talk about the effects or injured agents, it might be better to model these ideas as hidden variables that allocate more evidence in the holistic approach, instead of working in the goal of making them explicit.

To this moment, there is also a lack of established methodologies for evaluating disinformation detection systems able to consider all these levels of analysis. Developing such methodologies and organizing evaluation campaigns in different languages could be a first step in fostering a stronger interdisciplinary research community in Europe around the field of misinformation.

## 6   Conclusion

In this paper we have motivated the need of holistic methodologies for the identification of disinformation campaigns. The holistic integration of signals coming from message and network levels requires the modelling of implicit or hidden variables such as the types of narratives and their intentions or goals. At the end, what we need is to advance the state of the art towards methodologies aimed to reconstruct the communicative context of these campaigns.

Towards this goal, we really need to involve other disciplines such as journalism and communication, politics and sociology, or psychology.

We claim that the multiple interactions that take place within a holistic approach will give us the opportunity to evolve and achieve new results even if some attempts don't succeed.

## References

1. Benevenuto, F., Magno, G., Rodrigues, T., Almeida, V.: Detecting spammers on Twitter. In: Collaboration, Electronic Messaging, Anti-abuse and Spam Conference (CEAS), vol. 6, p. 12 (2010)

2. Butt, S., Sharma, S., Sharma, R., Sidorov, G., Gelbukh, A.: What goes on inside rumour and non-rumour tweets and their reactions: a psycholinguistic analyses. Comput. Hum. Behav. **135**, 107345 (2022)
3. Cao, Q., Sirivianos, M., Yang, X., Pregueiro, T.: Aiding the detection of fake accounts in large scale social online services. In: Presented as part of the 9th {USENIX} Symposium on Networked Systems Design and Implementation, {NSDI} 2012, pp. 197–210 (2012)
4. Chulvi, B., Toselli, A., Rosso, P.: Fake news and hate speech: language in common. arXiv preprint arXiv:2212.02352 (2022)
5. Cisneros-Velarde, P., Oliveira, D.F.M., Chan, K.S.: Spread and control of misinformation with heterogeneous agents. In: Cornelius, S.P., Granell Martorell, C., Gómez-Gardeñes, J., Gonçalves, B. (eds.) CompleNet 2019. SPC, pp. 75–83. Springer, Cham (2019). https://doi.org/10.1007/978-3-030-14459-3_6
6. Da San Martino, G., Yu, S., Barrón-Cedeno, A., Petrov, R., Nakov, P.: Fine-grained analysis of propaganda in news article. In: Proceedings of the 2019 Conference on Empirical Methods in Natural Language Processing and the 9th International Joint Conference on Natural Language Processing, EMNLP-IJCNLP, pp. 5636–5646 (2019)
7. Daley, D.J., Kendall, D.G.: Epidemics and rumours. Nature **204**, 1118 (1964)
8. Dhawan, M., Sharma, S., Kadam, A., Sharma, R., Kumaraguru, P.: Game-on: graph attention network based multimodal fusion for fake news detection. arXiv preprint arXiv:2202.12478 (2022)
9. Gencheva, P., Nakov, P., Màrquez, L., Barrón-Cedeño, A., Koychev, I.: A context-aware approach for detecting worth-checking claims in political debates. In: Proceedings of the International Conference Recent Advances in Natural Language Processing, RANLP 2017, pp. 267–276 (2017)
10. Ghanem, B., Glavaš, G., Giachanou, A., Ponzetto, S.P., Rosso, P., Rangel, F.: UPV-UMA at CheckThat! Lab: verifying Arabic claims using a cross lingual approach. In: CEUR Workshop Proceedings, vol. 2380, pp. 1–10. RWTH Aachen (2019)
11. Gupta, A., Kaushal, R.: Towards detecting fake user accounts in Facebook. In: 2017 ISEA Asia Security and Privacy (ISEASP), pp. 1–6. IEEE (2017)
12. Hassan, N., Li, C., Tremayne, M.: Detecting check-worthy factual claims in presidential debates. In: Proceedings of the 24th ACM International on Conference on Information and Knowledge Management, pp. 1835–1838 (2015)
13. Jiang, M., Cui, P., Beutel, A., Faloutsos, C., Yang, S.: Inferring lockstep behavior from connectivity pattern in large graphs. Knowl. Inf. Syst. **48**, 399–428 (2016)
14. Jin, F., Dougherty, E., Saraf, P., Cao, Y., Ramakrishnan, N.: Epidemiological modeling of news and rumors on Twitter. In: Proceedings of the 7th Workshop on Social Network Mining and Analysis, pp. 1–9 (2013)
15. Jin, Z., Cao, J., Guo, H., Zhang, Y., Luo, J.: Multimodal fusion with recurrent neural networks for rumor detection on microblogs. In: Proceedings of the 25th ACM International Conference on Multimedia, pp. 795–816 (2017)
16. Kazemi, A., Garimella, K., Gaffney, D., Hale, S.A.: Claim matching beyond English to scale global fact-checking. arXiv preprint arXiv:2106.00853 (2021)
17. Martino, G.D.S., Cresci, S., Barrón-Cedeño, A., Yu, S., Di Pietro, R., Nakov, P.: A survey on computational propaganda detection. arXiv preprint arXiv:2007.08024 (2020)
18. Mayank, M., Sharma, S., Sharma, R.: DEAP-FAKED: knowledge graph based approach for fake news detection. In: 2022 IEEE/ACM International Conference on Advances in Social Networks Analysis and Mining (ASONAM), pp. 47–51 (2022)

19. Moreno, Y., Nekovee, M., Pacheco, A.F.: Dynamics of rumor spreading in complex networks. Phys. Rev. E **69**(6), 066130 (2004)
20. Nikopensius, G., Mayank, M., Phukan, O.C., Sharma, R.: Reinforcement learning-based knowledge graph reasoning for explainable fact-checking. In: 2023 IEEE/ACM International Conference on Advances in Social Networks Analysis and Mining (ASONAM) (2023)
21. Patwari, A., Goldwasser, D., Bagchi, S.: TATHYA: a multi-classifier system for detecting check-worthy statements in political debates. In: Proceedings of the 2017 ACM on Conference on Information and Knowledge Management, pp. 2259–2262 (2017)
22. Ross, B., Pilz, L., Cabrera, B., Brachten, F., Neubaum, G., Stieglitz, S.: Are social bots a real threat? An agent-based model of the spiral of silence to analyse the impact of manipulative actors in social networks. Eur. J. Inf. Syst. **28**(4), 394–412 (2019)
23. Schütz, M., Schindler, A., Siegel, M., Nazemi, K.: Automatic fake news detection with pre-trained transformer models. In: Del Bimbo, A., et al. (eds.) ICPR 2021. LNCS, vol. 12667, pp. 627–641. Springer, Cham (2021). https://doi.org/10.1007/978-3-030-68787-8_45
24. Shaar, S., Martino, G.D.S., Babulkov, N., Nakov, P.: That is a known lie: detecting previously fact-checked claims. arXiv preprint arXiv:2005.06058 (2020)
25. Sharma, S., Agrawal, E., Sharma, R., Datta, A.: FaCov: Covid-19 viral news and rumors fact-check articles dataset. In: Proceedings of the International AAAI Conference on Web and Social Media, vol. 16, pp. 1312–1321 (2022)
26. Sharma, S., Datta, A., Shankaran, V., Sharma, R.: Misinformation concierge: a proof-of-concept with curated Twitter dataset on Covid-19 vaccination. In: CIKM (2023)
27. Sharma, S., Sharma, R.: Identifying possible rumor spreaders on Twitter: a weak supervised learning approach. In: 2021 International Joint Conference on Neural Networks (IJCNN), pp. 1–8. IEEE (2021)
28. Sharma, S., Sharma, R., Datta, A.: (Mis) leading the Covid-19 vaccination discourse on Twitter: an exploratory study of infodemic around the pandemic. IEEE Trans. Comput. Soc. Syst. (2022)
29. Shu, K., Cui, L., Wang, S., Lee, D., Liu, H.: dEFEND: explainable fake news detection. In: Proceedings of the 25th ACM SIGKDD International Conference on Knowledge Discovery & Data Mining, pp. 395–405 (2019)
30. Shu, K., Mahudeswaran, D., Wang, S., Lee, D., Liu, H.: FakeNewsNet: a data repository with news content, social context, and spatiotemporal information for studying fake news on social media. Big Data **8**(3), 171–188 (2020)
31. Tambuscio, M., Ruffo, G.: Fact-checking strategies to limit urban legends spreading in a segregated society. Appl. Netw. Sci. **4**, 1–19 (2019)
32. Tambuscio, M., Ruffo, G., Flammini, A., Menczer, F.: Fact-checking effect on viral hoaxes: a model of misinformation spread in social networks. In: Proceedings of the 24th International Conference on World Wide Web, pp. 977–982 (2015)
33. Thomas, K., McCoy, D., Grier, C., Kolcz, A., Paxson, V.: Trafficking fraudulent accounts: the role of the underground market in Twitter spam and abuse. In: USENIX Security Symposium, pp. 195–210 (2013)
34. Trpevski, D., Tang, W.K., Kocarev, L.: Model for rumor spreading over networks. Phys. Rev. E **81**(5), 056102 (2010)
35. Vasileva, S., Atanasova, P., Màrquez, L., Barrón-Cedeño, A., Nakov, P.: It takes nine to smell a rat: neural multi-task learning for check-worthiness prediction. arXiv preprint arXiv:1908.07912 (2019)

36. Vo, N., Lee, K.: Where are the facts? Searching for fact-checked information to alleviate the spread of fake news. arXiv preprint arXiv:2010.03159 (2020)
37. Vosoughi, S., Roy, D., Aral, S.: The spread of true and false news online. Science **359**(6380), 1146–1151 (2018)
38. Wu, Y., Zhan, P., Zhang, Y., Wang, L., Xu, Z.: Multimodal fusion with co-attention networks for fake news detection. In: Findings of the Association for Computational Linguistics, ACL-IJCNLP 2021, pp. 2560–2569 (2021)
39. Zaman, T., Fox, E.B., Bradlow, E.T.: A Bayesian approach for predicting the popularity of tweets. Ann. Appl. Stat. **8**(3), 1583–1611 (2014). https://doi.org/10.1214/14-AOAS741
40. Zhang, J., Zhang, R., Zhang, Y., Yan, G.: The rise of social botnets: attacks and countermeasures. IEEE Trans. Depend. Secure Comput. **15**(6), 1068–1082 (2016)
41. Zhang, Y., Yang, Q.: A survey on multi-task learning. IEEE Trans. Knowl. Data Eng. **34**(12), 5586–5609 (2021)
42. Zhao, L., Qiu, X., Wang, X., Wang, J.: Rumor spreading model considering forgetting and remembering mechanisms in inhomogeneous networks. Phys. A **392**(4), 987–994 (2013)
43. Zubiaga, A., Liakata, M., Procter, R.: Learning reporting dynamics during breaking news for rumour detection in social media. arXiv preprint arXiv:1610.07363 (2016)

# Towards Multimodal Campaign Detection: Including Image Information in Stream Clustering to Detect Social Media Campaigns

Lucas Stampe[ID], Janina Pohl[(✉)][ID], and Christian Grimme[ID]

Computational Social Science and Systems Analysis, University of Münster, Münster, Germany
{lucas.stampe,janina.pohl,christian.grimme}@uni-muenster.de

**Abstract.** This work explores the potential to include visual information from images in social media campaign recognition. The diverse content shared on social media platforms, including text, photos, videos, and links, necessitates a multimodal analysis approach. With the emergence of Large Language Models (LLMs), there is now an opportunity to convert image content into textual descriptions, enabling the incorporation of previously text-based methods into a multimodal analysis. We evaluate this approach by conducting a parameter study to assess the resulting differences in image captions and a case study to examine the contribution of textualized image information to campaign recognition. The results indicate that, using image captions separate from or alongside tweet texts, connections between campaigns can be identified, and new campaigns detected.

**Keywords:** Social Media · Multimodality · Campaign Detection · Image to Text

## 1 Introduction

The detection and analysis of campaigns in social media is an important and exciting research topic that has gained importance over recent years [2,6,8]. Besides advertising campaigns, especially disinformation campaigns, are new challenges by aiming for societal change [15,23] or even by supporting physical war efforts [16].

Social media are just as diverse as the content disseminated on them. In addition to often short textual messages, users share photos or videos. These additional data refine the context of messages, but sometimes, they also contradict the messages' content. Pictures or videos are either a supplementary

The authors acknowledge support by the European Research Center in Information Systems (ERCIS) and by the project HybriD (FKZ: 16KIS1531K) funded through the German Federal Ministry of Education and Research.

D. Ceolin et al. (Eds.): MISDOOM 2023, LNCS 14397, pp. 144–159, 2023.
https://doi.org/10.1007/978-3-031-47896-3_11

medium or the decisive focal point. In addition, references are often found as links pointing to information that can also represent contextual information. In this respect, it seems only logical to include this additional information together with text in the analysis of social media campaigns [10,11,21]. This approach - referred to as multimodal analysis - is an emerging but rather complex research topic. In particular, the problem is to find a suitable representation for the different types of content such that analysis procedures can process all modalities together. Early developed approaches relied on the forensic analysis of pictorial or audio-visual content to assess messages as correct or incorrect. Tools such as photo forensics[1] should be understood in this context. Later approaches fuse the multimodal information (e.g., into different representation vectors) to jointly detect these features in Deep Learning models for classifying (often event-based) campaign-like contexts [11,21].

With the advent of Large Language Models (LLMs) such as GPT, there exist reliable tools now to capture and describe image content textually. This opens up an interesting perspective to relying on previously text-based methods for multimodal analysis [2]. Thus, images can be converted into text and incorporated into stream clustering approaches to provide additional information and more meaningful clusters.

The subject of this paper is an evaluation of the potential of including image captions as one of several multimodal features to extend campaign-detection capabilities. To this end, we first conduct a detailed parameter study to investigate the quality differences depending on different parameters. These results are then incorporated into a case study investigating the contribution of textualized image information to campaign recognition. Our work is structured as follows: Sect. 2 provides background and related work on multimodal campaigns, image captioning, and our implemented approach. Section 3 describes the experimental setup, while Sect. 4 presents the results, and Sect. 5 discusses and concludes the work.

## 2   Background

### 2.1   Multimodal Campaign Detection

To date, most studies have disregarded image information when detecting coordinated campaigns within social media. Existing methodologies primarily concentrate on textual analysis [2] or various features associated with the user accounts [4,23], like investigating the user's activities to build user graphs [6,8].

For a long time, image fraud was considered separately from false information, e.g., by focusing on the identification of Deep Fakes [12,18]. However, with the increasing prominence of the term "fake news" on social media, researchers have begun incorporating images into their analysis of posts containing fraudulent information. Numerous methodologies developed so far leverage neural networks, specifically convolutional neural networks (CNNs), to process image data,

---

[1] https://fotoforensics.com/.

while another neural network or a transformer model like BERT is employed to extract information from texts. Subsequently, the information from these sources is either fused using a third neural network or directly inputted into a classifier [11,21]. In some experiments, researchers have supplemented the analysis with additional information, such as image-text similarities [9], deep fake classifier [24], or the output of image captioning models [20,26].

In their investigation of coordinated networks on Twitter, Pacheco et al. [15] incorporate the RGB color histogram of images. They extract behavioral data from accounts, including shared content, activities, and meta information, to identify users with similar features. Consequently, they successfully discern a network of interconnected accounts that engage in sharing identical images. Similarly, Erhard and Albassam [8] integrated image-sharing accounts into their influence analysis method. While these two papers incorporate image analysis to study network behavior, there remains an unexplored research opportunity to delve into the mechanisms and types of images shared within campaigns.

## 2.2    Image Captioning Models

Typically, models designed for image captioning either focus on particular tasks such as visual question answering or optical character recognition (OCR), while state-of-the-art vision-and-language transformers try to create a universal model suitable for dozens of tasks. Examples of such models include `Frozen` [19], `MAGMA` [7], and `Flamingo` [1]. These models are considered few-shot learners, offering the advantage of being primed for images they have yet to encounter. In contrast, `CLIP` [17] operates as a zero-shot learner, demonstrating how simplified training approaches can compete without further fine-tuning on new tasks or contexts. `BLIP` [14], and its subsequent iteration `BLIP2` [13] rely on synthetically generated captions and incorporate a filtering mechanism to remove incorrect captions, thereby refining the training data sourced from web images. `SimVLM` [22] employs weak supervision to simplify the training process while still achieving competitive performance compared to other state-of-the-art models. Similarly, `CoCa` [25] combines both approaches, yielding even better results in image captioning across multiple metrics and data sets compared to its predecessors. Additionally, there are training procedures based on those employed for language models, such as `BEiT` [3] or `ImageGPT` [5]. However, these models may require additional fine-tuning for tasks like image captioning.

For several reasons, our study will primarily focus on `BLIP2` [14]. Firstly, `BLIP2` stands out as a freely accessible and openly available model with comprehensive documentation. In contrast, models like `MAGMA` [7] or `Frozen` [19] would require the same level of availability and documentation. Furthermore, `BLIP2` is offered in various sizes, granting flexibility to select the most suitable model for a specific task. Importantly, `BLIP2` does not necessitate additional fine-tuning, unlike many alternatives, which were only accessible in relatively smaller sizes with fewer parameters. Consequently, during preliminary trials, the OPT-2.7B version of `BLIP2` exhibited superior performance compared to other models. A detailed comparison of models is omitted here due to space limitations.

### 2.3 Implemented Approach

In our experiments, we combine information from images with text information to explore coordinated behavior and campaigns on social media. As aforementioned, we use the `BLIP2` [14] model due to its compelling performance for this task. The two main components of `BLIP2` are a combination of an image encoder and a query transformer used to learn representations of visual features and language and an LLM-based generative model that creates captions based on these features. Pre-trained image and language models are thus connected via a Querying-Transformer, based on pre-trained `BERT` weights, consisting of two sub-modules, one transformer to extract visual features from the image encoder, and a text transformer to encode and decode text. It was trained to perform various vision-language tasks and outperforms other state-of-the-art models on tasks like visual question answering, image captioning, and image-text retrieval.

To detect multimodal campaigns, we extend a text-based campaign detection approach introduced by Assenmacher et al. [2]. The authors utilized the stream clustering algorithm `textClust` to group social media posts with similar texts into cohesive clusters. `textClust` is a one-pass algorithm that employs TF-IDF vectors and cosine similarity. Each text assigned to a cluster increases its weight, while an exponential fading function gradually diminishes it over time, allowing topics to fade away. By visualizing the temporal trends of these clusters, observers can identify anomalous patterns, such as abrupt spikes in cluster weight that deviate from the expected natural emergence of topics on social media platforms. These patterns serve as indicators of potential campaigns.

This study expands the analysis beyond social media texts and incorporates information from and about images. Consequently, we will investigate how the cluster trends are affected when this additional information is included.

## 3 Experimental Setup

In order to generate high-quality image captions, we first test and configure `BLIP2` for the task at hand (objective 1). Then, we generate one or several captions to include them in the stream clustering approach in various ways to test their influence on the clustering result (objective 2).

### 3.1 Objective 1 - Image Captioning Model Configuration

To create a diverse dataset for configuring BLIP2, we used a sample from ten different polarized topics on Twitter collected using `twarc` on the 5[th] of June 2023, namely *artificial intelligence, brexit, capitalism, censorship, climate change, communism, environment, free speech, migration,* and *ukraine war* which added up to 225 images and 167 after de-duplication.

BLIP2 combines image-based and language-based models to generate descriptive outputs. Configuring the language model is crucial for producing suitable captions that accurately correspond to the images. Two exclusive configuration approaches exist: deterministic (or "greedy") search and sampling.

The deterministic search involves the model predicting the most probable token successively in a greedy manner. However, this token-by-token process may overlook better captions. To address this, the search requires setting the beam width, which determines the number of token candidates evaluated in parallel. Ultimately, the caption with the highest overall likelihood is chosen.

In contrast, sampling considers the likelihood of each candidate, favoring those with higher probabilities. Two parameters can be configured for this method: temperature or top-$k$/top-$p$. Temperature modifies the candidate likelihood distribution, balancing the probabilities. Consequently, previously highly likely candidates become less probable and vice versa. Alternatively, the top-$k$ parameter restricts the candidates to the top-$k$ with the highest probabilities. This exclusion prevents less appropriate candidates, often found in the "long tail" of unlikely options. Additionally, the top-$p$ parameter restricts the number of candidates by including only candidates making up at least $p\%$ of the total likelihood. Combining these parameters offers a means to restrict potentially unsuitable captions while allowing for creative outputs.

In our evaluation, we tested both deterministic and sampling options. Refer to Table 1 for a comprehensive overview of tested parameters. The parameter settings in this exploratory study are chosen as a subset of a grid search approach based on preliminary experiments for finding reasonable scales and stepsizes. Additionally, we tested three different options for prompting: (a) no prompts, (b) "This is a picture of" and c) "This image shows" to see the impact of priming the model. Further, to prevent captions with repetitions, we set the parameter *no_repeat_ngram_size* to 2. Finally, we tested two different output lengths, i.e., once with a maximum number of tokens of 20 and once with 40.

To evaluate the output of these different configurations, we manually and automatically checked all the captions generated for the images. Manually, we checked whether the captions contained all the information in the image (but not more) and whether one configuration led to obviously misleading captions.

**Table 1.** Tested parameter configurations for BLIB2

|  | Parameter | Configurations |
|---|---|---|
| Deterministic | beam width | [1, 2, 3, 4, 5, ..., 16, 17, 18, 19, 20] |
| Sampling | temperature | [0.2, 0.4, 0.6, 0.8, 1, 1.5, 2, 2.5, 3, 3.5, 5, 10, 15, 20, 25, 30, 35, 40, 45, 50, 60, 70, 80, 90, 100] |
|  | top-$k$/top-$p$ | [100/1, 100/0.8, 100/0.6, 100/0.4, 100/0.2, 80/1, 80/0.8, 80/0.6, 80/0.4, 80/0.2, 60/1, 60/0.8, 60/0.6, 60/0.4, 60/0.2, 40/1, 40/0.8, 40/0.6, 40/0.4, 40/0.2, 20/1, 20/0.8, 20/0.6, 20/0.4, 20/0.2] |

## 3.2    Objective 2 - Image Information for Campaign Detection

To evaluate the potential impact of adding image-based information to stream clustering approaches to detect campaigns, we used a Twitter streaming dataset collected February 11-13, 2023. We selected climate change as a topic since we expect it to be controversial on Twitter, thus incorporating many images to support the argument. In total, the dataset comprises 112 000 tweets with over 18.000 including images, of which multiple users referenced 6400.

The tweet texts were fed into `textClust` first without any image-based information to identify campaign-like activities. `textClust` was configured with its standard parameter, i.e., with active preprocessing, real-time fading, auto-radius, and $\lambda = 0.001$ and $tgap = 100$. Next, we conducted several experiments: We ran `textClust` with only the text without image captions to see which topics were discussed and when. Then, we created the image captions using the results of objective 1. We then included the caption either in the tweet to which it belongs or – in a separate experiment – added them as stand-alone posts to the dataset. We also let solely the captions run in `textClust` to see whether any clusters emerged purely based on image information.

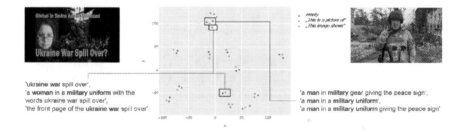

**Fig. 1.** Exemplary image captions with their corresponding embeddings reduced to two dimensions by using `t-sne`.

## 4    Results

### 4.1    Objective 1 - Image Captioning Model Configuration

**Prompting.** Across all configurations, it becomes apparent that using different prompts results in variation between captions, indicating the potential to use different prompts instead of sampling to capture more visual information. An example can be seen in Fig. 1, where the paraphrase embedding `paraphrase-MiniLM-L6-v2` was used, and dimensionality reduction was applied via `t-sne`.

One can see that each triplet of captions, one for each prompt, is generally positioned in direct vicinity to each other. However, as in the case of the left-hand image, one prompt favored OCR-only captions over those combining OCR with regular descriptions. Consequently, the captions, including OCR, are semantically more similar, while the caption "a woman ... military" is next to the description of the right-hand image. Although no pattern was discernible, this might be a concern for the TF-IDF-based textClust algorithm.

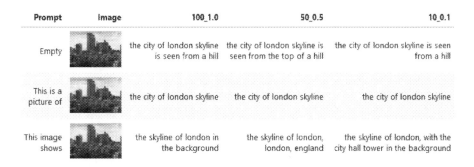

| Prompt | Image | 100_1.0 | 50_0.5 | 10_0.1 |
|---|---|---|---|---|
| Empty | | the city of london skyline is seen from a hill | the city of london skyline is seen from the top of a hill | the city of london skyline is seen from a hill |
| This is a picture of | | the city of london skyline | the city of london skyline | the city of london skyline |
| This image shows | | the skyline of london in the background | the skyline of london, london, england | the skyline of london, with the city hall tower in the background |

**Fig. 2.** Captions for different configurations (top-$k$_top-$p$) and different prompts.

**Deterministic - Beam Width.** In our experimental findings, increasing the beam width improved captions in some cases. These captions generally contained more information; however, instances including non-image-related information were rare. Conversely, utilizing a smaller beam width led to highly repetitive and monotonous captions that often lacked the specificity required to represent the image accurately. Thus, in the experiments for objective 2, we will use a beam width of 20.

**Sampling - Temperature.** Generally, we observed that the higher the temperature, the more creative – and misleading – the outputs were. Specifically, as the temperature increased beyond 3.5, the model produced captions that included information unrelated to the input images, such as fictitious dates, locations, authors, or copyright holders. As a result, considering the potential inclusion of misleading information in captions, we decided to exclude the temperature parameter from further evaluation.

**Sampling - Top-$k$ and Top-$p$** As presented in Table 1, we tested a variety of values for these two parameters. An example of selected top-$k$ and top-$p$ values can be found in Fig. 2. The first manual analysis reveals much higher consistency between the captions compared to the temperature parameter. We observed only slight variations in the created captions, as anticipated in a sampling-based approach. A difference in quality in terms of correctness and completeness across configurations cannot be observed. In most cases, the generated captions effectively conveyed the essential visual information contained within the images. Notably, the generation of either OCR-only or mixed captions varied with different top-$k$ and top-$p$ configurations as well, although again without any apparent pattern. This once again highlights the potential for merging multiple captions into one output. We further use quantitative metrics to capture hidden differences between configurations automatically. First, we compared the number of unique bigrams, the text length in words, and finally, the number of unique captions across samples, once with a maximum number of tokens of 20 and once with 40. The result can be seen in Fig. 3.

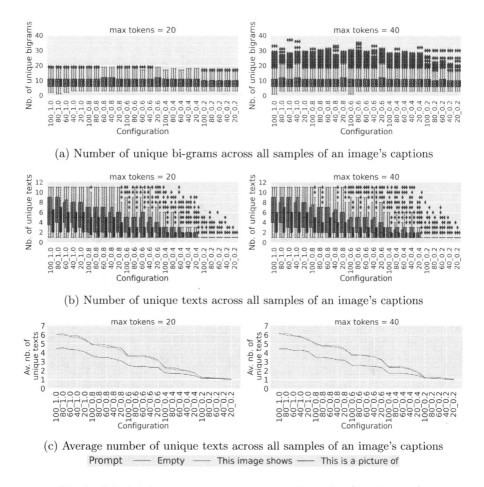

(a) Number of unique bi-grams across all samples of an image's captions

(b) Number of unique texts across all samples of an image's captions

(c) Average number of unique texts across all samples of an image's captions

Prompt ——— Empty ——— This image shows ——— This is a picture of

**Fig. 3.** Calculated metrics per parameter configuration (top-$k$_top-$p$).

We found a strong correlation between text lengths and the count of unique bigrams. Therefore, we only depict the latter in Fig. 3a, where similarpatterns across the three prompts can be observed. While a minor trend is noticeable, indicating a slight reduction in unique bigrams with lower parameter values, these variations are insignificant. However, we noticed disparities in output length: when employing a maximum token length of 40, outliers with more unique bigrams were noted. This suggests that increasing the number of generated tokens does not consistently result in longer output sequences and might bias the stream clustering algorithm.

In contrast, Fig. 3b provides insight into the number of unique captions generated across configurations. The plot illustrates a decline in unique texts as parameter values decrease. Eventually, a point is reached where, for most images, all samples produce identical captions. Notably, as per Fig. 3c, we observe an almost step-like decrease of the average, revealing that "This image shows" and using no prompt produce more varied captions than "This is a picture of".

Next to the pure occurrence of words, we also check the semantic similarity of the created captions. Thus, we use sentence embeddings created with the T5-large embeddings. We then calculated a cluster centroid based on these numerical vectors, from which we computed the average distance from all captions' points in the multidimensional space to this centroid. Figure 4 illustrates how much the sampled captions vary semantically.

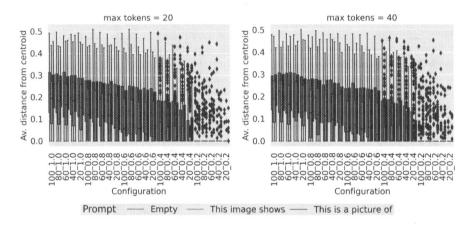

**Fig. 4.** Boxplots of distances of an image's captions from their centroid per parameter configuration (top-$k$_top-$p$).

The results indicate that lower parameter configurations yield an average distance converging to 0 as top-$p$ decreases, while top-$k$ has only a minor impact. Similar to previous findings, the choice of prompts appears to be influential. Comparing the number of unique texts in Fig. 3b to the distance to cluster centroids in Fig. 4, we see that for some configurations and prompts, the number of unique texts is high. Simultaneously, their semantic difference might be comparatively small and vice-versa. This suggests that only because the captions differ syntactically does not necessarily imply that they are different semantically and, thus, do not necessarily contain more information. Thus, we observe how semantically similar outputs balance out the variations in the number of unique texts generated per configuration and prompt.

Since neither the average distance from the centroid nor the number of unique texts or bigrams differs much for the maximum tokens, we set the maximum tokens to 20 instead of 40. Additionally, since the higher the parameter values, the higher the number of unique texts and the distance from the centroid, we set the values for top-$k$ and top-$p$ to $80/0.8$, respectively. Thus, we clip the long tail but keep the benefits of having a greater variety in generated captions.

## 4.2   Objective 2 - Image Information for Campaign Detection

The result of applying the clustering algorithm `textClust` to the datasets with and without captions can be seen in Fig. 5. In order to assess the impact of the captions, we first cluster the dataset without any captions (Fig. 5a). Then, we added captions using the configurations we identified as most promising in Sect. 4.1. To test the effects of adding captions, we examined different setups: (1) adding single captions, (2) combining three captions from different prompts, and (3) combining up to three sampled captions from one prompt. The captions were included in the data set in three ways: as part of the tweet text (Fig. 5b), as an additional, stand-alone "post" (Fig. 5c), or as a tweet without the original tweet text (Fig. 5d), resulting in nine combinations. We only kept an image's unique captions when using multiple prompts or sampling. This de-duplication meant that for some images, only one or two captions remained. When sampling captions, for some images, receiving three different captions was so unlikely that we needed to set a stopping criterion to a maximum number of tries, for the model would otherwise create captions endlessly for some non-specific images.

**Baseline and General Observations (Fig. 5a)** Clusters of similar shape and content are portrayed using the same color across all plots in Figs. 5a, 5b, and 5c, and again across all plots in Fig. 5d to match them as closely as possible for the following analysis. As new clusters form, `textClust` incrementally assigns them new IDs. Thus, different IDs are assigned to similar clusters across the different runs, although they are mostly the same content-wise. Of course, the addition of captions also results in new clusters, as discussed below. To focus on the most promising clusters, we selected the top 10 according to their maximum achieved weight at one time during the entire time for analysis. The baseline results with only the tweet texts can be observed in Fig. 5a, illustrating how each cluster's weight changes over time. With few exceptions, the clusters show peaks at some point and remain flat otherwise, representing a coherent topic Twitter users discussed over a more extended period.

By examining the tweets and the accounts behind them, the analysis of the clusters in the baseline approach reveals three types of clusters formed by `textClust`. Four of the clusters (15, 94, 2714, 5061) contain mostly authentic behavior with peaks created by bots posting weather announcements (e.g., "MARTINSBURG WV Feb 13 Climate: High: 54 Low: 28 Snow: Missing [link]")), while five clusters (2069, 4671, 4012, 4284, 6161) contain peaks that are mainly due to one user responsible for campaigning many similar tweets in a short amount of time (e.g., "@[user] go #Vegan for #Mercy #Health #ClimateCrisis #Justice [link] #SuperBowl"). Two of these clusters' peaks were also increased due to further actors joining the activity and repeatedly posting similar content. Finally, one cluster (4421) reveals more coordinated activities, where multiple

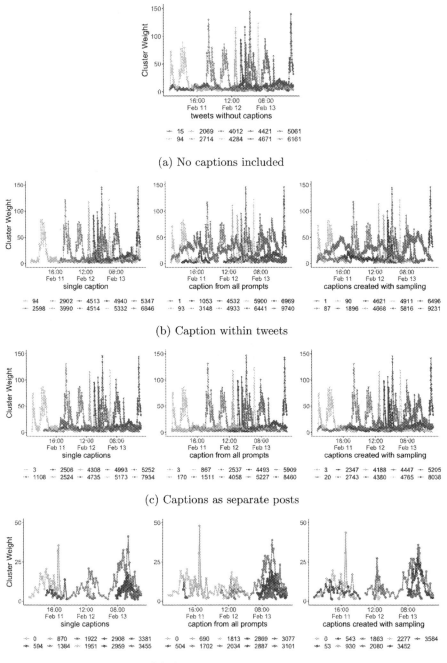

(a) No captions included

(b) Caption within tweets

(c) Captions as separate posts

(d) Captions without tweets

**Fig. 5.** Clustering results for only tweets (a), adding captions to tweets in various ways (c/d), and only captions (d).

users posted similar tweets, mainly using the same texts ("Can We Fight Climate Change By Giving the Ocean an Antacid?: [link]"), during a short time frame. When examining only the tweets' texts, various orchestrated and systematic activities can be observed, which may further be influenced by adding captions.

**Captions as Part of Tweet Text (Fig. 5b)** We observe that the clusters make no significant changes compared to the baseline clustering result when using simple captions. When using multiple captions, be it via prompts or sampling, a new cluster that follows the day and night cycle (cluster 1 in Fig. 5b 2/3) appears next to the previous ones. In this cluster, most of the texts containing image information were summarized. The rest of the images are attached to other clusters. As a result, clusters 2069 and 4671 that initially existed in the baseline merged into 4933 and 4668 in Fig. 5b 2/3. Many of the tweets with images that were part of the original clusters of the baseline are no longer part of these merged clusters, raising the question of how desirable this behavior is. On the cluster level, the overall impact of adding captions to tweet texts is relatively fractional. Apart from more expressive tweet texts themselves, a potential reason for this could be hashtags and user references.

Generally, many captions contain common entities, which form clusters based on these central features. Examples are people ("a man...", "a woman...", "a group of people", ...), advertising material ("a poster", "a logo", "a flyer",) or graphs. Consequently, many clusters also formed due to the inclusion of the type of image captioned ("a screenshot", "an image", "an aerial view", ...), which surprisingly happened regardless of the prompt. Consequently, about 25 % of cluster 1 is made up of posts with images of people, potentially taking away helpful information from other clusters, revealing a caveat to adding captions to tweet texts.

**Captions Added as Additional "Posts" (Fig. 5c)** When handling captions separately from their original tweets, adding single captions or only prompts resulted in a few clusters receiving a significant number of image captions. To get further insight into the issue, we looked at the distribution of images across clusters. As shown in Fig. 6, few clusters receive many image captions, while most obtain only a few, if any, reminiscent of a power law distribution. In the case of adding single captions, the two clusters with the most images among the top ten, 1108 and 5252, contain posters advertising an event by a Ugandan governmental organization and, therefore, do not constitute an inauthentic campaign. For prompts, over 17 % of cluster 3 consists of image captions. This cluster mainly contained texts related to weather announcement activities, and the captions do not add to its peaks, instead forming a tail that starts a few hours after the second peak ends. Similarly, the peaks for clusters 5909, 4058, and 1511 contain almost no image captions. If at all, these captions contain very general image descriptions. In the case of sampling, over 65 % of cluster 20 consists of image captions that revolve mainly around general descriptions of people and groups of them. Cluster 4447 still contains the previously identified campaign from the baseline (6161) but now also contains the advertisement from the single captions approach. All in all, adding posts as additional tweets did not result in meaningful changes to the top clusters analyzed here.

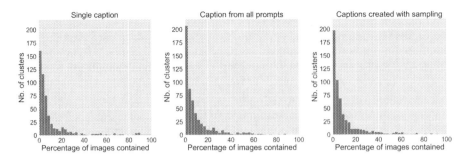

**Fig. 6.** Percentage of images contained in clusters for simple captions, three prompts, sampling when using captions as separate posts.

**Captions Without Tweet Text (Fig. 5d)** When considering the clustering results of only the captions, overall comparable results can be observed when considering single captions, captions containing all three prompts, and sampled captions. All three approaches lead to the formation of clusters that follow time patterns, temporally limited but dense occurrences, and high peaks. Using sampling, the variance in captions led to combining the various smaller clusters towards the end of the timeline on February 14.

The effect of images including common entities (like a graph, a logo, or a person) can be observed more strongly here since clusters form primarily on that basis. Some clusters consist solely of these descriptions, containing, for example, people or groups of them. However, a few peaks are discernible in each of the three approaches. In the light-blue cluster, a climate change activist posted the same graph on the rise in atmospheric carbon dioxide and global temperature, accompanied by different tweet texts each time. This user would not have stood out in the baseline experiment despite posting almost 250 times, over 100 times said graph, meaning this imaged-based campaign would have gone unnoticed. Considering images as separate from a post's text thus reveals campaigns that are not apparent in the text-based clustering mainly due to their volume, as less than 20% of all tweets contain images. Similarly, the dark-pink cluster had its peak on February 12 at approximately 12 p.m. contains posts created by a climate change denier posting another graph with information in favor of global warming accompanied by different texts. This user did not appear in the baseline's top 10 clusters, although he posted 35 times in total and over 20 times on said graph. In these cases, images were used to support an argument with data presented in graphs. Various other types of use could be imagined, such as loading images emotionally, which might not be detected via text-based methods.

## 5    Conclusion

In this initial study, we presented the complex task of including textual image representations in social media campaign detection approaches. The results indicate that next to sampling, multiple prompts can be used to capture various image information. A high degree of creativity, expressed by high-temperature values during sampling, must be avoided to ensure that a caption reflects the image's content. Instead, when sampling via top-$k$/top-$p$, different configurations did not result in any significant quality changes but did impact the variance between samples and should, thus, not be too conservative.

The findings were applied to a case of English tweets surrounding climate change through various experiments where captions were either included in the respective tweet, added as a new "post", or included without the original text. They revealed that combined captions have a more significant impact than single captions when used as part of the text. Albeit in all cases, there were only minor effects on the overall cluster formation, merges of similar clusters could be observed, facilitating campaign detection. Using captions without the original tweet texts enabled the identification of particular users posting images in a campaign-like manner. Thus it was the most promising of the three approaches. Finally, as sampling did not produce insights compared to deterministic approaches, models that provide the user with more configuration options, particularly to further specify prompts, which could allow for more holistic image descriptions and enhance their potential for campaign detection.

Future work could enhance captions with, e.g., entity recognition to make them more expressive, in particular by naming entities such as people or landmarks to avoid too general descriptions. Further, visual information could be extended to include videos and even supplementary information attached to tweets, like comments, and others include types of social media elements or even refer back to the original sources to extract further information. Finally, embeddings could be utilized to capture the semantic similarity between texts and images, and more advanced analysis tools could reveal more profound insights into the formation of clusters and, thus, underlying campaigns.

# References

1. Alayrac, J.B., et al.: Flamingo: a visual language model for few-shot learning. Adv. Neural. Inf. Process. Syst. **35**, 23716–23736 (2022)
2. Assenmacher, D., Clever, L., Pohl, J.S., Trautmann, H., Grimme, C.: A two-phase framework for detecting manipulation campaigns in social media. In: Meiselwitz, G. (ed.) HCII 2020. LNCS, vol. 12194, pp. 201–214. Springer, Cham (2020). https://doi.org/10.1007/978-3-030-49570-1_14
3. Bao, H., Dong, L., Piao, S., Wei, F.: Beit: BERT pre-training of image transformers. arXiv:2106.08254 (2021)
4. Bellutta, D., Carley, K.M.: Investigating coordinated account creation using burst detection and network analysis. J. of Big Data **10**(1), 1–17 (2023)
5. Chen, M., Radford, A., Child, R., Jun, H., Luan, D., Sutskever, I.: Generative pretraining from pixels. In: Proceedings of the 37th International Conference on Machine Learning, PMLR, pp. 1691–1703 (2020)
6. Cinelli, M., Cresci, S., Quattrociocchi, W., Zola, P.: Coordinated inauthentic behavior and information spreading on twitter. Decision Support Systems **160**, 113819 (2022)

7. Eichenberg, C., Black, S., Weinbach, S., Parcalabescu, L., Frank, A.: MAGMA - multimodal augmentation of generative models through adapter-based finetuning. arXiv: 2112.05253 (2021)
8. Erhardt, K., Albassam, D.: Detecting the hidden dynamics of networked actors using temporal correlations. In: Companion Proceedings of the ACM Web Conference 2023, pp. 1214–1217. WWW 2023 Companion, ACM, Austin, TX, USA (2023)
9. Giachanou, A., Zhang, G., Rosso, P.: Multimodal multi-image fake news detection. In: 2020 IEEE 7th International Conference on Data Science and Advanced Analytics (DSAA), pp. 647–654. IEEE, Sydney, Australia (2020)
10. Guo, B., Ding, Y., Yao, L., Liang, Y., Yu, Z.: The future of false information detection on social media. ACM Comput. Surv. **53**(4), 1–36 (2020)
11. Jin, Z., Cao, J., Guo, H., Zhang, Y., Luo, J.: Multimodal fusion with recurrent neural networks for rumor detection on microblogs. In: Proceedings of the 25th ACM International Conference on Multimedia, pp. 795–816. ACM, New York, NY, USA (2017)
12. John, J., Sherif, B.V.: Multi-model deepfake detection using deep and temporal features. In: Chen, J.IZ., Tavares, J.M.R.S., Shi, F. (eds.) Third International Conference on Image Processing and Capsule Networks. ICIPCN 2022. Lecture Notes in Networks and Systems, vol. 514, pp. 672–684. Springer, Cham (2022). https://doi.org/10.1007/978-3-031-12413-6_53
13. Li, J., Li, D., Savarese, S., Hoi, S.: BLIP-2: bootstrapping language-image pre-training with frozen image encoders and LLM. arXiv:2301.12597 (2023)
14. Li, J., Li, D., Xiong, C., Hoi, S.: BLIP: bootstrapping language-image pre-training for unified vision-language understanding and generation. In: International Conference on Machine Learning, pp. 12888–12900 (2022)
15. Pacheco, D., Hui, P.M., Torres-Lugo, C., Flammini, A., Menczer, F.: Uncovering coordinated networks on social media: methods and case studies. In: Proceedings of the 14th International Conference on Web and Social Media, pp. 455–466. AAAI Press, Online (2021)
16. Pohl, J.S., Markmann, S., Assenmacher, D., Grimme, C.: Invasion@Ukraine: providing and describing a twitter streaming dataset that captures the outbreak of war between Russia and Ukraine in 2022. In: Proceedings of the 17th International Conference on Web and Social Media, pp. 1093–1101. AAAI Press, Limassol, Cyprus (2023)
17. Radford, A., et al.: Learning transferable visual models from natural language supervision. In: International Conference on Machine Learning, pp. 8748–8763 (2021)
18. Rafique, R., Gantassi, R., Amin, R., Frnda, J., Mustapha, A., Alshehri, A.H.: Deep fake detection and classification using error-level analysis and deep learning. Sci. Rep. **13**, 7422 (2023)
19. Tsimpoukelli, M., Menick, J.L., Cabi, S., Eslami, S., Vinyals, O., Hill, F.: Multimodal few-shot learning with frozen language models. Adv. Neural. Inf. Process. Syst. **34**, 200–212 (2021)
20. Uppada, S.K., Patel, P., B., S.: An image and text-based multimodal model for detecting fake news in OSN's. J. Intell. Inf. Syst. (2022). https://doi.org/10.1007/s10844-022-00764-y
21. Wang, Y., Ma, F., Jin, Z., Yuan, Y., Xun, G., et al.: EANN: event adversarial neural networks for multi-modal fake news detection. In: Proceedings of the 24th International Conference on Knowledge Discovery & Data Mining, pp. 849–857. ACM, NY, USA (2018)

22. Wang, Z., Yu, J., Yu, A.W., Dai, Z., Tsvetkov, Y., Cao, Y.: SimVLM: simple visual language model pretraining with weak supervision. arXiv:2108.10904 (2021)
23. Weber, D., Neumann, F.: Amplifying influence through coordinated behaviour in social networks. Soc. Netw. Anal. Min. **11**, 111 (2021)
24. Xue, J., Wang, Y., Tian, Y., Li, Y., Shi, L.: Detecting fake news by exploring the consistency of multimodal data. Inf. Process. Manage. **58**(5), 102610 (2021)
25. Yu, J., Wang, Z., Vasudevan, V., Yeung, L., Seyedhosseini, M., Wu, Y.: CoCa: contrastive captioners are image-text foundation models. arXiv:2205.01917 (2022)
26. Zhang, X., Dadkhah, S., Weismann, A.G., Kanaani, M.A., Ghorbani, A.A.: Multimodal fake news analysis based on image-text similarity. IEEE Trans. Comput. Soc. Syst., pp. 1–14 (2023)

# ChatGPT as a Commenter to the News: Can LLMs Generate Human-Like Opinions?

Rayden Tseng, Suzan Verberne$^{(\boxtimes)}$ ⓘ, and Peter van der Putten ⓘ

LIACS, Leiden University, Leiden, The Netherlands
{s.verberne,p.w.h.van.der.putten}@liacs.leidenuniv.nl

**Abstract.** ChatGPT, GPT-3.5, and other large language models (LLMs) have drawn significant attention since their release, and the abilities of these models have been investigated for a wide variety of tasks. In this research we investigate to what extent GPT-3.5 can generate human-like comments on Dutch news articles. We define human likeness as 'not distinguishable from human comments', approximated by the difficulty of automatic classification between human and GPT comments. We analyze human likeness across multiple prompting techniques. In particular, we utilize zero-shot, few-shot and context prompts, for two generated personas. We found that our fine-tuned BERT models can easily distinguish human-written comments from GPT-3.5 generated comments, with none of the used prompting methods performing noticeably better. We further analyzed that human comments consistently showed higher lexical diversity than GPT-generated comments. This indicates that although generative LLMs can generate fluent text, their capability to create human-like opinionated comments is still limited.

**Keywords:** Large language models · opinion generation · generative content detection

## 1 Introduction

Since the public availability of GPT-3.5, its capabilities have been researched for a wide range of tasks [2]. It has shown remarkable performance in text summarization [17], machine translation [6] and classification, such as hate speech detection [3] and sentiment analysis [16]. GPT-2 has previously been used for generating fake product reviews [1,10], and GPT-3.5 to generate Tweets [14]. To our knowledge, there is no research into to what extent GPT-3.5 can generate human-like opinions on news articles.

In this paper, we present a small-scale study investigating the capability of GPT-3.5 to produce opinionated text, and more specifically, comments on news articles. For the purpose of this study, we loosely define 'human-like' as 'not distinguishable or difficult to distinguish from human'. We crawled human comments from a Dutch newspaper website, and generated opinions by prompting GPT with

D. Ceolin et al. (Eds.): MISDOOM 2023, LNCS 14397, pp. 160–174, 2023.
https://doi.org/10.1007/978-3-031-47896-3_12

two different generated personas. We supplied just the title or additional context from the article, and in zero-shot and few-shot settings. Subsequently, we analyze to what extent the GPT-3.5 generated comments can be distinguished from human comments, using a fine-tuned Dutch BERT model. As additional analysis, we use other metrics to investigate the differences between the outputs, such as type-token ratio and qualitative analysis of misclassifications with SHAP.

## 2   Related Work

### 2.1   Large Language Models and GPT-3.5

Large Language Models are Transformer-based language models, which enables them to capture contextual dependencies and generate human-like text. It was shown that when models with a large amount of parameters are trained on large amounts of text, they can solve problems for a wide range of tasks. The Generative Pre-trained Transformer 3.5 (GPT-3.5) from OpenAI has 175 billion parameters, and is trained on approximately 499 billion tokens [2]. Its companion GPT-4 model is even more powerful, even though architectural details have not been made public. The architecture of GPT is decoder-only, which allows for open-ended generation. Unlike encoder-decoder architectures, the output of decoder-only models is less scoped by the input, which enlarges the space of acceptable output generations and therefore increases its potential for more diverse and creative responses [7]. Without any fine-tuning or gradient updates, it has shown strong performance in many NLP tasks on many datasets.

### 2.2   BERT

In 2019, Devlin et al. introduced a Transformer-based language model called BERT, which stands for Bidirectional Encoder Representations from Transformers [5]. In contrast to GPT, the BERT model is a transformer *encoder*, without a decoder component. BERT's pre-training makes use of a Masked Language Modeling (MLM) objective. It randomly masks some tokens from the input, after which its objective is to predict the original token based on the context. in addition, it uses Next Sentence Prediction (NSP), which, given two sentences, determines whether the second sentence follows the first. MLM and NSP help BERT understand context across different sentences. BERT models can be fine-tuned for specific tasks, creating new state-of-the-art models for supervised learning tasks.

RobBERT is a large pre-trained general Dutch language model that can be fine-tuned on a given dataset to perform a wide range of NLP tasks [4]. It uses a RoBERTa architecture and pre-training with a Dutch tokenizer. RoBERTa, a Robustly Optimized BERT Pre-training Approach has some modified key hyperparameters, such as removing the NSP objective in pre-training, having much larger batches and training on longer sequences [8]. It has shown state-of-the-art results for various tasks, especially compared to other models when applied to smaller datasets [4]. In this research, we use the Dutch RobBERT model to fine-tune for our specific use case, classifying comments as GPT- or human-generated.

## 2.3   Previous Research on GPT-3.5's Capabilities

Since the public release of GPT-3.5 its capabilities have been researched extensively. For summarization, it was shown that its extractive summarization performance is inferior compared to existing methods [17], but other research showed that GPT models have competitive translation performance for high-resource languages, while still being limited for low-resource languages [6]. In addition to its capabilities to produce text, GPT has also been evaluated for its ability to classify. Chiu et al. used zero-shot and few-shot prompting techniques to investigate whether GPT-3 can identify sexist or racist text. They found an average zero-shot accuracy between 55% and 67%, whereas few-shot learning achieved an accuracy that can be as high as 85% [3]. Another study has shown that Chat-GPT exhibits impressive zero-shot performance in sentiment classification tasks and can rival a fine-tuned BERT model. Few-shot learning further enhances its performance, even surpassing fine-tuned BERT models in some cases [16].

In terms of language generation in online media, GPT-3 has also been evaluated on whether it could write human-like content on social media through the form of tweets. In this research, human participants were asked to determine whether tweets were human-written or machine-generated. This has shown that GPT-3, in comparison with humans, can produce accurate (dis)information that is easier to understand and that humans could not distinguish whether tweets were generated or written by humans [14]. A task even closer to our use case is the generation of fake product reviews, and it was demonstrated that GPT-2 can already be used to generate such reviews, but also that in some cases classifiers could be built to detect these reviews more successfully than humans [1,10].

## 3   Methods

In this paper, we address the capabilities of GPT-3.5 for producing opinionated comments on news articles. We evaluate this by fine-tuning a BERT model on the task of classifying comments as either Human- or GPT-generated. In this section, we describe the methods that were used for this research. This includes (1) collecting news articles and human comments from an online platform; (2) generating opinions with GPT-3.5 using two generated personas, zero-shot and few-shot settings, and using just the article title or also the introduction as context in the prompt; (3) assessing the quality of the output by evaluating how well a fine-tuned Dutch-based BERT model is able to detect generated opinions. All code is written in Python.

### 3.1   Data Collection

In order to compare human to artificial opinions, we collect opinions on news articles from *NU.nl*, a major online news channel in the Netherlands, with a politically centrist and reporting oriented positioning. It features an integrated comment system *NUjij*. We collected a total of ten articles, each containing at least a hundred comments. The articles and their corresponding numbers of

**Table 1.** Titles of articles with number of comments and publication dates

| Number | Title | Opinions | Date |
|---|---|---|---|
| 1 | Avondklok besproken als 'serieuze optie'. maar invoering nog niet aan de orde | 103 | 12/01/2021 |
| 2 | Burgemeester Parijs: 'Geen Russische atleten op Spelen zolang oorlog woedt' | 143 | 03/02/2023 |
| 3 | EU adviseert QR-code tot 9 maanden na laatste prik te laten gelden voor reizen | 101 | 25/11/2021 |
| 4 | Feyenoord-aanvoerder Kökçü weigert vanwege religie regenboogband te dragen | 194 | 16/10/2022 |
| 5 | Jumbo stopt per direct met WK-reclamespot na storm van kritiek | 144 | 02/11/2022 |
| 6 | Minister rekent op 1.400 euro vergoeding voor studenten uit 'pechgeneratie' | 104 | 25/03/2022 |
| 7 | Rusland valt Oekraïne aan. oorlog breekt uit | 105 | 24/02/2022 |
| 8 | Rutte biedt excuses aan voor slavernijverleden: 'Aan alle nazaten tot hier en nu' | 160 | 19/12/2022 |
| 9 | Studentenorganisaties willen tijdelijke rem op komst internationale studenten | 122 | 02/02/2023 |
| 10 | Talpa wist volgens BOOS mogelijk al veel langer van misstanden bij The Voice | 110 | 25/08/2022 |

comments (opinions) are shown in Table 1. The main requirement of an appropriate article was that it discussed a topic on which opinions generally differ. We selected articles with at least 100 comments. Since an account was required to access the comments, each HTML page needed to be downloaded manually. For this research, the Chrome extension Save Page WE was used after having registered to the platform.[1]

**Human Opinions.** Once the articles had been downloaded and stored in the same directory, we parsed the HTML content to extract the article text and comments. Our implementation only included parent comments since sub-comments might deviate from the initial topic. We found that the comments were contained in the *coral-comment-content* class and the text in the *textblock paragraph* class. Firstly, using the BeautifulSoup[2] library, the text was extracted and secondly the comments. Subsequently, both the text and comments were individually written to files in newly created directories. It appeared that the comments inside the HTML pages had an inconsistent structure, resulting in varying outcomes during scraping. While some articles were scraped without any issues, others showed HTML tags or unusual punctuation. This includes unusual `<br>`, `<br/>`, `<div>` or `<p>` tags for no apparent reason, alongside inconsistent use of ' or ". Since there was no other way to resolve this, all inconsistencies had to be corrected manually. All ten articles had between 100 and 200 comments. Since GPT-3.5's pre-training data is from before September 2021, an important remark here is that all articles except for article 1 were published after this date.

## 3.2 Generating Opinions with GPT-3.5

After correctly parsing the text and opinions of the articles, opinions were generated. Using the *gpt-3.5-turbo* model, we were able to take advantage of a longer input context and incorporate human responses into the conversation as examples, whereas earlier models like *text-davinci-003* could not. Since each article

---

[1] https://chrome.google.com/webstore/detail/save-page-we/
dhhpefjklgkmgeafimnjhojgjamoafof.

[2] https://www.crummy.com/software/BeautifulSoup/bs4/doc/.

contains at least 100 human opinions, the goal was to generate 100 artificial opinions per article.

**Prompts and Personas.** First of all, prompts had to be constructed. By providing the title of the article in the prompt, we first ran a set of test prompts to explore the quality of the responses of the model. It became evident that the model mostly gave formal, boring and factual perspectives on the subject.

To generate more opinionated and human-like content, we used GPT-3.5 to generate personas, such that subsequently we could generate opinions through a specific perspective, expecting more personalization in the opinions. Two random personas were generated in advance and provided in this new contextual model. Obviously, two is a limited number of personas, but we wanted to explore the potential of persona-based opinion generation, and also see whether both the output as well as the detection would vary across personas.

This was accomplished by appending the personas to the `system role`, such that the model knew how to 'behave'. Every time the experiments were run, we prompted GPT-3.5 to generate these random personas. We ultimately came up with the following prompt: `Generate a persona. Use three sentences. Start with 'You are'`. This prompt was constructed based on several criteria. Firstly, it was necessary to be concise and easily be easily understood. Secondly, since it would be used in other prompts to experiment with other settings, the output had to start with '`You are`'. Other options such as providing more information about what kind of persona it had to generate were also taken into consideration. We tried to provide the information that this persona likes to read an online news platform. However, after evaluating this, it became evident that it resulted in a more general persona based on the fact that it likes to read, rather than characteristics which would influence its opinion. It was nevertheless important to provide this information. We appended '`You comment on an online newsplatform`' to the output manually. At last, we could pass this information to the other settings by appending the persona to the `role` contents. In Sect. 4, these personas are referred to as 1 and 2 or P1 and P2.

Another observation after analyzing the test completions was that it consisted of opinions that were significantly shorter in length than human opinions. To address this, we provided an approximate length for each opinion in the prompt, calculated for each individual article. We used the average length of human comments on the article for determining the comment length. In total, we investigated four settings, described below.

**Zero-Shot.** The first setting was designed to utilize zero-shot learning. Recent work has shown that large language models exhibit the ability to perform reasonable zero-shot generalization to new tasks [11]. In this case of generating human-like perspectives, the model was solely prompted to generate opinions, with the title of the article as additional information. With this approach, we could examine GPT's creativity to the fullest. However, depending on the topic of the article, the model generally has the least amount of context with this prompt. This led to the following prompt:

```
Give a list of 100 varied and critical opinions on the
following news article: 'w', where each opinion has an
approximate length of 'x' words.
```

Here, w refers to the title of article and x to the approximate length of the comment. In Sect. 4, the zero-shot prompt is referred to as ZS.

**Few-Shot.** In the second setting, a few examples of human opinions were provided. The aim was to give the model more context and guidance to generate opinions similarly. Due to the limitations discussed in Sect. 3.2, only four examples are provided. Assuming the relevance is high, the comments with the most likes were selected. This method was most likely to perform best. It first of all learned directly from real examples and therefore might adapt its style and tone more accurately. This setting resulted in the following prompt:

```
Give a list of 100 varied and critical opinions on the
following news article: 'w', where each opinion has an
approximate length of 'x' words. Here are four examples: 'y'.
```

In the prompting script, the variable y was replaced by the first four examples of the article. Later on, the few-shot approach is described as FS.

**Context.** In the third setting the experiments were run with is additional context. In addition to the zero-shot prompt, the introduction of the article was provided. The model, therefore, had more context to work with. This method may be beneficial since GPT-3.5 can produce more in-depth opinions, whereas the zero-shot prompt or few-shot can not. A potential downfall is that the introduction might not always contain any relevant or additional information. This resulted in the final prompt:

```
Give a list of 100 varied and crital opinions on the following
news article: 'w', where each opinion has an approximate length
of 'x' words. This is the introduction of the article: 'z'.
```

The z variable was substituted by the introduction of the corresponding article. The context prompt is later described as CL. We utilized ten different articles and three different prompting techniques, each with two different personas. Therefore, the number of total prompts is equal to 60 ($10 \times 3 \times 2$).

**Limitations.** In practice however, there were some limitations. Language models read text in chunks called tokens. Tokenization is the process of splitting text into smaller units called tokens, which is a fundamental preprocessing step for almost all NLP tasks [13]. Due to a maximum request of 4,096 tokens, which includes both the prompt and completion, the model would stop generating when that limit was reached. This, in particular for the few-shot and context prompt, resulted in unfinished completions. This limitation was also the reason we could not provide more examples or even the entire article in the prompt, which in theory would perform better. We came up with a solution by reducing the request of opinions to 25 (and 20 for the few-shot setting), such that the request was more likely to stay within the limit and increasing the number of requests per prompt to 4 (5 for few-shot).

### 3.3    Evaluation Through Classification

After we successfully prompted GPT-3.5, with 6 modes and ten articles we ideally would have 6000 generated opinions. To best evaluate the difference between
the output of the prompts, different classification models were built. The data
first needed to be correctly formatted such that the BERT model could process it. A small Python script was written, which iterates over all the outputs
and then formats them to a readable database format. For this implementation,
the .csv file format was chosen. An important remark here is that each record
consists of a text *comment* and a *human* column, indicating the boolean value
for Human- (1) or AI-generated (0). The data must be split into train and test
sets. We split the data on article level, keeping all comments to the same article
together in one partition. We processed the data in such a way, that we could
examine an individual setting with every possible article as a test set. This in
total, resulted in 120 files, where each file was either a train or test set, given
a setting and article. Due to the lack of computational power available, the
classification phase is performed using Google Colab.

**Fine-Tuning.** We analyze the human likeness of the generated comments by
classifying them. We fine-tuned *robbert-v2-dutch-base*, which is the state-of-the-
art Dutch BERT model [4]. The goal of the models was to predict whether a given
opinion is human-generated or GPT-3.5-generated. To ensure the models were
properly trained, as mentioned earlier, we fine-tuned them via 10-fold cross-
validation. Here for each fold, we trained the model on the other 9 of the 10
article sets and evaluated its performance on the remaining set. In this research,
10 models were trained for each setting, rather than a single model. We made
this choice to prevent the model from overfitting the training data and to ensure
it could generalize well to unseen data.

To fine-tune the BERT model, several steps had to be taken. First, the generated train and test sets needed to be imported. In order for the model to read
the input, the input text needed to be tokenized using the tokenizer from the
pre-trained model. Since we did not use an existing dataset from the Hugging-
Face library, our tokenized data had to be converted to a suitable *Dataset* object,
in order for the trainer to run without errors.

Before training the model, the *TrainingArguments* needed to be initialized.
TrainingArguments are a subset of arguments that relate to the training process.
For this analysis, we used the default values provided by the HuggingFace tuto-
rial.[3] Specifically, the learning rate at which the model adapts its parameters
while training was set to $2 \times 10^{-5}$ and the batch size per training core to 8.
The weight decay was set to 0.01, while the evaluation and save strategies were
configured to epoch. The number of training epochs was set to 3.

To evaluate the model, we used the F1 score, recall and precision as metrics.
These methods can be imported via the Python *evaluate* library. In addition to
these metrics, we also created a confusion matrix.

---

[3] https://huggingface.co/docs/transformers/training.

# 4   Results

The results of the research are discussed in this section. It contains an overview of the output of the prompts and the metrics of the fine-tuned models. Also, we analyze the lexical diversity of the output discuss two examples qualitatively.

## 4.1   Output

Before utilizing all prompts, the two personas were generated, which resulted in the following two completions (translated to English):

```
    You are a middle-aged man, married and father of two children.
You have worked as an accountant at a large company for 20 years
and you enjoy playing tennis in your spare time. You comment on an
online news platform.
```

and

```
    You are a 32-year-old marketing executive who loves
socialising and travelling. You have a busy job, but find it
important to spend time with family and friends. In your spare
time, you like to be outdoors and do running and yoga. You have a
passion for cooking and are always trying out new recipes. You
comment on an online news platform.
```

Ideally, the methods described in Sect. 3.2 would result in 100 comments per setting per article. In practice, a total of 5855 generated comments were generated, where a few prompts did not result in the full completion due to the limitations. As a consequence, balanced datasets could not be generated in some cases. We wanted to achieve this anyway, so in some cases, we had to generate the remaining responses manually, by prompting GPT-3.5 separately from the script. In Table 2, the article, setting and number of generated comments are shown. We also released all generated comments on github.[4]

On preliminary manual analysis of the completions, a few things immediately stood out. Firstly, it became evident that each prompt did not complete in a single run. Each prompt, despite being the same, consisted of multiple requests, resulting in multiple batches. This was evident as there was less variation within one batch than between different batches. Batches showed clear differences in overall writing style. It appears that the output relies on earlier produced tokens in the same request. A second preliminary observation we made was the nature of the generated comments. While these could be classified as opinions, they exhibited mostly factual text or reasoned arguments rather than expressing emotional viewpoints, even having utilized the few-shot prompt. Besides, the comments looked rather formal, as opposed to the human-written comments which often contained more informal language and slang.

## 4.2   Classification Results

Our main results are presented in Table 3. Each row contains a single setting. The columns represent the average and standard deviation of metrics of all the

---

[4] https://github.com/raydentseng/generated_opinions.

**Table 2.** Amount of generated comments per setting. A setting consists of a prompt and a generated persona. ZS refers to the zero-shot prompt, FS to few-shot and CL to the context prompt. For instance, FS-2 indicates few-shot with persona 2.

| Article | ZS-1 | FS-1 | CL-1 | ZS-2 | FS-2 | CL-2 | Total |
|---|---|---|---|---|---|---|---|
| 1 | 100 | 92 | 100 | 100 | 73 | 100 | 565 |
| 2 | 100 | 95 | 100 | 100 | 100 | 100 | 595 |
| 3 | 100 | 71 | 100 | 100 | 75 | 100 | 546 |
| 4 | 100 | 73 | 100 | 100 | 100 | 100 | 573 |
| 5 | 100 | 88 | 100 | 100 | 100 | 100 | 588 |
| 6 | 100 | 100 | 100 | 100 | 100 | 100 | 600 |
| 7 | 100 | 100 | 100 | 100 | 88 | 100 | 588 |
| 8 | 100 | 100 | 100 | 100 | 100 | 100 | 600 |
| 9 | 100 | 100 | 100 | 100 | 100 | 100 | 600 |
| 10 | 100 | 100 | 100 | 100 | 100 | 100 | 600 |
| Total | 1000 | 919 | 1000 | 1000 | 936 | 1000 | 5855 |

**Table 3.** Results per setting for both classes Human and GPT-3.5. Lower scores mean that classification was more difficult, meaning that the GPT-generated comments were more human-like.

| Setting | F1 | GPT-3.5 | | Human | |
|---|---|---|---|---|---|
| | | Precision | Recall | Precision | Recall |
| ZS-1 | **0.912 ± 0.047** | 0.926 ± 0.055 | 0.924 ± 0.084 | 0.931 ± 0.065 | 0.912 ± 0.065 |
| FS-1 | 0.936 ± 0.032 | 0.943 ± 0.039 | 0.914 ± 0.082 | 0.939 ± 0.065 | 0.940 ± 0.044 |
| CL-1 | 0.925 ± 0.043 | 0.932 ± 0.046 | 0.922 ± 0.103 | 0.932 ± 0.080 | 0.928 ± 0.056 |
| ZS-2 | 0.923 ± 0.024 | 0.937 ± 0.041 | 0.918 ± 0.039 | **0.913 ± 0.038** | 0.936 ± 0.045 |
| FS-2 | 0.934 ± 0.027 | 0.962 ± 0.027 | **0.896 ± 0.074** | 0.915 ± 0.056 | 0.962 ± 0.030 |
| CL-2 | 0.920 ± 0.034 | **0.888 ± 0.047** | 0.966 ± 0.071 | 0.969 ± 0.062 | **0.873 ± 0.090** |

fine-tuned models. All values in Table 3 are relatively high. Initially, this seems positive. However, we are most interested in the lowest scores, since it reveals the cases where the model encountered the most challenges in distinguishing human-written comments from machine-generated comments. Lower values therefore indicate better performance of that setting. In terms of the F1-score, which represents the overall performance of the model, there is little difference, with the ZS-1 setting having the lowest of 91.2%. However, it does not have the lowest precision and recall of both classes, and the differences to other settings are small.

In Table 4, the metrics are shown per article. Just like in Table 3, all values are close to each other. The F1 scores are again all around 90%. Overall, models which used article 1 as test set resulted in the lowest F1 score of 89.2%. This is interesting because article 1 is the only article that was published before the pre-training date of GPT-3.5. In other words, the article is the only topic (Covid regulations in the Netherlands) that GPT-3.5 likely has covered in its pre-training data.

**Table 4.** Metrics per article. Lower scores mean that classification was more difficult, meaning that the GPT-generated comments were more human-like.

| Article | F1 | GPT-3.5 | | Human | |
|---|---|---|---|---|---|
| | | Precision | Recall | Precision | Recall |
| 1 | **0.892 ± 0.029** | 0.971 ± 0.008 | **0.812 ± 0.085** | **0.843 ± 0.061** | 0.975 ± 0.008 |
| 2 | 0.928 ± 0.008 | 0.906 ± 0.028 | 0.958 ± 0.025 | 0.957 ± 0.024 | 0.898 ± 0.036 |
| 3 | 0.931 ± 0.023 | 0.947 ± 0.019 | 0.913 ± 0.050 | 0.919 ± 0.044 | 0.948 ± 0.019 |
| 4 | 0.945 ± 0.017 | 0.930 ± 0.031 | 0.965 ± 0.008 | 0.963 ± 0.010 | 0.925 ± 0.037 |
| 5 | 0.913 ± 0.028 | 0.954 ± 0.019 | 0.870 ± 0.083 | 0.887 ± 0.066 | 0.957 ± 0.019 |
| 6 | 0.937 ± 0.021 | 0.979 ± 0.016 | 0.893 ± 0.067 | 0.907 ± 0.055 | 0.980 ± 0.017 |
| 7 | 0.926 ± 0.014 | 0.886 ± 0.026 | 0.982 ± 0.024 | 0.981 ± 0.024 | 0.872 ± 0.034 |
| 8 | 0.927 ± 0.019 | 0.910 ± 0.037 | 0.952 ± 0.028 | 0.951 ± 0.028 | 0.903 ± 0.043 |
| 9 | 0.914 ± 0.010 | **0.867 ± 0.028** | 0.980 ± 0.017 | 0.978 ± 0.018 | **0.848 ± 0.038** |
| 10 | 0.948 ± 0.013 | 0.961 ± 0.035 | 0.938 ± 0.045 | 0.943 ± 0.0395 | 0.958 ± 0.039 |

### 4.3 Lexical Diversity

Another quantitative method to analyze the different outputs is the *Type-Token Ratio* (TTR). TTR is the ratio calculated by dividing the types ($t$), which are the unique words occurring in a text, by its tokens ($n$), the total number of words. This, therefore, measures the lexical diversity, given multiple texts. After some preliminary observations of the generated output, we noticed that it seemed that GPT-3.5 used a lot of the same words. By utilizing the LexicalRichness[5] Python package [12], the lexical variety between human comments and GPT-3.5 generated comments can be quantitatively measured. Since not all generated comments equalled as many tokens as human comments and longer texts tend to have higher TTR values because they have more opportunities for unique words to occur, we used the *Corrected Type-Token Ratio* (CTTR) [15] metric. CTTR normalizes the TTR by using the square root, providing a more accurate measure by considering the potential effect of the text length, and is calculated as $\frac{t}{\sqrt{2n}}$, where $t$ is the number of unique terms in a text and $n$ is the total number of tokens. We computed the CTTR value over the total text of concatenated comments. In Table 5, the CTTR of all human and generated comments are shown. Since the number of human comments differs significantly per article, the first 100 are taken into account. The highest calculated GPT-3.5 CTTR per article is boldfaced. It appears the human text consistently has a higher value, compared to all the different settings. None of the settings matches the value of the human CTTR. From all generated completions, the few-shot completion of article 5 had the highest calculated CTTR value.

### 4.4 Qualitative Analysis

Aside from the quantitative analysis, we can also analyze the output qualitatively. Since our fine-tuned model classified 0 as *AI* (*GPT-3.5*) and 1 as *Human*,

---

[5] https://github.com/lsys/lexicalrichness.

**Table 5.** CTTR values per article. Boldface indicates the value for the GPT-3.5 model that is closest to the Human value for the article.

| Article | Human | ZS-1 | FS-1 | CL-2 | ZS-2 | FS-2 | CL-2 |
|---|---|---|---|---|---|---|---|
| 1 | 14.422 | 8.892 | 8.707 | 9.104 | 8.664 | **9.794** | 9.218 |
| 2 | 13.043 | **9.103** | 8.559 | 7.531 | 7.569 | 8.650 | 7.940 |
| 3 | 13.192 | 9.062 | 9.893 | **9.833** | 9.442 | 8.973 | 9.196 |
| 4 | 10.581 | 7.778 | 8.697 | **8.970** | 8.493 | 7.822 | 8.198 |
| 5 | 12.457 | 9.018 | 9.503 | 8.302 | 8.302 | **10.191** | 9.641 |
| 6 | 13.657 | 8.126 | 9.334 | 7.458 | 8.671 | **10.027** | 7.751 |
| 7 | 14.436 | 9.043 | **9.056** | 8.620 | 8.370 | 8.247 | 7.837 |
| 8 | 12.963 | 7.831 | 7.878 | 7.768 | 7.221 | **8.674** | 6.738 |
| 9 | 13.552 | 9.296 | 8.643 | 7.341 | **9.334** | 8.133 | 6.862 |
| 10 | 13.440 | 6.330 | 7.639 | 7.318 | 7.410 | **8.093** | 6.819 |

a false positive is considered a GPT-3.5-written comment classified as a human. A false negative is a human-written comment which got classified as GPT-3.5. The analysis is done using SHAP [9]. SHAP is a game theoretic approach to explain the output of any machine learning model.[6] While any instance can be analyzed, in this section we consider two misclassified instances, differing in setting and type of misclassification.

**False Positive.** The first example is a comment on article 1 generated by zero-shot GPT-3.5 as persona 1. In Fig. 1, the instance is visualized with SHAP. The model predicted that this particular instance was human-written, but in fact, was generated by GPT-3.5. Especially the first two sentences immediately stand out. The content seems rather personal and sentimental, which is most likely to cause the incorrect classification. This is the perfect example of the model utilizing the given persona, which was the initial intention of providing one. In the original Dutch output it also stood out that GPT-3.5 made a spelling mistake by generating `tenniser` instead of `tennisser`.

As we have selected the assigned human class at the top, the contribution of each token to the human class is shown. The individual contribution of a token is determined by calculating the difference between the total classification and the classification with a single token masked. Tokens in red suggest a positive contribution to the selected class, while tokens in blue suggest a negative contribution. It is evident that tokens in the first two sentences such as `fanatieke`, `het seizoen al voor me.` and `eigen` positively contribute to the classification. The third sentence, which has a rather formal tone, barely contributes positively to the classification. This is in line with our earlier observation. Our model does not associate tokens such as `als`, `tennis`, `sport`, `sector` and `?` with a human-written comment, suggesting these are more GPT-3.5 like.

---

[6] https://shap.readthedocs.io/en/latest/.

**Fig. 1.** False positive: a GPT-generated comment (ZS-1) that was classified as human. *"As an avid tennis player, I can already see the end of the season ahead of me. This is bad news not only for my own enjoyment, but also for the sports club where I play. Why are we hitting the sports and cultural sector so hard?"*

**Fig. 2.** False negative: a human comment on article 7 that was classified as GPT-3.5 (CL-2) *"Sad that as a world, we are slipping away like this. Not even capable of dialogue. I am genuinely worried about the future of my children."*

**False Negative.** A false negative in our case is a human-written comment on article 7 classified as GPT-3.5. In Fig. 2, the SHAP values for this instance are shown. It is noticeable that the comment has a rather formal structure. Rather than a strong opinion accompanied by personal motivation, the comment presents a rather impersonal perspective through factual statements. The last sentence exhibits the same personal characteristics of P1, which the model potentially associates with GPT-3.5-like opinions. The human class is again selected, meaning that in this scenario all blue tokens contribute positively and all red tokens negatively to the AI class. The first thing that stands out is that almost every token contributes positively to the AI class. It is remarkable that the first word is split into two tokens, which individually do not have a meaning. The token `riest` has the strongest negative contribution of the entire comment. The last sentence has GPT-3.5-like characteristics: Apart from the token `echt`, it strongly contributes to the AI classification.

## 5  Discussion

The results of the fine-tuned BERT models were all very high. This tells us the capabilities of GPT-3.5 are quite limited. Our findings do not suggest that a specific prompting technique (zero-shot, few-shot, or context) results in more human-like outputs. This suggests that capturing the complexity of human-natured comments is still a challenging task for GPT-3.5. The F1 scores are not different enough to make statements about which setting can best reproduce human opinions on news articles. We observe that regardless of the specific prompt, GPT-3.5 generally outputs comments which had a rather factual and boring tone of style. We tried to counter this by providing a persona, but this had little to no effect. This was probably because the generated personas were narrowly described and therefore the model had a limited idea about its beliefs and motivations, especially on multiple topics. In terms of future work, it will be interesting to experiment with larger amounts of personas, and evaluate the impact compared to not using personas at all.

As we observed earlier that GPT-3.5 generated comments seemed rather formal and often had the same structure, we analyzed the lexical diversity by calculating the CTTR values. We found that human opinions consistently exhibited higher CTTR values, meaning that the ratio of unique words to total words was greater than that of machine-generated comments. We saw that few-shot learning resulted in the highest lexical diversity, followed by zero-shot completions. It makes sense that the few-shot setting has the highest value since it directly learns from real-world instances and therefore copies such words more easily. Another finding is that providing the introduction of the article in the prompt reduces the variety of words the model used. However, the difference in diversity among the output of the prompts was much smaller than the difference between human-written or machine-generated comments.

We encountered several limitations during our research. As mentioned in Sect. 3.2 the API, in fact, had some flaws. On some days, a single completion would take much longer than usual or even not even be generated due to overloaded servers. Another issue we had was the token per request limit, not allowing a prompt to run successfully at once. As mentioned earlier, we managed to counter this by catching possible errors in our script. At first, this does not seem like a major issue. However, we found differences in the outputs of the prompt. While being prompted the same, the output differed between requests due to the probabilistic behaviour of the generative model. Within one request batch, the style was consistent though, e.g. the adding of quotation marks or starting every comment with the same words.

## 6   Conclusion

The goal of this research was to investigate to what extent GPT-3.5 can generate human-like comments on Dutch news articles and how to best generate these. We answered this question by experimenting with multiple prompting techniques, after which we could analyze the different outputs. In particular, the zero-shot, few-shot and context prompts were utilized, corresponding with a generated persona. We fine-tuned the pre-trained RobBERT-v2 model to classify whether unlabeled comments were human-written or generated by GPT-3.5.

While in previous research zero-shot and few-shot learning had shown remarkable performances, it does not so in our case. We found that the BERT models we fine-tuned were able to achieve high classification scores. We can conclude that GPT-3.5 is still limited in generating human-like comments on Dutch news articles, regardless of which prompting setting. It suggests that capturing the complexity of human-nature comments, even with real examples, is still a challenging task.

One of the findings from our analysis is that human-written comments generally have a much higher lexical diversity than GPT-3.5-generated comments. Although the differences are small, few-shot prompts averaged the highest lexical diversity but still lower than human comments. The manual analysis of individual misclassifications led to additional insights that GPT-3.5 very often tends to generate comments in a rather formal and factual style and less opinionated than humans.

During our research, OpenAI publicly announced GPT-4.[7] This may be an advantage in future studies on opinionated text generation. Instead of the current limit of 4,096 tokens, GPT-4 is capable of handling 25,000 tokens per request. This is a major improvement and can be used to run prompts at once, instead of running them in batches. Apart from GPT-4, we encourage follow-up research with open-source LLMs such as BLOOM. Secondly, it can be used to provide more context such as the entire article in the prompt, which would possibly lead to more in-depth comments. At last, a lot more human-written examples can be provided in the prompt, which may positively influence the human-likeness of the output. Other potential further research direction is the investigation of to what extent the pre-training date of GPT-3.5 influences its performance, experimenting with subjects from different time periods before and after this date.

# References

1. Adelani, D.I., Mai, H., Fang, F., Nguyen, H.H. Yamagishi, J., Echizen, I.: Generating sentiment-preserving fake online reviews using neural language models and their human- and machine-based detection. In: Advanced Information Networking and Applications, pp. 1341–1354 (2020)
2. Brown, T., et al.: Language models are few-shot learners. In: Advances in Neural Information Processing Systems, vol. 33, pp. 1877–1901 (2020)
3. Chiu, K.-L., Collins, A., Alexander, R.: Detecting hate speech with GPT-3. arXiv preprint arXiv:2103.12407 (2021)
4. Delobelle, P., Winters, T., Berendt, B.: RobBERT: a Dutch RoBERTa-based language model. In: Findings of the Association for Computational Linguistics: EMNLP 2020, pp. 3255–3265. Association for Computational Linguistics, November 2020
5. Devlin, J., Chang, M.-W., Lee, K., Toutanova, K.: BERT: pre-training of deep bidirectional transformers for language understanding. In: Proceedings of the 2019 Conference of the North American Chapter of the Association for Computational Linguistics: Human Language Technologies, Volume 1 (Long and Short Papers), pp. 4171–4186 (2019)
6. Hendy, A.: How good are GPT models at machine translation? A comprehensive evaluation. arXiv preprint arXiv:2302.09210 (2023)

---

[7] https://openai.com/gpt-4.

7.  Holtzman, A., Buys, J., Du, L., Forbes, M., Choi, Y.: The curious case of neural text degeneration. In: International Conference on Learning Representations (2020)
8.  Liu, Y., et al.: RoBERTa: a robustly optimized BERT pretraining approach (2019)
9.  Lundberg, S.M., Lee, S.-I.: A unified approach to interpreting model predictions. In: Advances in Neural Information Processing Systems, vol. 30 (2017)
10. Salminen, J., Kandpal, C., Kamel, A.M., Jung, S.G., Jansen, B.J.: Creating and detecting fake reviews of online products. J. Retail. Consum. Serv. **64**, 102771 (2022)
11. Sanh, V., et al.: Multitask prompted training enables zero-shot task generalization. In: The Tenth International Conference on Learning Representations, ICLR 2022, Virtual Event, 25–29 April 2022 (2022)
12. Shen, L.: LexicalRichness: a small module to compute textual lexical richness (2022)
13. Song, X., Salcianu, A., Song, Y., Dopson, D., Zhou, D.: Fast WordPiece tokenization. In: Proceedings of the 2021 Conference on Empirical Methods in Natural Language Processing, Punta Cana, Dominican Republic, pp. 2089–2103. Association for Computational Linguistics, November 2021
14. Spitale, G., Biller-Andorno, N., Germani, F.: AI model GPT-3 (dis)informs us better than humans. Sci. Adv. **9**(26), eadh1850 (2023)
15. Torruella, J., Capsada, R.: Lexical statistics and tipological structures: a measure of lexical richness. Procedia. Soc. Behav. Sci. **95**, 447–454 (2013)
16. Wang, Z., Xie, Q., Ding, Z., Feng, Y., Xia, R.: Is ChatGPT a good sentiment analyzer? A preliminary study. arXiv preprint arXiv:2304.04339 (2023)
17. Zhang, H., Liu, X., Zhang, J.: Extractive summarization via ChatGPT for faithful summary generation. arXiv preprint arXiv:2304.04193 (2023)

# Is Foreign Language News More or Less Credible Than Native Language News? Examining the Foreign Language Effect on Credibility Perceptions

Magdalena Wischnewski[1]([✉]) [iD] and Anna Wermter[2]

[1] Research Center for Trustworthy Data Science and Security, Dortmund, Germany
magdalena.wischnewski@tu-dortmund.de
[2] University of Duisburg-Essen, Duisburg, Germany

**Abstract.** In this study, we examine whether perceived news credibility is affected when reading news in a foreign language. In addition, we investigate whether a possible effect might be the result of (a) the attenuation of emotional responses in a foreign language and whether (b) it affects individuals depending on their need for cognition. In an online experimental study with N = 134 participants, we presented a news article either in the participants' native language or in a foreign language. Controlling for individuals' need for cognition, we assessed participants' emotional reactions and their perceived credibility. Results indicate that, for participants with a high need for cognition, the native language article was rated as more credible than the foreign language article. Participants with a low need for cognition perceived the foreign news article as similarly credible as compared to the native news. The language condition did not affect emotional responses.

**Keywords:** news credibility · foreign language effect · need for cognition · emotions

## 1 Introduction

Among many benefits and promises, online platforms, particularly social media platforms, enable an increasingly internationalized online news ecology, making news easily and instantaneously accessible across borders [3]. With the increased accessibility of and demand for international news, the internationalization of news readerships similarly expands. In Germany in 2020, for example, roughly 10% of the citizens consumed news in English (IfD Allensbach, 2021). Moreover, 54% of Spanish dominant Hispanics in the USA read news in English and Spanish (Pew Research Center, 2012), and roughly 27% Swedish nationals consume transnational news [41]. Especially migrants are likely to consume news in their native language but also in the language of the country they migrated to [1].

D. Ceolin et al. (Eds.): MISDOOM 2023, LNCS 14397, pp. 175–189, 2023.
https://doi.org/10.1007/978-3-031-47896-3_13

While the upsides of increasingly globalized online and social media platforms allow individuals to access and consume (international) news easier and quicker than ever before, one of the downsides is the amplified reach of misleading and false information [14]. Although news fabrication is not a new phenomenon [10], previous research of the last years connects online platforms with the increased dissemination of misinformation [40]. Consequently, individuals are increasingly challenged to decide whether news they encounter are credible or not.

In the light of both an increased international readership and an increased circulation of misinformation, it is important to ask whether reading news in a foreign language affects individuals' credibility perceptions. We argue that, in a first step, it is important to determine whether such an effect exists. In a second step, implications based on the direction of the effect need to be considered. Theoretically, two outcomes are possible: if news in a foreign language is more credible than news in one's native language, this makes consumers more vulnerable to misleading claims. In contrast, if news in a foreign language is less credible, factual information might be perceived as less credible, putting people at risk to discredit facts.

In particular, previous research on the foreign language effect (FLE) suggests that individuals process information differently when information is presented in a foreign language (L2) as compared to their native language (L1). Effects have been found, for example, for moral dilemmas [13] and risky choices [26]. Relying on previous theoretical and empirical insights on credibility perceptions and the foreign language effect, we investigate whether news in a foreign language improves or deters credibility perceptions about news.

## 2    Theoretical Background

### 2.1    Credibility Perceptions of News

Encountering information, individuals commonly assume information to be accurate and credible [20]. Explaining this initial accuracy assumption, previous studies point to higher base rates of true events, suggesting that in everyday life, most events are mundane and accurate [8]. Some research even proposes that individuals must, at least temporarily, accept information as accurate to comprehend the information [20]. However, under which circumstances do individuals reject information as incredible?

Applying dual-processing theories, such as the heuristic-systematic model [12] or the elaboration-likelihood model [38], suggests that two possible routes lead to the rejection of information due to a lack of credibility. First, individuals conclude to reject information based on thoughtful evaluation of its credibility. Thoughtful evaluations require effortful deliberation, which, in turn, requires sufficient cognitive resources and motivation. Second, dual-processing theories suggest that individuals rely on peripheral or heuristic processing strategies to arrive at the rejection of information.

While both routes offer theoretically plausible explanations as to why individuals reject information, empirical results by Metzger and colleagues [33] suggest that, instead of relying on effortful deliberation, individuals commonly employ heuristics to judge the credibility of information on the web (see also, [31]). Several credibility cues have been identified, such as the source credibility [28], content coherence, consensus effects but also compatibility with prior beliefs and expectancy violations concerning the appearance of information such as professionalism or typos [29].

The preference of heuristic strategies over deliberative reasoning strategies has been, on the one hand, associated with a general information overload on the web [28]. In other words, due to the mere quantity of information, it is not feasible for individuals to engage in effortful deliberation whenever they are confronted with a new piece of information. On the other hand, previous research suggests that individuals often behave like cognitive misers, preferring heuristics as mental shortcuts to avoid cognitive efforts [16]. In doing so, heuristic processing can, in some cases, even match the accuracy of deliberate processing [19].

Despite its feasibility which can compete with deliberate processing, in the context of credibility judgements, it was found that people who rely more on heuristic processing were more likely to rate misinformation as accurate [37]. In contrast, Muda et al. [34] found that people who rely more on deliberative processing were more likely to rate accurate information as such. Going beyond correlational evidence, Bago et al. [4] experimentally manipulated the degree to which participants engage in deliberative processing by adding a cognitive load task as well as a time constraint. The authors found that deliberative processing significantly reduced belief in misinformation but did not increase the belief in accurate information.

To conclude, while individuals, by default, generally tend to accept incoming information, such initial credibility judgments are predominantly revoked by effortless, heuristic processing of credibility cues such as the credibility of the sources. However, given enough resources and motivation, individuals can also engage in effortful, deliberative processing to arrive at a credibility judgment. Furthermore, previous research indicates that reliance on deliberative processing can decrease the credibility of misinformation and increase the credibility of accurate information.

However, which factors influence whether an individual engages in heuristic or deliberative processing? In other words, what makes news more or less credible? Especially environments in which factul and false information is circulated, it is important to investigate news credibility questions and factors that affect perceived credibility. While some individual factors (e.g., individual differences in need for cognition), as well as contextual factors (sufficient cognitive resources), have been identified, in the following, we investigate a possible foreign language effect on news credibility perceptions. In doing so, as a starting point, we are mainly interested in the possible effects of a foreign language on factual news.

## 2.2   The Foreign Language Effect

The foreign language effect (FLE) generally refers to differences in judgement and decision making due to the use of a non-native language (L2). In different studies, it has been observed that individuals' decision-making results depend on the language in which information is presented. For example, in three studies, Keysar et al. [26] found that when individuals were presented with information in an L2, decision biases were reduced compared to participants presented with information in their native language (L1). The authors suggest two possible explanations for this decrease of decision biases: increased deliberation and increased emotional distance resulting from L2 reasoning. Moreover, Hadjichristidis and colleagues [22] found that participants judged risks and benefits differently when information was presented in L2. Judgments became less risk-averse, and benefits were judged more pronounced. Testing the causal effect of emotions on the FLE, Hadjichristidis et al. [22] found that emotional responses mediated the effect of a language condition on risk perceptions. In particular, the authors found that displaying information in a foreign language decreased negative affect and increased positive affect. However, similar to Keysar et al. [26], the authors concede that increased deliberation due to L2 reasoning explains the results.

Investigating the increased deliberation hypothesis in more depth, Costa et al. [13] suggest in a theoretical paper that the disfluency of a second language increases overall deliberation. In other words, this disfluency explanation proposes that information in a foreign language signals that a person cannot rely on intuitive, heuristic responses, but that effortful deliberation is needed. Research on disfluency supports this view [2].

While there is empirical and theoretical support for the increased deliberation hypothesis, other studies examine the attenuation of emotion hypothesis in-depth. To that end, Caldwell-Harris [11] found, for example, that reading words in a foreign language elicited less negative affect. Explaining this result, Cladwell-Harris [11] theorizes that the most important factor which connects a language with emotional responses "is the context in which a language is learned and used" (p. 2). Using a language early on in emotional contexts creates strong associative pathways to the emotional regulation system. In contrast, a second language learned in a classroom has less association with the emotional regulation system.

However, both hypotheses, increased deliberation and attenuation of emotional responses, have been challenged. Białek et al. [6] found, for example, that participants' performance decreased when reasoning about logical syllogisms in a second language. The authors suggest that participants were less able to engage in reflective processing when information was presented in L2. In addition, the authors also propose a metacognitive approach to the FLE, arguing that the FLE affects individuals' ability to either detect conflicting signals or stun reliance on intuitions. Similarly, results by Geipel et al. [18] challenge the attenuation of emotion hypothesis. In their experimental study, the authors found no differences in affective responses between two language conditions. Instead, Geipel and colleagues [18] suggest that the FLE results from decreased accessibility of social and moral norms.

Furthermore, some studies found no difference between information presented in L1 or L2. For example, the difference between L1 and L2 presentations were neither found in intertemporal choice paradigms [5], gambling decisions [35], nor for logical reasoning in the cognitive reflection tasks [30]. While both explanations, the attenuation of emotions and increased deliberation as a consequence of foreign language use, are independent of each other, it has been argued that they can, of course, also cooccur [6].

## 2.3  Credibility Perceptions and the FLE

While the above-reported studies predominantly investigate the effects of a foreign language on judgement and decision making, central to this investigation is whether the FLE can also be found for credibility perceptions about news. First empirical studies investigating the FLE on credibility perceptions yielded mixed results. For example, Fernández-López and Perea [15] asked participants to read false news articles and judge the credibility and emotionality of the presented articles. Contrary to their predictions, the authors found no difference between news presented in participants' mother tongue and news in a foreign language. Instead, Fernández-López and Perea [15] found that emotionality drove credibility perceptions equally in each language condition, with higher emotionality increasing the overall credibility perception. Moreover, in a similar study, Muda et al. [34] asked participants to discern true from false news, which was presented in both participants' native language and a foreign language. Results indicated that the FLE reduced individuals capacity to differentiate true from false news by decreasing the credibility of factual news and increasing the credibility of false news. Similar to Fernández-López and Perea [15], Muda et al. [34] found that emotionally arousing articles were perceived as more credible. In addition, Muda and colleagues found that individuals' inclination for deliberative thinking increased credibility independent of language condition but did not interact with the language condition.

In light of these as well as previous results, different predictions about credibility perceptions can be made. As described above, individuals commonly rely on cognitive heuristics to judge the credibility of information, "minimize[ing] their cognitive effort and time, through the use of cognitive heuristics" [32, p. 214]. However, previous results show that individuals who rely less on such heuristic processing and more on deliberative processing perceived news as more credible [34]. In addition, both Fernández-López and Perea [15] and Muda et al. [34] found that increases in emotionality positively predicted the perceived credibility of news. Hence, we predict:

H1: Individuals' inclination for deliberative thinking affects the perceived credibility of news so that a higher need for deliberative thinking increases the perceived credibility of news.

H2: Emotionality drives the credibility of news, with news that are higher in emotionality are perceived as more credible.

Moreover, the increased deliberation hypothesis of the FLE suggests that, besides the trait level disposition to engage in effortful deliberation, foreign language reasoning should increase the state level of effortful deliberation in a way that individuals momentarily rely more on deliberative and less on heuristic processing. Hence, foreign language reasoning should increase the perceived credibility of news by promoting the credibility of news via effortful deliberation.

However, following empirical findings by Muda et al. [34] contradict these the-oretical claims: foreign news was perceived as less credible than news in the native language. Because of these divergent predictions, we pose the following non-directional research question:

RQ1: What is the effect of a foreign language on credibility perceptions?

Going beyond the mere occurrence of the FLE, predictions can also be made about the underlying processes which lead to the FLE. As reported above, both Fernández-López and Perea [15] and Muda et al. [34] found that increases in emotionality positively predicted the perceived credibility of news. In both stud-ies, this effect was independent of the language condition. However, these results contradict previous findings that foreign language reasoning leads to the atten-uation of emotional responses. Because of these contradicting findings, we pose another non-directional research question:

RQ2: If an FLE for credibility perceptions is found, can it be explained by the attenuation of emotionality (i.e., lower emotionality of the foreign language condition)?

Reviewing the previous literature on the FLE, it remains unclear whether the FLE affects individuals differently, depending on their individual inclination for deliberative processing. To that end, previous empirical findings by Hayakawa et al. [23] and Muda et al. [34] suggest that the FLE affected individuals indepen-dent of their inclination for deliberative processing. Resting on the premise that reasoning in a foreign language increases deliberative processing, we hypoth-esize that if an FLE can be found, it should affect individuals depending on their inclination for deliberative processing. Credibility ratings of individuals with low dispositional levels of deliberative processing should increase due to the disfluency of the foreign language, signalling that reliance on heuristics is not appropriate. In contrast, credibility ratings of individuals with high disposi-tional levels of deliberative processing should be unaffected by foreign language reasoning as they already display increased readiness for deliberative processing. Hence, we predict:

H3: The effect of the FLE is moderated by individuals' inclination for delib-erative processing, increasing credibility perceptions only for individuals with a low dispositional inclination for deliberative reasoning.

## 3  Method

This study received ethical approval from the ethics committee of the University of Duisburg-Essen. All hypotheses and analyses were preregistered.

### 3.1  Sample and Procedure

We applied a two group (native language vs foreign language) between-subject design. In an online experiment, we asked 134 (89 female) from the age of 18 to 55 years (M = 24.93, SD = 6.56) to read a news article in either their native lan-guage (here: German) or a foreign language (here: English). All participants were instructed to read the article carefully. A timer was set to 20 s so participants could not immediately jump to the next page but instead spent time reading the article. Immediately after being presented with the article, participants were asked to rate how they felt after reading the news article and rate how credible they found the article. Participation was restricted to participants who were at least 18 years, had at least B1[1] skills of the foreign language, and whose native language was German. Bilingual participants were also allowed to participate if their second language was not English.

The news article was taken from a small local newspaper (Donaukurier) and discussed Covid-19 vaccinations. The original native language article was translated to English and back-translated to German to ensure the articles in both languages displayed the same information.

### 3.2 Dependent Variables

We used Gaziano and McGrath's [17] credibility scale to assess participants' credibility judgments, measuring credibility through ten items on a 5-point Likert scale. The scale's reliability was sufficient (Cronbach's alpha = .86) so that items were summarized into one mean score, with higher scores indicating higher credibility.

### 3.3 Independent Variables

Emotions were assessed through the native language version of the positive and negative affect schedule (PANAS) by [9]. The PANAS consists of 20 items (10 positive affect ratings & 10 negative affect ratings), such as nervous, angry, relaxed, and enthusiastic, measured on a 5-point Likert scale. For the analysis, emotions were summarized into two variables, negative affect (Cronbach's alpha = .85) and positive affect (Cronbach's alpha = .89). Higher numbers indicate higher levels of negative and positive affect, respectively.

To assess individuals' inclination for deliberation, we used the abbreviated version of the Need for Cognition (NfC) scale by [7], consisting of 16 items such as "I enjoy cognitively challenging tasks". The NfC was measured on a 7-point Likert scale, with higher values indicating a higher need for cognition. All items were summarized into a mean score (Cronbach's alpha = .80).

We also controlled for source credibility and language proficiency. Including a measure of source credibility helped us parse out variance related to the source credibility and enabled us to examine the distinctive effects of language. Hence, we measured in one 7-point Likert item how credibly participants rated the source (1 = not at all credible; 7 = highly credible). Similarly, we included language proficiency to account for possible confounding effects due to a lack of

---

[1] The B1 proficiency level follows the Common European Framework of Reference for Language (CERF) (see more here https://bit.ly/3mn129y). B1 describes the independent user stage, an intermediate stage of language proficiency, which students commonly achieve after their graduation (after 10 years of schooling).

understanding. Proficiency was measured through one self-report item in which participants could indicate their level of proficiency (1 = B1, 2 = B2, 3 = C1, 4 = C2).

## 4  Results

To answer the overarching research question of whether credibility is perceived differently when information is presented in a foreign language, we conducted a multiple linear regression with perceived credibility of the article as the dependent variable and language condition (dichotomous variable), need for cognition, emotions and the control variables (age, gender, education, foreign language skills, source credibility) as predictors. The descriptive statistics of the dependent variable credibility and the independent variables can be found in Table 1. Results of the multiple linear regression can be found in Table 2.

**Table 1.** Mean scores and standard deviations of the variables of interest.

|  | M | SD |
|---|---|---|
| Credibility | 2.64 | 0.70 |
| Positive affect | 2.42 | 0.77 |
| Negative Affect | 1.58 | 0.58 |
| NfC | 4.83 | 0.74 |
| Source credibility | 4.05 | 1.26 |

**Table 2.** Results of the multiple linear regression with perceived credibility as the criterium, including the control variables age, gender, education, and foreign language skills.

|  | Beta | t | p | 95% CI | |
|---|---|---|---|---|---|
| Language* | -0.165 | -2.196 | .030 | −0.436 | −0.023 |
| Positive Affect | 0.046 | 0.595 | 0.553 | −0.095 | 0.177 |
| Negative Affect | 0.193 | 2.656 | .009 | 0.064 | 0.438 |
| Need for Cognition | 0.075 | 0.994 | 0.322 | −0.070 | 0.021 |
| Source Credibility | 0.510 | 6.546 | <.001 | 0.197 | 0.367 |

Adjusted R2 = .365, (F(9, 120) = 9.23, p < .001). * Coded as: Native language = 1, foreign language = 2

The multiple linear regression results indicate that, as predicted, the most significant contribution to the overall credibility perceptions was due to the perceived credibility of the source ($\beta = 0.51$, $p < .001$). However, after parsing out variance associated with the source's credibility, we found that language significantly affected credibility ratings ($\beta = -0.165$, $p = -.030$). The results imply that participants who viewed the article in their native language rated the credibility of the article higher than participants who viewed the article in a foreign language, which supports previous empirical findings [34].

Furthermore, H1, which proposed that individuals' need for cognition would positively predict credibility perceptions, was not supported, indicating that credibility perceptions were independent of participants' need for cognition ($\beta = 0.075$, $p = -.322$), contradicting previous findings [4]. Supporting H2, the multiple linear regression results indicate that negative affect drove credibility perceptions-increased negative affect led to higher perceived credibility, supporting previous findings [15].

In a second research question, we wanted to know whether, if an FLE is found, it could be attributed to the attenuation of emotional responses. To answer RQ2, we conducted a parallel mediation analysis with model 4 of the Process Macro by [24], using bootstrapping procedures, computing 10000 bootstrapped samples with a confidence interval of 95%. The language condition was set as our independent variable, and credibility ratings as the dependent variable. Both emotion ratings, positive and negative, were entered as mediator variables. All standardized coefficients are reported in Fig. 1. Results of the mediation analysis support the findings of a foreign language effect on credibility perceptions found in the regression analysis. However, we found no support for the attenuation of emotion hypothesis. There was no indirect effect of language on credibility perceptions mediated by positive (beta = -.06, LLCI = $-.16$ & ULCI = .01) and negative emotions (beta = .02, LLCI = $-.05$ & ULCI = .13).

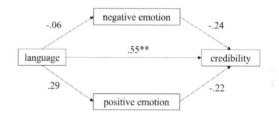

**Fig. 1.** Results of the mediation analysis with relevant path standardized coefficients. Significant path coefficients are marked as followed: ***p < .001, ** p < .01, *p < .05.

To conclude, while we found an FLE for credibility perceptions with the native language receiving higher credibility scores than the foreign language condition, decreased emotionality could not explain this difference.

Instead of the attenuation of emotions approach, another possible explanation for the found FLE is that the foreign language impacted information processing. We ran another multiple linear regression to test H3, which suggested that the FLE should affect individuals depending on their inclination for deliberation (as reported before). We added an interaction term of language condition and NfC (see Table 3 for the results).

First, when including the interaction term, explainable variance increased by roughly 4%. Second, the effect of language reversed, indicating that participants reading the foreign language article rated it more credible than participants who

**Table 3.** The multiple linear regression results with credibility as the criterium, including the interaction term of individuals' inclination for deliberation (NfC) and the language condition as well as the control variables age, gender, education, and foreign language skills.

|  | $\beta$ | $t$ | $p$ | 95% CI | |
|---|---|---|---|---|---|
| Language | 1.122 | 2.456 | .015 | 0.302 | 2.811 |
| Positive Affect | 0.032 | 0.462 | 0.671 | −0.104 | 0.161 |
| Negative Affect | 0.205 | 2.903 | .004 | 0.085 | 0.499 |
| Need for Cognition | 0.666 | 3.033 | 0.003 | 0.217 | 1.032 |
| Source Credibility | 0.508 | 6.712 | <.001 | 0.198 | 0.364 |
| Language*Need for Cognition | −1.434 | −2.855 | .005 | −0.623 | −0.113 |

$R2 = .400$, $(F(10, 119) = 9.585, p < .001)$. * Coded as: Native language = 1, foreign language = 2

read the native language article. Whereas the effect of negative affect remained the same (higher levels of negative affect increased credibility ratings), the effect of NfC was now significant. Scrutinizing the effect more closely indicated that individuals with a higher need for cognition perceived the article as more credible, as predicted in H1.

The results of the interaction effect suggested that the FLE affected individuals depending on their inclination for deliberation (NfC). While we predicted that the effect of language should only affect participants with low levels of need for cognition (H3), our results indicate otherwise: When information was presented in the native language, higher NfC scores positively influenced credibility perceptions. In contrast, when information was presented in the foreign language, higher NfC scores negatively influenced credibility perceptions. Moreover, Participants with low need for cognition differentiated less between native and foreign language news, whereas participants with high need for cognition differentiated more between native and foreign news.

## 5    Discussion

This study aimed to examine whether a foreign language effect (FLE) for credibility perceptions of news exists. Our results suggest that, indeed, news in a foreign language were perceived different than news in one's native language. The direction of this effect was, however, somewhat difficult to ascertain. While in the first analysis, foreign news was perceived as less credible than native news, a second analysis revealed that foreign news was perceived as more credible than native news. However, the results of the second analysis were dependent on individuals' level of need for cognition: the higher individuals' need for cognition was, the lower they perceived the credibility of foreign news. It was also found that the lower individuals' need for cognition was, the higher they perceived the credibility of foreign news. The contrasting effect was found for native language news: The higher (lower) the individuals' need for cognition, the higher (lower) the credibility perceptions. The found interaction of the language effect and individuals' need for cognition contradicts previous findings by Muda et al. [34], who found no such interaction effect.

To understand these contradicting findings, let us first point to the differences between Muda et al. [34] and our study. While Muda et al. [34] conducted a within-subjects study design, our design was a between-subjects experiment. However, the choice of study design has been found to impact state processing. Stanovich and West [39] propose that within-subjects designs possibly increase participants' awareness of variables of interest. In turn, participants are more likely to decontextualize information presented, and more deliberative processing is cued, reducing the impact of naturally occurring individual differences. Hence, the null findings for the interaction of language and inclination for deliberation by Muda et al. [34] might result from the selected within-subjects design.

Another explanation for the observed interaction is that our results were confounded by a reduced understanding of the foreign language condition by people with a low need for cognition. However, because we controlled for individual differences concerning language proficiency, this explanation seems less plausible.

Instead, we suggest examining the effect of need for cognition separated by language condition. First, the finding that low scoring NfC individuals increased their credibility ratings for the foreign news article supports previous FLE findings. In particular, these findings suggest that, as a result of the disfluency cued by the foreign language, individuals who are less inclined to engage in effortful deliberation become more inclined to engage in effortful deliberation, which is reflected by increased perceived credibility of foreign news as compared to native news.

Moreover, findings for individuals with a high need for cognition yielded precisely the opposite results we anticipated. Because, theoretically, individuals high in need for cognition should be more likely to engage in effortful deliberation, we expected to find no effect of language. Instead, we found that the higher individuals' need for cognition, the lower they perceived the credibility of the foreign news article. This suggests that engaging in effortful deliberation undermined the ability to judge the credibility of the news article. We suggest that thinking too much might have negatively affected the perceived credibility of the foreign news.

Indeed, previous research has found that overthinking can affect individuals' judgement and decision making. Different explanations account for this effect, such as considering too many attributes or overweighting the importance of one attribute over others. Transferring these results to our findings, we suggest that foreign language reasoning could have resulted in overthinking for those participants who already show a high inclination for deliberation, leading to decreased perceived credibility. Alternatively, we suggest that the foreign language itself (in this case, English specifically) served as a credibility heuristic that was perceived differently, depending on individuals' need for cognition. Previous studies have already found that individuals differ in their attitudes about certain languages. For example, Kobayashi [27] found a gender effect for attitudes towards English, with Japanese females holding more positive attitudes. However, to better gauge the effect of individual differences in need for cognition and how such differences affect the processing outcome, future studies should focus on unpacking the underlying psychological mechanisms of credibility perceptions by focusing on information processing and elaboration measures.

Furthermore, the observed effects of emotionality were less ambiguous. Similar to previous results by Fernández-López and Perea [15] as well as Muda et al. [34], we found no effect of the foreign language on emotionality. Hence, it seems unlikely that the FLE for credibility perceptions resulted from the attenuation of emotions and was instead driven by the difference in information processing. Nevertheless, emotional responses shaped participants' credibility perceptions. The more negative the article was perceived, the more credible it became. This is in line with previous findings concerning the relationship between emotionality and credibility [15].

## 5.1   Limitations and Future Studies

Although we see good reason to assume that differences in processing depth are at the heart of the effects we found, we did not implement explicit measures of processing style. To ascertain a causal relationship, future studies should focus on measures and paradigms that allow to gain more insights into the processing style. To achieve this, previous studies have, for example, employed self-report scales of processing style [21], thought-listing [25], and perceived argument strength [36]. Affecting the general processing depth, the viewing time of the article, which was set to 20 s, cued more deliberate processing that would not occur naturally.

Moreover, as discussed above, specific attitudes towards the foreign language could have affected the perceived credibility. Hence, it is possible that high need for cognition participants perceived foreign news sources as generally less credible. To rule out the possibility that the foreign language itself served as a credibility cue, future studies should also include measures of perceived credibility of foreign than national/native news sources.

In addition, we would also like to point to limitations related to the selected stimulus design. First, while all text was translated to the foreign language (here: English), we did not change the source, which remained in its native language (here: German). Consequently, in the foreign language condition, it appeared that a native language source published news in the foreign language. Although two previous studies by both Fernández-López and Perea [15] and Muda et al. [34] used a similar set-up, we suspect that this discrepancy could have also served as a credibility cue which was only evaluated as a negative cue for participants with a high need for cognition. Solving this issue is not straightforward. One possible solution would be to choose a source that publishes in both languages, which must also be known by the participants.

# 6   Conclusion

In this investigation, we were interested in finding a foreign language effect for the perceived credibility of news. Showing participants news either in their native language (German) or in a foreign language (English), we found that the native language article was rated as more credible than the foreign language article. However, this was only true for participants with a high need for cognition. Participants with a low need for cognition perceived the foreign news article similar to the native news. Trying to explain these findings, we suggest that the foreign news condition promoted individuals with a high need for cognition to think too much (overthinking) which ultimately decreased the perceived credibility. In addition, we found no effects which indicated that the foreign language effect was due to reduced emotional responses. Although increased negative emotional responses increased the perceived credibility of the news article, this was true for both language conditions.

While our study does not allow us to make strong assumptions as to why we find a foreign language effect for perceived credibility, we would like to emphasize that the mere occurrence of the effect is, nevertheless, very imporant. As described in the introduction, the foreign language effect can possibly threaten news consumers in two ways by either increasing the credibility of misinformation or decreasing the credibility of factual information. As more and more people consume news in a foreign language, it is likely that negative consequences occur, like an increased belief in false claims or the rejection of factual information. Because the potential consequences of a foreign language effect can be very severe, we strongly encourage future studies to investigate the foreign language effect on perceived credibility in further depth.

# References

1. Alencar, A., Deuze, M.: News for assimilation or integration? examining the functions of news in shaping acculturation experiences of immigrants in the netherlands and spain. Eur. J. Commun. **32**(2), 151–166 (2017). https://doi.org/10.1177/026732311768999
2. Alter, A.L., Oppenheimer, D.M., Epley, N., Eyre, R.N.: Overcoming intuition: metacognitive difficulty activates analytic reasoning. J. Exp. Psychol. Gen. **136**(4), 569–576 (2007). https://doi.org/10.1037/0096-3445.136.4.569
3. Athique, A.: Transnational Audiences: Media Reception on a Global Scale. Wiley, Hoboken (2017)
4. Bago, B., Rand, D.G., Pennycook, G.: Fake news, fast and slow: deliberation reduces belief in false (but not true) news headlines. J. Exp. Psychol. Gen. **149**(8), 1608–1613 (2020). https://doi.org/10.1037/xge0000729
5. Białek, M., Domurat, A., Paruzel-Czachura, M., Mud, R.: Discounting in a foreign language, pp. 1–36 (2021)
6. Białek, M., Muda, R., Stewart, K., Niszczota, P., Pieńkosz, D.: Thinking in a foreign language distorts allocation of cognitive effort: evidence from reasoning. Cognition **205**, 104420 (2020). https://doi.org/10.1016/j.cognition.2020.104420

7. Bless, H., W"anke, M., Bohner, G., Fellhauer, R.F., Schwarz, N.: Need for cognition: Eine skala zur erfassung von engagement und freude bei denkaufgaben. Zeitschrift F"ur Sozialpsychologie **25**(2), 147–154 (1994)
8. Brashier, N.M., Marsh, E.J.: Judging truth. Annu. Rev. Psychol. **71**, 499–515 (2020). https://doi.org/10.1146/annurev-psych-010419-050807
9. Breyer, B., Bluemke, M.: Deutsche version der positive and negative affect schedule panas (gesis panel). Zusammenstellung Sozialwissenschaftlicher Items Und Skalen (ZIS). Burkhardt, J. M. **53**(8), 5–8 (2016), https://doi.org/10.6102/zis242
10. Burkhardt, J.M.: Combating fake news in the digital age, vol. 53. American Library Association Chicago, IL, USA (2017)
11. Caldwell-Harris, C.L.: Emotionality differences between a native and foreign language: theoretical implications. Front. Psychol. **5**, 1–4 (2014). https://doi.org/10.3389/fpsyg.2014.01055
12. Chaiken, S.: The heuristic model of persuasion. In: Zanna, J.O., Herman, C. (eds.) M, pp. 3–39. The Ontario symposium 5th ed., Lawrence Erlbaum, Social influence (1987)
13. Costa, A., Vives, M., Corey, J.D.: On language processing shaping decision making. Curr. Dir. Psychol. Sci. **26**(2), 146–151 (2017). https://doi.org/10.1177/0963721416680263
14. Del Vicario, M., Bessi, A., Zollo, F., Petroni, F., Scala, A., Caldarelli, G., Stanley, H.E., Quattrociocchi, W.: The spreading of misinformation online. Proc. Natl. Acad. Sci. **113**(3), 554–559 (2016)
15. Fernández-López, M., Perea, M.: Language does not modulate fake news credibility, but emotion does. Psicologica **41**(2), 84–102 (2020). https://doi.org/10.2478/psicolj-2020-0005
16. Fiske, S.T., Taylor, S.E.: Social cognition. McGraw-Hill, New York (1991)
17. Gaziano, C., McGrath, K.: Measuring the concept of credibility. Journal. Q. **63**(3), 451–461 (1986). https://doi.org/10.1177/107769908606300301
18. Geipel, J., Hadjichristidis, C., Surian, L.: The foreign language effect on moral judgment: the role of emotions and norms. PLoS ONE **10**(7), 1–17 (2015). https://doi.org/10.1371/journal.pone.0131529
19. Gigerenzer, G., Gaissmaier, W.: Heuristic decision making. Annu. Rev. Psychol. **62**, 451–482 (2011). https://doi.org/10.1146/annurev-psych-120709-145346
20. Gilbert, D.T.: How mental systems believe. Am. Psychol. **46**(2), 107–119 (1991). https://doi.org/10.1037/0003-066X.46.2.107
21. Griffin, R.J., Neuwirth, K., Giese, J., Dunwoody, S.: Linking the heuristic-systematic model and depth of processing. Commun. Res. **29**(6), 705–732 (2002). https://doi.org/10.1177/009365002237833
22. Hadjichristidis, C., Geipel, J., Savadori, L.: The effect of foreign language in judgments of risk and benefit: the role of affect. J. Exp. Psychol. Appl. **21**(2), 117–129 (2015). https://doi.org/10.1037/xap0000044
23. Hayakawa, S., Tannenbaum, D., Costa, A., Corey, J.D., Keysar, B.: Thinking more or feeling less? explaining the foreign-language effect on moral judgment. Psychol. Sci. **28**(10), 1387–1397 (2017)
24. Hayes, A.F.: Introduction to mediation, moderation, and conditional process analysis: a regression-based approach. Guilford publications (2017)
25. Jain, S.P., Maheswaran, D.: Motivated reasoning: a depth-of-processing perspective. J. Consum. Res. **26**(4), 358–371 (2000). https://doi.org/10.1086/209568
26. Keysar, B., Hayakawa, S.L., An, S.G.: The foreign-language effect: thinking in a foreign tongue reduces decision biases. Psychol. Sci. **23**(6), 661–668 (2012). https://doi.org/10.1177/0956797611432178

27. Kobayashi, Y.: The role of gender in foreign language learning attitudes: Japanese female students' attitudes towards English learning. Gend. Educ. **14**(2), 181–197 (2002). https://doi.org/10.1080/09540250220133021

28. Lang, A.: The limited capacity model of mediated message processing. J. Commun. **50**, 46–70 (2000). https://doi.org/10.1111/j.1460-2466.2000.tb02833.x

29. Lewandowsky, S., Ecker, U.K.H., Seifert, C.M., Schwarz, N., Cook, J.: Misinformation and its correction: continued influence and successful debiasing. Psychol. Sci. Public Interest **13**(3), 106–131 (2012). https://doi.org/10.1177/1529100612451018

30. Mækelæ, M.J., Pfuhl, G.: Deliberate reasoning is not affected by language. PLoS ONE **14**(1), 1–13 (2019). https://doi.org/10.1371/journal.pone.0211428

31. Metzger, M.J.: Making sense of credibility on the web: models for evaluating online information and recommendations for future research. J. Am. Soc. Inform. Sci. Technol. **58**(13), 2078–2091 (2007). https://doi.org/10.1002/asi.20672

32. Metzger, M.J., Flanagin, A.J.: Credibility and trust of information in online environments: the use of cognitive heuristics. J. Pragmat. **59**, 210–220 (2013). https://doi.org/10.1016/j.pragma.2013.07.012

33. Metzger, M.J., Flanagin, A.J., Medders, R.B.: Social and heuristic approaches to credibility evaluation online. J. Commun. **60**(3), 413–439 (2010). https://doi.org/10.1111/j.1460-2466.2010.01488.x

34. Muda, R., Pennycook, G., Pieńkosz, D., Białek, M.: People are worse at detecting fake news in their foreign language (2021)

35. Muda, R., Walker, A.C., Pieńkosz, D., Fugelsang, J.A., Białek, M.: Foreign language does not affect gambling-related judgments. J. Gambl. Stud. **36**, 633–652 (2020)

36. Nabi, R.L.: Anger, fear, uncertainty, and attitudes: a test of the cognitive-functional model. Commun. Monogr. **69**(3), 204–216 (2002). https://doi.org/10.1080/03637750216541

37. Pennycook, G., Rand, D.G.: Lazy, not biased: susceptibility to partisan fake news is better explained by lack of reasoning than by motivated reasoning. Cognition **188**, 39–50 (2019). https://doi.org/10.1016/j.cognition.2018.06.011

38. Petty, R.E., Cacioppo, J.T.: The elaboration likelihood model of persuasion. In: Advances in Experimental Social Psychology, vol. 19, pp. 123–205 (1986). https://doi.org/10.4148/1051-0834.1183

39. Stanovich, K.E., West, R.F.: Natural myside bias is independent of cognitive ability. Thinking Reasoning **13**(3), 225–247 (2007)

40. Tandoc, E.C., Lim, Z.W., Ling, R.: Defining "fake news": a typology of scholarly definitions. Digit. J. **6**(3), 1–17 (2017). https://doi.org/10.1080/21670811.2017.1360143

41. Widholm, A.: Transnational news consumption and digital content mobility: insights from Sweden. J. Stud. **20**(10), 1472–1490 (2019). https://doi.org/10.1080/1461670X.2018.1526642

# Author Index

D. Ceolin et al. (Eds.): MISDOOM 2023, LNCS 14397, p. 191, 2023.
https://doi.org/10.1007/978-3-031-47896-3